Getting Started with Forex Trading Using Python

Beginner's guide to the currency market and development of trading algorithms

Alex Krishtop

BIRMINGHAM—MUMBAI

Getting Started with Forex Trading Using Python

Copyright © 2023 Packt Publishing

Publishing Product Manager: Apeksha Shetty

Senior Editor: Tazeen Shaikh

Technical Editor: Kavyashree K S

Copy Editor: Safis Editing

Project Coordinator: Farheen Fathima

Proofreader: Safis Editing

Indexer: Sejal Dsilva

Production Designer: Vijay Kamble

Marketing Coordinator: Nivedita Singh

First published: March 2023

Production reference: 2200323

Published by Packt Publishing Ltd.

Livery Place

35 Livery Street

Birmingham

B3 2PB, UK.

ISBN 978-1-80461-685-7

www.packtpub.com

To my loving wife, Emily, without whose perpetual kicking I would have never accomplished this book.

And to my son, Daniel, who is making his first steps in the weird world of data science and Python programming.

– Alex Krishtop

Contributors

About the author

Alex Krishtop is a quantitative trader and researcher with 20 years of experience in developing automated trading solutions. He is currently the head of trading and research at Edgesense Technologies and CTO at Econq Ltd. He develops market models and trading algorithms for FX, commodities, and crypto. He was one of the first traders who started using Python as the ultimate environment for quantitative trading and suggested a few approaches to developing trading apps that, today, have become standard among many quant traders. He has worked as a director of education with the Algorithmic Traders Association, where he developed an exhaustive course in systematic and algo trading, which covers the worlds of both quantitative models and discretionary approaches.

About the reviewer

Andrey Lyashenko is a VP quantitative analyst at one of the largest investment banks in Eastern Europe and has around 20 years of experience in information technologies and finance in various roles. He has worked primarily in the development of high-availability and high-performance systems (including trading platforms) and has experience in private equity and leveraged algorithmic trading in financial markets. In trading, he takes a systematic, science-based approach to developing and implementing investment strategies.

Table of Contents

3

FX Market Overview from a Developer's Standpoint   29

Part 2: General Architecture of a Trading Application and A Detailed Study of Its Components

4

Part 3: Orders, Trading Strategies, and Their Performance

9

Trading Strategies and Their Core Elements   197

10

Types of Orders and Their Simulation in Python   223

11

Backtesting and Theoretical Performance   237

Part 4: Strategies, Performance Analysis, and Vistas

12

Sample Strategy – Trend-Following   281

13

14

Preface

Forex trading has been popular for the last 20 years and its popularity is only growing. This market attracts new traders mostly because of huge potential profits and the ability to start with a relatively small amount of initial capital. However, at the same time, it is known to be one of the most dangerous markets, as according to the statistics of most regulators, more than 75% of forex traders completely lose their money.

This happens for a number of reasons. Some newcomers to forex tend to treat it the same as stock trading and try to invest in a market that doesn't have an intrinsic upside potential. Others want to take advantage of high leverage, being inspired by multiple "get rich quick" books to hunt for legendary profits, incorrectly calculating their exposure, and then quickly losing their entire deposit.

But the main problems for all beginner forex traders are a lack of trading ideas and a lack of understanding of why the market may do this or that, when it may be reasonable to place a trade, when it may be problematic, and when to stay away from the market entirely to avoid almost inevitable losses.

Algorithmic trading can provide a solution to this problem because it's based on rules that can be tested before any real money is put at stake. Beyond that, trading automation helps to mitigate operational risks and provides full control over execution, which is not achievable with manual order placement.

This book bridges the gap between the "easy forex" advertised by many retail brokers and the real forex market, with all its caveats and pitfalls, from the perspective of a professional algo trader. It guides the reader through all the necessary steps in developing automated trading strategies that have at least a chance of survival in this controversial market. It is not a collection of ready-made recipes for you to copy, paste, and run: the markets are constantly changing and you will have to adapt and re-adapt your strategies to them as they change.

The main goal of the book is to provide a clear understanding of what is possible, what is not, and what to realistically expect from algorithmic trading in forex. By the end of the book, you will have the essential knowledge of the forex market at the level of a professional desk trader. At the same time, you will have developed practical skills for implementing trading algorithms in Python. Although this book is only the first step for beginners into the world of forex trading, it can help you not only get started as a retail trader but also eventually find a job in this industry.

Who this book is for

This book is for anyone familiar with Python programming who wants to test the waters of algo trading. This is not a Python tutorial: I assume that you are well familiar with the language and object-oriented programming. No special knowledge in programming is required though, and any time a new type of object or structure is used, it is explained in detail.

No knowledge about markets and trading is required and nor is any prior experience in trading. I tried to explain the contents in the most simple terms but without simplifying the subject itself to help you expand your trading vocabulary and get a clear understanding of the meaning of the most essential terms.

At the same time, Python is used only to provide working examples of the concepts considered in the book. No special programming techniques specific to Python are used. This means that you can easily port the code or develop something on your own in other languages, so the book can also be quite useful for traders who use other platforms, such as MetaTrader.

What this book covers

Chapter 1, *Developing Trading Strategies – Why They Are Different*, introduces the concept of trading strategies and automated trading and highlights the main components of a trading application, such as receiving market data, making trading decisions, and executing orders.

Chapter 2, *Using Python for Trading Strategies*, focuses on using Python for market analysis, modeling, and actual trading.

Chapter 3, *FX Market Overview from a Developer's Standpoint*, explains how markets operate, focuses on the different kinds of market participants and the way they affect the price, and introduces core terminology essential for any further study.

Chapter 4, *Trading Application – What's Inside?*, expands the first draft of a trading app architecture that was proposed in *Chapter 1* and provides a more detailed view of its main components.

Chapter 5, *Retrieving and Handling Market Data with Python*, provides practical examples of manipulating ticks and order book data, explains the use of data compression, and introduces the concept of a universal data connector.

Chapter 6, *Basics of Fundamental Analysis and Its Possible Use in FX Trading*, explains the difference between fundamental and technical analysis and shows examples of the most important fundamental events and the way they impact the market price.

Chapter 7, *Technical Analysis and Its Implementation in Python*, considers a number of the most well-known and typical technical studies, explains their relationships with the underlying price time series, and suggests possible implementations in Python.

Chapter 8, *Data Visualization in FX Trading with Python*, introduces basic plotting, which is used to visualize price time series and other graphical objects, such as equity curves and drawdowns.

Chapter 9, Trading Strategies and Their Core Elements, introduces alpha and beta as the key performance metrics, explains benchmarking in capital management, and discusses the most popular alpha-generating trading strategies.

Chapter 10, Types of Orders and Their Simulation in Python, introduces the concept of a trading order, explains the main types of orders, and emphasizes the risks associated with each of them.

Chapter 11, Backtesting and Theoretical Performance, discusses backtesting as the core of any trading strategy development, reviews the architecture of a trading application, introduces multithreading and provides a detailed use case of it to organize communication between the parts of an app, explains the logic involved, and proposes working code solutions for a trading app using live market data for backtesting.

Chapter 12, Sample Strategy – Trend-Following, carefully considers all the steps necessary to develop a simple trading strategy from scratch and provides some working Python code.

Chapter 13, To Trade or Not to Trade – Performance Analysis, introduces the very basic metrics used to assess the performance of a trading strategy and gives practical examples using the theoretical performance of the strategy developed in *Chapter 12*.

Chapter 14, Where to Go Now?, offers a collection of trading ideas, technical setups, and code snippets that you can use for your own development.

To get the most out of this book

Please remember that the code printed in the book is interwoven with explanations: this is intentionally done to comment on most of the lines so that no important action remains unexplained. Therefore, it is advised to first read the entire code with explanations, follow the logic, understand how it works, and only afterward copy the code from the book or GitHub and run it. Otherwise, there's a risk that you will attempt to run only a part of the code, which may not work without the context.

Software/hardware covered in the book	Operating system requirements
Python 3.10 or above	Windows, macOS, or Linux

If you are using the digital version of this book, we advise you to type the code yourself or access the code from the book's GitHub repository (a link is available in the next section). Doing so will help you avoid any potential errors related to the copying and pasting of code.

Download the example code files

You can download the example code files for this book from GitHub at `https://github.com/PacktPublishing/Getting-Started-with-Forex-Trading-Using-Python`. If there's an update to the code, it will be updated in the GitHub repository.

We also have other code bundles from our rich catalog of books and videos available at `https://github.com/PacktPublishing/`. Check them out!

Conventions used

There is a number of text conventions used throughout this book.

`Code in text`: Indicates code words in text, database table names, folder names, filenames, file extensions, pathnames, dummy URLs, user input, and Twitter handles. Here is an example: "Mount the downloaded `WebStorm-10*.dmg` disk image file as another disk in your system."

A block of code is set as follows:

```
html, body, #map {
  height: 100%;
  margin: 0;
  padding: 0
}
```

When we wish to draw your attention to a particular part of a code block, the relevant lines or items are set in bold:

```
[default]
exten => s,1,Dial(Zap/1|30)
exten => s,2,Voicemail(u100)
exten => s,102,Voicemail(b100)
exten => i,1,Voicemail(s0)
```

Bold: Indicates a new term, an important word, or words that you see onscreen. For instance, words in menus or dialog boxes appear in **bold**. Here is an example: "Select **System info** from the **Administration** panel."

> **Tips or important notes**
> Appear like this.

Get in touch

Feedback from our readers is always welcome.

General feedback: If you have questions about any aspect of this book, email us at `customercare@packtpub.com` and mention the book title in the subject of your message.

Errata: Although we have taken every care to ensure the accuracy of our content, mistakes do happen. If you have found a mistake in this book, we would be grateful if you would report this to us. Please visit `www.packtpub.com/support/errata` and fill in the form.

Piracy: If you come across any illegal copies of our works in any form on the internet, we would be grateful if you would provide us with the location address or website name. Please contact us at `copyright@packt.com` with a link to the material.

If you are interested in becoming an author: If there is a topic that you have expertise in and you are interested in either writing or contributing to a book, please visit `authors.packtpub.com`.

Share Your Thoughts

Once you've read *Getting Started with Forex Trading Using Python*, we'd love to hear your thoughts! Scan the QR code below to go straight to the Amazon review page for this book and share your feedback.

https://packt.link/r/1-804-61685-0

Your review is important to us and the tech community and will help us make sure we're delivering excellent quality content.

Download a free PDF copy of this book

Thanks for purchasing this book!

Do you like to read on the go but are unable to carry your print books everywhere?

Is your eBook purchase not compatible with the device of your choice?

Don't worry, now with every Packt book you get a DRM-free PDF version of that book at no cost.

Read anywhere, any place, on any device. Search, copy, and paste code from your favorite technical books directly into your application.

The perks don't stop there, you can get exclusive access to discounts, newsletters, and great free content in your inbox daily

Follow these simple steps to get the benefits:

1. Scan the QR code or visit the link below

https://packt.link/free-ebook/9781804616857

2. Submit your proof of purchase
3. That's it! We'll send your free PDF and other benefits to your email directly

Part 1:
Introduction to FX Trading Strategy Development

Success in any software development project is determined by two main factors – how fluent you are with the technology and how proficient you are in the subject domain.

Part 1 gives an essential overview of today's FX markets, focusing on their peculiarities, which determine the choice of solutions used in developing actual code. By the end of *Part 1*, you will have gained a conceptual understanding of the market structure, its operations, and the key risks, and at the same time, you will have learned about approaches to designing the architecture of trading applications, which address specific market-related issues.

This part comprises the following chapters:

- *Chapter 1, Developing Trading Strategies – Why They Are Different*
- *Chapter 2, Using Python for Trading Strategies*
- *Chapter 3, FX Market Overview from a Developer's Standpoint*

1
Developing Trading Strategies – Why They Are Different

For many years, I traded in various markets, educated developers in trading, and taught some essential programming and algorithm (algo) development to traders. Eventually, I concluded that the main problem for both groups (the developers and traders) was not a lack of knowledge in programming, but an incorrect or insufficient understanding of the subject domain, that is, financial markets and their mechanics.

This was quite a surprise for me. I thought that coding, debugging, and handling errors should be the main obstacle, but in reality, the problem is in finding useful, correct, and adequate information about markets, their structure, and operations, especially in regard to algo trading. I don't mean that it's somehow undisclosed or otherwise hidden from the general audience – not at all. The problem is that it's really hard to find a source that not only covers everything – from the market structure to money and risk management – but also shows clear connections between very specific features of a market and less-specific features that a trading algorithm should have in order to be successful in this market.

For example, many authors consider entries and exits in a trading strategy as something that can be executed immediately and with equal success at any moment, any time of the day. However, in the real market, this is not the case. I saw lots of strategies that only worked *on paper* because their developers didn't take into consideration the fact that they were dealing with a real, complex structure with lots of limitations and shortcomings, and not with an abstract idealistic model.

This example is really primitive, but I hope it explains the most important point that is missed by many researchers and developers: we do not deal with abstract datasets and time series where each data point has an equal value and where any action can be taken at any moment with equal possibility; we work with a very complex structure that has lots of features that make this structure a *dynamic non-stationary system*. And to be successful in algo trading, these features should be accounted for.

Without knowing how markets are organized and how they operate, our trading algorithms will inevitably fail sooner or later.

If put in a more positive manner, understanding the market will help us in making trading algorithms more robust.

This book is my humble attempt to bridge the gap between the world of quantitative trading (driven by numbers) and the real market (driven by humans). I am convinced that today, any long-term success in trading can be achieved only with good knowledge of both.

Let's begin with the basics. We will learn about the very basic market terminology and the essential concept of a trading strategy, get familiar with the risk in various forms and aspects with a special focus on ordering and transactional risk, and also mention market data processing in a very general sense.

In this chapter, we will discuss the following topics:

- Trading strategies – it's all about how you manage risk

- Automated trading – operational risk and regulatory limitations

- Making actual trading decisions – trading logic and credit risk

- Ordering – transactional risk

- The general architecture of a trading application

Trading strategies – it's all about how you manage risk

Let's start from the beginning by giving definitions. I know it sounds like an academic textbook, but I promise that it's going to get more and more interesting very quickly.

According to the definition provided by Cambridge Dictionary, trade is *"the activity of buying and selling, or exchanging, goods and/or services between people or countries."* This means that if I exchange my money for meat or vegetables, then I am at a grocery market. If I exchange my money for obligations to buy or sell live cattle or wheat in the future, then I am in a derivatives market. And if I exchange my money for another type of money, I am in the **foreign exchange**, **forex or FX market**.

What I buy and sell in a particular market is called an **asset**. If I buy or sell something that can be delivered (wheat, gold, stocks, or even money) it's called the **underlying**. If I buy or sell an obligation or the right to buy or sell the underlying at a certain price in the future, then it's called a **derivative**.

Underlying and derivatives are traded at **trading venues** – previously, physical locations such as exchanges, but today, more electronic networks where traders, liquidity providers, market makers, and other market participants match their orders.

If I went to a grocery market to sell potatoes, then I am on the **sell side**. If I came to buy potatoes, I am on the **buy side**. In financial markets, buy-side market participants are mostly referred to as **price takers** (because they can only take prices offered by the sell side), and sell-side market participants are referred to as **price givers**.

Not all trading venues welcome everyone as a direct participant. Most of them work via a network of **brokers** – entities that accept orders from their clients and route them to one or more trading venues, possibly internally netting client positions and sometimes even acting as the counterparty for their clients.

In *Chapter 3, FX Market Overview from a Developer's Standpoint*, we will consider all these entities in more detail to see why we should pay particular attention to their behavior and how to actually use them to make our trading strategies more robust.

Let's proceed with a very quick look into the essence of a trading strategy and see the main risks that are natural to the systematic or algo trading business.

Trading strategies – how we make money in financial markets

A trading strategy is a set of rules that tells me when to buy and when to sell the asset if I am on the buy side, or when and how much to offer to the market if I am on the sell side. But in any case, *the ultimate goal of a trading strategy is to make money.*

If I am on the buy side, I can make money only in the following two ways:

- I buy low and I sell high, or vice versa (earning on the price difference)
- I buy and receive dividends

The former is called **active trading**, and the latter is normally called **investing**, or getting passive income. In this book, we will consider only active trading.

There are two major classes of active trading strategies on the buy side. The first one is called **directional trading** and in essence, it's when we buy, wait, and sell. If we manage to sell at a price greater than the price at which we bought, we make money.

The second class of buy-side trading strategies is **arbitrage**. Such a strategy identifies moments when the same asset is priced differently at different trading venues (so-called *real* or *pure* arbitrage), or when there is a tradable difference between the price of the underlying and a derivative, different derivatives, or even more complex setups that consist of multiple instruments (so-called **statistical arbitrage** or **stat arb**).

Sounds a bit overwhelming? Don't worry, we will now consider each case in more detail.

Trading app – what can be simpler?

At this point, if you have sufficient experience in application development and a reasonable knowledge of markets, you might exclaim the following:

"Why do we need all this? It is so easy to build a trading application: you only need to get market data, calculate entry and exit orders, and send them to the broker!"

So, the suggested general architecture of a trading application from that standpoint may look as simple as this:

Figure 1.1 – Initial architecture of a trading application

However, as we will see very soon, this is an overly simplified view and it lacks at least one key feature that makes developing trading strategies different from developing other applications: it doesn't include risk management.

So, what about that risk?

Before discussing ways to make money in trading, let's first pay closer attention to avoiding losses – at least because according to all statistics, more than 70% of active traders, unfortunately, lose money.

Before we proceed, let me note that the following classification of risks does not fully correspond to official legal and academic classifications. This informal classification is used here for the sake of simplicity, to sort out rather complex matters quickly and with an acceptable degree of comfort.

All risks in active trading can be generally put into three major categories, as follows:

- **Operational risks** are those associated with how you place trades and depend on your own business procedures as well as third parties, such as brokers, trading venues, and regulators.

- **Systemic risks** are those pertaining to the very market itself and the logic of a trading strategy.

- **Transactional risks** are those that make the execution of orders different from expectations; this is the main reason why many strategies that work *on paper* are unable to make money in reality.

Now that we are a bit more familiar with the idea of a trading strategy and know that the main problem any systematic trader should solve is risk mitigation, let's dive a little deeper into risks specific to the algo trading business.

Automated trading – operational risk and regulatory limitations

Operational risk is the risk of direct or indirect loss resulting from inadequate or failed internal procedures, people, and systems, or from external events (Bank for International Settlements, *Basel Committee on Banking Supervision, Operational Risk Supporting Documentation to the New Basel Capital Accord* (Basel: BIS, 2002), p. 2, https://www.bis.org/publ/bcbsca07.pdf).

Since, in this book, we will talk mostly about developing trading algos with Python and not about running a trading business, the main operational risk in this context could be that you don't follow your own strategy or intervene in the algorithmic trading process discretionarily.

Another risk that may be considered operational (although it is normally considered as money management) is the improper use of leverage. In essence, leverage is a credit line provided by the broker that allows you to buy more than you have in your account. If the leverage is too high, you are at risk of being unable to enter the market, or in certain cases, even worse – liquidating your positions that are rapidly losing money.

Broker risk can also be attributed to operational risks as the broker is the very entity that provides you with access to the market, gives you a credit line to open positions, and does the clearing and settlement. Some brokers also act as market makers for their clients, netting their positions internally and acting as the counterparty for their own clients, which may lead to a conflict of interest, and even worse – loss of money if the broker didn't have sufficient capital to perform these operations.

Last, but not least, we should note that algorithmic and/or automated trading may be fully or partially prohibited in certain jurisdictions. So always check with the respective market regulators to make sure you can run your algo trading at all.

> **Key takeaways**
> Always perform a background check of all counterparties, especially your broker. Be careful with leverage and check local regulatory documents on algo trading.

Enough on operational risk – at least for a quick start – and let's move on to another kind of risk that is common for any trading activity but becomes particularly problematic for algo trading: the risk of basing trading decisions on incorrect market data.

Retrieving market data – quality and consistency as keys to success

Market data is often considered something that cannot contribute to the overall risk in systematic trading. However, this is a massive mistake. There are two key risks associated with market data:

- Issues with receiving data
- Issues with received data

In the next two subsections, we will dive deeper into the preceding risks.

Receiving data – when size does matter

There are two forms in which we get market data: real-time or historical. In both cases, we obtain it from a data vendor, a broker, or directly from an exchange. The difference is that real-time data is used for actual trading (as it reflects what is going on in the market right now) and historical data is used only for research and development, to rebuild hypothetical trades and estimate the theoretical performance of a trading algorithm.

The issues with receiving data are mostly related to real-time data.

Let's now add some more definitions as we need to acquire some common terminology to move on with market data and ordering.

A request to buy an asset at a certain price is called a **bid**. It's like you go to a market and shout, *"I want to buy this asset at this price. Is anyone willing to sell it to me?"*

A request to sell an asset at a certain price is called an **ask** or **offer**. It means that you are ready to sell it to anyone willing to accept your price.

In financial markets, both requests are realized by buy side traders with a **limit order** (see *Chapter 10, Types of Orders and Their Simulation in Python*, for a detailed discussion on types of orders).

When another counterparty agrees to place a trade at the order price, a new trade is registered and its information is included in the data stream and distributed across data vendors, brokers, and other recipients. Such a record is called a **tick**. In other words, a tick is a minimal piece of information in the market data and normally consists of the following fields:

- `date`
- `time`
- `price`
- `traded volume`
- `counterparty1`
- `counterparty2`

The last two fields contain information about actual counterparties and are normally not disclosed or distributed to protect the market participants. Traded volume means the amount of the asset that was traded (number of contracts, or just the amount of money if we are talking about forex).

The main problem with receiving market data in its raw form is that it's simply overwhelmingly huge. There are so many market participants and so many trading venues that streaming all transactions for just one asset (which is also called a "financial instrument") may easily reach megabytes per second – receiving it is already a challenge by itself (don't worry, we are not going to work with data feeds of this sort in this book). Next, even if we are able to receive a data stream with such a throughput, we need to store and handle this data somehow, and thus a very fast database is required. And finally, we need to be able to process this amount of data at an adequate speed, so we need blazingly fast computers.

But there is good news. Despite some strategies (mostly arbitrage and high-frequency trading) do require raw market data in the format just described (also frequently referred to as **time and sales** data) to identify trading opportunities, most directional trading algorithms are far less sensitive to lack of information about each and every trade. So, data vendors provide data in a compressed format. This becomes possible because most of the raw market data contains sequences of ticks with identical prices, and removing them won't distort the price movements. This happens because there may be many market participants placing trades at the same price at almost the same time, so by excluding these sequences, we lose information about each transaction but retain information about any change in price. Such a market data stream is often referred to as *filtered* or *cleaned*. Besides that, some trades are made at bids, others at asks, and while both bids and asks remain the same, these trades form sequences of trades where prices seem to be different. However, in reality, they are always at the distance of the difference between bids and asks. This difference doesn't mean that the market price changes. Such a phenomenon is called a **bounce** and is normally also excluded from cleaned data.

Some vendors and brokers go even further and send *snapshots* of the market data instead of a filtered data stream. A snapshot is sent at regular time intervals, for example, 100 ms or 1 s, and contains only the following information:

- Date
- Time
- Price at the beginning of the interval (also known as *open*, or just *O*)
- Maximum price during the interval (also known as *high*, or *H*)
- Minimum price during the interval (also known as *low*, or *L*)
- Price at the end of the interval (also known as *close*, or *C*)
- Traded volume

Therefore, instead of thousands of ticks, we receive only one tick with seven data fields. This approach dramatically reduces the throughput but is obviously somewhat destructive to the data, and snapshot data may not be suitable for some strategies.

Key takeaway

Be careful with choosing the source of data, especially for live trading, and always make sure it contains sufficient information for your strategy.

Received data – looking at it from a critical angle

After we have successfully received the data, we should make sure it makes sense. Often, data, especially tick data, contains erroneous prices. These prices may be received due to a number of reasons, which we will discuss in detail in *Chapter 5, Retrieving and Handling Market Data with Python*.

Erroneous, otherwise known as *non-market*, prices may cause trouble for systematic traders because a single *wrong* quote may trigger an algorithm to buy or sell something, and such a trade should not have happened according to the strategy logic.

Sometimes, these incorrect quotes can be seen if plotted on a chart. The human eye intuitively expects data points to be within a certain reasonable range and easily catches the outliers, as can be seen in the following chart:

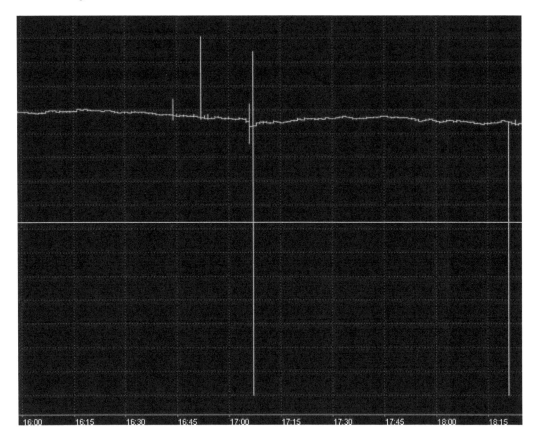

Figure 1.2 – Non-market prices seen on a tick chart

In case we receive snapshots or other compressed data, there could be missing intervals when we receive no quotes. It can happen because of the following:

- The market is closed (scheduled or due to an emergency)
- The data server is down
- The connection is broken

> **Key takeaway**
>
> A robust trading app should have a module capable of checking data consistency and connection persistence.

Alright, we are now aware of the operational risks and know how harmful incorrectly handling market data could be. Anything else? Of course, here comes the main risk: systemic.

Making actual trading decisions – trading logic and credit risk

In directional trading, systemic risks are mostly realized when you or your trading strategy supposed the price would go in one direction, but in reality, it went in the opposite direction. Don't worry, this situation is absolutely normal for systematic trading, and no one can guarantee that any strategy will generate a win rate of 100%.

There are two major types of trading strategies: data-driven and event-driven. **Data-driven** strategies analyze the price time series (which we discussed in the *Retrieving market data – quality and consistency as keys to success* section) in order to find a certain pattern or sequence that then triggers an order. Event-driven strategies wait for a certain event to happen – for example, a new tick at a certain price and with a certain volume, or a release of political news or economic indicators. In both cases, a trading app should have rules to not only open positions but also to liquidate them – again, based on price data or events (or both).

In general, if a strategy generates *some* wins and *some* losses, there are only two ways for it to make money:

- Generate more wins than losses
- Have the average win greater than the average loss

If your trading algorithm does not have a routine that handles situations when the market goes against the position, then most likely, the average loss across a statistically significant number of trades will be greater than the average win, and it will become really problematic to make money with such a strategy.

Don't forget that forex is traded using leverage, which means the ability to trade much greater amounts of money than you actually have in your account. In the case that your trading algorithm has poor risk management logic and incorrect position sizing, an open position may quickly drain your account to zero if the price goes the opposite way, and even worse – some brokers will even let you go negative and you will be left with debt instead of profit.

> **Key takeaway**
> Systemic risk management and position sizing algorithms are crucial parts of an algo trading application.

Systemic risk is very important, but there's good news for systematic traders: it is possible to mitigate this risk by carefully testing the strategy before going to production and adjusting it so the systemic risk is minimized. But there is one more risk that is hard to mitigate during the research and development phase: transactional risk.

Ordering – transactional risk

Transactional risks are the real problem in the first place for arbitrage, but they also affect directional strategies. In simple terms, this is a risk of the following:

- Entering or exiting the market at a wrong price

- Entering or exiting the market at a wrong time

- Entering or exiting the market with a wrong trading size

- Not entering or exiting the market at all

All four situations are more than possible in all markets and are even quite frequent during periods of insufficient liquidity (see *Chapter 3, FX Market Overview from a Developer's Standpoint*, for a more detailed discussion of liquidity issues).

> **Key takeaway**
> Transactional risks are managed by a set of algorithms that are also an essential part of any trading application.

Well, it's been quite a trip across the various risks, and we now understand that the initial idea of a trading application with a simple and straightforward linear logic definitely won't work in real life. Now, we can suggest something (unfortunately) more complex, but (fortunately) more realistic.

The general architecture of a trading application

Now, we can improve our initial diagram (see *Figure 1.1*) representing the architecture of a trading application. Although it is still very general and high level, it now radically differs from what we suggested in the beginning:

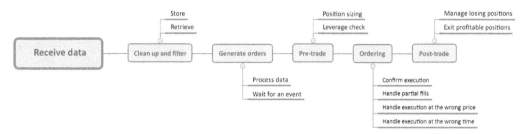

Figure 1.3 – More complete general architecture of a trading app

Here, we can see that the real trading application features a number of blocks or modules, and some of them receive feedback from others. After we have received market data, we should clean it up and add storage and retrieval facilities, as pieces of data may be reused in the following code. Then, we generate trading signals according to the strategy logic. But before sending these signals to the market in the form of orders, we should do some checks to make sure that the order size is comfortable for both the strategy and the market. After that, we actually trade – send orders to the market controlling their execution. And finally, we track the open positions and manage exposure according to the running profit or loss.

Summary

In this chapter, we familiarized ourselves with the core terminology and key concepts of FX markets, learned about counterparties and transactions, understood the intrinsic issues with market data, reviewed various risks, and drafted the first mockup of a trading application's architecture. We now know that a robust trading app is more about risk management, checking various situations that may happen in real life before and after the trade, and making corrections on the fly. This is what makes the development of trading apps different.

In the next chapter, let us see how using Python in algo trading helps improve the research and development of trading applications.

2

Using Python for Trading Strategies

Python has gained a reputation as the language of choice for the development of a wide range of applications in the financial industry and has become a de facto industry standard for the research phase of trading strategy development. However, as with any other language or, better put, programming ecosystem, it has its advantages and disadvantages. So, as with any tool, it is essential to understand its strong and weak points to use the tool properly (not trying to hammer nails with a microscope, so to say).

In this chapter, not only will we consider using Python for algorithmic trading strategy development but we will also learn about the essential steps in the research and development process, discuss the difference between market modeling and event-based trading, and point to the mistakes most typically made in the research and development process. Finally, we will see the limitations of using Python for algo trading so our expectations always meet reality.

We will quickly dive a bit deeper than just a surface overview to see how the strongest advantages of Python, such as native language structures and efficient **object-oriented programming** (OOP), help make the code transparent and keep the architecture of a trading app modular, flexible, and scalable.

By the end of this chapter, you will be familiar with the key concepts of trading and algo trading, applications of Python, and various **integrated development environments** (IDEs) for the research and development of trading strategies, and you will know the limits beyond which using Python is not efficient.

In this chapter, we will cover the following topics:

- The advantages of using Python in trading strategy development
- Modeling – forecasting the future doesn't necessarily mean practical benefits
- Paper trading and backtesting – an essential part of a systemic trader's risk management

- The disadvantages of using Python in trading strategy development
- Live trading – where Python faces its limits

Technical requirements

You will need Python 3.10 or higher to run the code in this chapter.

The advantages of using Python in trading strategy development

Today when we say *Python*, we most likely mean not only the most flexible object-oriented programming language but also the most powerful and convenient interactive IDEs, such as Spyder or PyCharm, along with the vast collection of libraries that extend this language to fit virtually any domain of applied and fundamental research, from medicine to astronomy. There is no surprise that the Python ecosystem has become the de facto standard in the financial industry where numbers play a decisive role.

The advantages of using Python for the development of trading strategies are obvious and we will look into a few of these advantages in detail in the following sections.

Memory management

Python is one of the few interpreters that has robust built-in memory management services such as garbage collection and reference counting. Essentially, this means that you don't have to care about any complex object you work with and the amount of data processed by your code. Of course, this dramatically increases the development speed, especially if you work with large datasets – and trading applications work with large datasets.

Interactive computing

Python is an interpreted language and this means two important things.

First, you can stop executing the code at any moment and check the environment at runtime, including all variables, functions, and objects – which is convenient for debugging.

Second, you can work with Python interactively. This means that in all Unix-like systems, we run Python in a console where we can send commands one by one and immediately get responses from the interpreter. If you develop trading applications, this allows you to quickly test some modules on small datasets before integrating them into the final code. It also allows you to quickly visualize any portion of a data set on the fly without rewriting and rerunning any code, which is invaluable for developing any applications that work with time series.

Working in a native console is not as convenient as in IPython – a command shell that supports introspection, rich media, syntax highlighting, tab completion, and history. Released in 2001 as an open source project, IPython quickly transformed Python into a direct competitor to Matlab, and thanks to the open source status and enormous community of contributors we can say that today, Python has won the competition. In 2014, a spin-off project based on IPython started with the idea of developing a universal interactive computing environment suitable not only for Python but also for other languages. This project was called Jupyter and today this is probably the most popular notebook-style interactive computing environment. Sometimes Jupyter is even considered a replacement for IPython; however, this is not really correct. DataCamp published an excellent article that explains the difference: `https://www.datacamp.com/blog/ipython-or-jupyter`.

Ease of integration and routing

If the previous two advantages are not specific to the development of trading applications, then what makes Python the preferred language for both trading research and development is the ease with which you can switch between *research mode* and *production mode*.

If you have carefully planned your data structures and codes (and this is what we will be learning to do throughout this book), then all essential modules of the trading app (which we drafted in the previous chapter) will be independent and replaceable. What advantage does this give you as a developer? The advantages are as follows:

- It allows you to develop the trading logic using historical data and then replace the data source with a live stream from the broker.

- It allows you to fine-tune and debug your application by simulating order execution and letting you switch to production using the same code you used for development. This reduces the risk of errors.

- It allows you to scale your trading business by adding more execution venues, protocols, APIs, and trading accounts, keeping the rest of the code the same.

Besides that, thanks to the interactivity of the Python environment, you can even intervene in the trading process manually. For example, you can send a `FIX` message to close all open positions in case of an emergency. Of course, this is *not* the best practice, or even something that can be recommended, but knowing that even in the worst unexpected scenario you can take urgent action straight from the familiar development environment adds to peace of mind.

Native language structures – lists and dictionaries

One of the key advantages of using Python for data processing is that it natively implements two powerful structures: lists and dictionaries.

Trading applications work with time series, and having convenient tools to read, access, compress, and process this data is crucial. Using lists and dictionaries along with objects becomes quite efficient. Let's consider an example.

Imagine we have tick data and want to transform it into OHLC data points (see the previous chapter for an explanation of OHLC). We can define such a data point, which in trading is normally called a *bar*, as follows:

```
class OHLC:
        def __init__(self, O, H, L, C):
                self.open = O
                self.high = H
                self.low = L
                self.close = C
```

Then, we can create storage for our bars:

```
class time_series:
        def __init__(self):
                self.ts = []
                self.last = -1
        def add(self, bar):
                self.ts.append(bar)
        def read(self):
                self.last += 1
                return self.ts[self.last]
```

Here, we can define a native Python list where we store OHLC bars and the `self.last` pointer, which points to the last element that was read from the list. Then, we will add the `read` method, which returns the element to which the `self.last` pointer points.

Then, instead of retrieving OHLC bars by index in the production code as follows:

```
data = time_series()
i = some_index
price = data.ts[i].close
```

We will retrieve closing prices without direct reference to the index:

```
data = time_series()
price = data.read().close
```

This streamlines working with time series (or any data series) dramatically as we no longer need to store indices in the main code and even more importantly – we reduce the risk of *peeking ahead*. Peek ahead is a common error in trading strategy development. While doing backtests, the strategy code must use only past and current price data for each emulated trade. For example, if the strategy emulates the market on April 1st, it should not refer to price data from April 2nd. The same is applied to any time resolution, down to milliseconds. Strategies that use future data in the research phase, normally, are unable to work in real life (see *Chapter 5, Retrieving and Handling Market Data with Python,* for a detailed discussion on proper data handling when performing backtests). It is impossible to overvalue the convenience with which Python allows you to avoid critical errors such as this, as these errors may cost real and substantial money.

Dictionaries offer another way to store and process series data in Python. As each data point, be it a tick or a bar, has a timestamp, we can use timestamps as keys in a dictionary:

```
class OHLC:
        def __init__(self, dt, O, H, L, C):
                self.datetime = dt
                self.open = O
                self.high = H
                self.low = L
                self.close = C
class time_series:
        def __init__(self):
                self.ts = {}
        def add(self, bar):
                self.ts[bar.datetime] = bar
```

Then, retrieving a particular `close` price by its `timestamp` value will be simple with the following code:

```
price = data.ts[timestamp].close
```

So, even native Python language structures offer a quick, simple, and extremely efficient way to handle data specific to trading. However, it is libraries that make Python the definite choice for quantitative trading.

Libraries

The ultimate success of Python as the environment for quantitative finance and trading is determined by a number of libraries, which today are de facto industry standards and sometimes are so tightly associated with the language itself that many developers do not think about them separately. Let us look into some of these libraries.

NumPy

Originally released in 1995 as Numeric Python, this library is used today in virtually any application that uses mathematics. It was the very library that transformed Python from just a programming language into a Matlab-like, powerful, number-crunching suite.

NumPy offers implementations for a number of core objects from linear algebra such as vectors, arrays, and operations with them. It offers comprehensive mathematical functions, random number generators, Fourier transforms, and more. Best of all – its core is written in C, so all native numpy methods work blazingly fast.

Matplotlib

Matplotlib was released in 2003 as the universal plotting library for Python and NumPy. It recognizes native NumPy objects and produces print-quality images of almost any type of chart used in mathematics.

What makes Matplotlib especially attractive for trading app development are the following features:

- It automatically scales data series to fit the chart, so it's extremely easy to visualize any market or trading data with a single command

- The charts are embeddable and can be output in consoles such as IPython or Jupyter

- The charts are interactive, so you can zoom in, zoom out, and drag to explore details without needing to write your own image-handling tools

pandas

It is believed that the name **pandas** is derived from **panel data**, a term used in econometrics. It can also be understood as **Python Analysis of Data**. This is a library that introduces the concept of DataFrames. You can think about a DataFrame as a hybrid of a Python dictionary, list, and database. It uses keywords to access records but preserves the order of items so data can be retrieved by indexing. At the same time, it features routines typical for databases, such as making subsets or slices.

On top of DataFrames, pandas offers tools to read and write data between in-memory structures and different file formats, including CSV, JSON, SQL queries and tables, and MS Excel, which covers virtually all formats used today by data vendors, brokers, and exchanges.

If we also take into consideration the fact that pandas offers a variety of powerful functions that can rebuild missing data, generate datetime ranges, convert sampling frequencies, support sliding window statistics, and many more – you understand that you get the ultimate toolbox for developing any kind of trading application.

While covering pandas in all its powerful aspects is well beyond the scope of this book, we will consider a few useful applications of pandas in *Chapter 8, Data Visualization in FX Trading with Python*.

NumPy and matplotlib are parts of SciPy – a comprehensive library for any applied mathematics, from optimization and linear algebra to signal processing and multidimensional image processing.

Modeling – forecasting the future doesn't necessarily mean practical benefits

In order to keep the discussion consistent, we need to draw a thin but solid line between trading and modeling. Sometimes, these two terms are seriously confused and may lead not only to misunderstanding but also to losing money.

Modeling is a research activity that aims at building a model that explains the observed data. For example, Ptolemy developed a geocentric model of the Solar System, whereas Nicolaus Copernicus suggested a model of the Earth spinning around its own axis and traveling around the Sun on an elliptical orbit – now known as the heliocentric model. Both models explain the observed data: that the Sun visually moves around the Earth, that day follows night, and that seasons change in order. However, the heliocentric model proved to be far more precise and easy to use, so the other one was abandoned.

In the financial world, modeling a market means finding a set of quantitative rules that explain the observed price behavior. At first glance, it looks like modeling any other physical process, for example, the same solar motion. The main problem with financial modeling, especially in trading, is that the modeled process is non-stationary.

In very simple terms, a **non-stationary process** doesn't have a constant mean value or consistent distribution of values across time. This is the very reason for the eventual failure of any attempt to use classical statistics, from averages to Gaussian distribution, to calculate fair prices or predict anything in the future. This is the very reason why many modern approaches that involve elements of machine learning, especially based on linear regression, also fail in practical trading.

If you are interested in learning more about non-stationary processes, including what they are and what makes successful statistics-based trading so problematic, then I'd recommend starting with a basic article from Investopedia: https://www.investopedia.com/articles/trading/07/stationary.asp. Or, if you are more advanced in mathematics, there is an excellent book by M. B. Priestley, *Non-linear and Non-stationary Time Series Analysis*.

Back to the point – modeling non-stationary data is not only problematic but also often provides practically useless results. In the case of a stationary process, such as the Earth going around the Sun, we can use our model to predict the future – and will be correct in the absolute majority of cases. But with a non-stationary process, most models will perfectly explain past data, data that had already been observed, but will have problems forecasting future observations. So, in my opinion, the realm of market modeling is academic research, and using it for practical active trading is questionable. I know that there are opposite opinions, but nevertheless, in this book, we will focus only on event-driven trading.

The difference in approaches is that with market modeling, we try to predict future price movements and then follow the forecast to make trading decisions while in event-driven trading, we wait for a certain event to happen and then react immediately by placing an order. For example, if we run an arbitrage strategy, then we wait for the (rare) moment when the asset is mispriced. If we run a directional trading strategy, we wait for a moment when certain economic news is released or prices start to change rapidly, or vice versa – when the market is slow, but anyway – the strategy reacts to what is going on in the market *right now*, without *predicting* or *forecasting* anything.

scikit-learn

Nevertheless, some of the inventory traditionally used in market modeling, especially machine learning, can be quite useful in event-driven trading strategies as part of data pre-processing. Therefore, we should mention at least one more Python library that is another de facto industry standard for data science.

scikit-learn or **sklearn** is a library with implementations of the most popular techniques used in data science and machine learning. It includes easy-to-use implementations of classification, regression, clustering, and preprocessing along with model selection algorithms (cross-validation, grid search, and more). Having such a robust library also adds to the choice of Python as the preferred ecosystem for the development of trading strategies.

Now that we have familiarized ourselves with the diversity of powerful features offered by Python and numerous libraries, it's time to dig a bit deeper into the process of research and development that is typical for any kind of algo trading strategy.

Paper trading and backtesting – an essential part of a systemic trader's risk management

Imagine that we have used all the power of Python and developed a trading application. Now what? Is it time to immediately launch it and try earning some money? No! Before jumping in the pool, it's essential to make sure there's water in it, and in our case before putting the app into production, it's essential that it can make money, at least in theory.

In this section, we'll consider paper trading and backtesting – two cornerstones of systematic trading that help us understand potential pitfalls with the newly developed strategy. We will learn about historical data, trade simulation, and ordering, and we'll also quickly consider some ready-made packages that simplify this part of the development.

What are paper trading and backtesting?

After we have developed a trading algorithm, connected to the data source, and are ready to send orders, it's time to test our setup. Such a test validates the following crucial points:

- The consistency of the trading logic
- Risk management
- Ordering interface and handling errors

If a test is performed using past market data (mostly referred to as **historical data**) with orders sent to a simulation engine, then it is called **backtesting**. If the test is performed using live market data with orders sent to the UAT environment (provided by the broker, trading venue, or again emulated locally), then it is called **paper trading**.

The purpose of backtesting is to see how our strategy would have reacted to various market situations in the past. This is absolutely essential because all systematic trading is built around the idea that if a certain situation happened in the past, then most likely it will repeat in the future. For example, if the non-farm payroll is way lower than expectations, stock prices go down for some time. This is confirmed by many years of historical data. So, we may assume that next time it is too low, stock prices will go down again.

Paper trading is essential because this is the only test that may prove that the strategy is able to practically make money, not only in theory. Remember our discussion regarding modeling and forecasting in the previous sections? It is possible (and not really difficult) to build a model that perfectly trades in the past but is helpless in production. So, any trading app requires a certain period of paper trading to check whether it can make money in real life.

Backtesting and paper trading in Python

Python itself is very convenient for backtesting and paper trading because of its capabilities for interactive computing and ready-made libraries for data handling and visualization. We can write an order execution simulator and collect cumulative data about returns from our trades in a dataset – this will take some time and effort, but is then so easy to analyze: from statistical methods to visual representation, which is most widely known as **equity curve**. All this can be done interactively by issuing a single command in the console.

In this book, we will focus on the architecture of trading applications and, therefore, mostly consider solutions based on native Python structures as our goal is to understand all stages of developing a trading app going down to the core logical structures. However, as is the case with data handling, there are open source and free libraries and frameworks that facilitate backtesting in Python, making it even more attractive for the development of trading strategies. A detailed review or tutorial on any of these products is beyond the scope of this book but you will be able to easily incorporate any of them into your workflow once you understand the research and development process.

PyAlgoTrade

PyAlgoTrade is a framework with which you can develop full-featured trading strategies. It is quite a mature product, as it was one of the first in this class, and it is still actively maintained and developed. It follows the modular ideology of designing a trading application. So, you can first develop a strategy, backtest it, then switch the data source to live data, paper-trade, and finally switch the output from emulated order execution to the broker of your choice and trade live. It supports free data sources such as Yahoo! Finance and Google Finance, but if you want to use PyAlgoTrade for forex trading, you will have to obtain data from a third party source, save it in CSV format, and only then use the data with this framework.

It's important to note that PyAlgoTrade supports real-time Twitter event handling, which means that you can use rules based on non-price data for your strategies (such as *"when an ECB member says something, sell the euro"*).

You will find the project page located here: `github.com/gbeced/pyalgotrade`.

bt – backtesting for Python

bt is another framework for backtesting that is more focused on portfolio trading (running many different strategies and trading many different markets in parallel).

This approach brings bt close to various visual constructors of trading strategies that were popular some time ago. Of course, this speeds up the development process dramatically as you don't need to code the algos on a low level; you only select the most appropriate from the inventory. However, this advantage is clearly a shortcoming as well because you are limited to using what the developers of the framework considered suitable.

However, the good news here is that, unlike visual constructors, you can modify anything in bt and write your own *building blocks*, which gives you almost the same freedom as writing your own strategies from scratch.

bt also offers a comprehensive suite of statistical tools to analyze the strategy or portfolio performance and also to quickly try various combinations of trading algorithms to discover the one that works best in the particular market.

This framework is predominantly focused on backtesting and paper trading, so you will need to develop your own order generation and submission module if you plan to trade live from the same application.

You will find the project page located here: `pmorissette.github.io/bt`.

Zipline

Zipline is probably the most well-known research and development tool for trading strategies. It was developed by Quantopian, the famous project that offered any developer an opportunity to become a quantitative trader by providing them with an environment for developing trading strategies. It even allocated some capital to them in case the strategy performance was proven to be acceptable.

Zipline can be used as a framework and as a standalone application, an algorithmic trading constructor and simulator with paper and live trading capabilities. You can interact with it using the browser-based iPython Notebook interface.

Zipline comes with 10 years of 1-minute-resolution historical US stock data. This is not much, and definitely not relevant to forex trading, but it supports importing data in various formats so you can use third-party data, for example, from your broker.

As Zipline was designed as part of Quantopian's ecosystem, its live trading capabilities are limited.

Despite the initial success of Quantopian and quite some hype in the media, in 2020, the company went bankrupt and shut down all operations. Zipline was then sold to Robinhood. But the new owners were not interested in the development of the product as much as its creators, so the project now exists mainly in form of enthusiast-supported forks, the "official" version not being supported any longer.

You will find the project page located here: `zipline.io`.

You will find the GitHub source here: `github.com/quantopian/zipline`.

QSTrader

QSTrader was developed by QuantStart. It is, again, a framework for research and development with live trading capabilities.

This framework strictly follows the modular principle of building trading applications that we already saw in the previous chapter, which is the main focus throughout this book. This helps streamline the general development process – **research | backtesting | paper trading | live trading** – because the code responsible for the strategy logic remains the same.

Currently, QSTrader supports bar-based data but tick data can also be used.

You will find the project page located here: `https://www.quantstart.com/qstrader/`.

You will find the Github source here: `github.com/mhallsmoore/qstrader`.

The disadvantages of using Python in trading strategy development

Having praised the advantages of using Python in algo trading, it's time to mention its important shortcomings. As with many robust and universal ecosystems, these shortcomings are the other side of its advantages.

By any means, the most annoying thing about Python is speed, or, rather, the lack of it. Partly this is pre-determined by the fact that Python is an interpreted language; however, a much greater contribution to the overall slowness is made by weak typing and the same advanced memory management that we love so much when we develop code.

For readers who are not familiar with memory management, I'd recommend starting with a simple article at `https://www.geeksforgeeks.org/memory-management-in-python/`, which also has references for further reading. In brief, if the language relieves the coder of the burden of declaring variables, then every time the variable is referenced, a number of routines are executed to make sure the reference is done correctly. Of course, this slows down the execution of the entire code.

The main part of trading strategy development where insufficient speed of code execution becomes apparent is backtesting. During a backtest, we should process all historical data at a resolution granular enough for the specific strategy, and sometimes, this may be as low as raw tick data. As you may remember, the amount of such data may reach thousands of ticks per second, so just imagine how many times we would repeat the entire strategy logic in a loop processing each tick received in the last year!

But during the research and development phase, this slowness may be just annoying: indeed, no one is happy to wait for minutes, sometimes hours, and, in the worst cases, days to see the theoretical performance of their strategy. However, waiting too long is one thing, and being unable to place trades in production is completely different, and live trading is exactly where Python faces its limits.

Live trading – where Python faces its limits

Thus said, trading applications written in pure Python are not suitable for any live trading activity that assumes the minimization of time from the moment market data is received to the moment an order is sent. Therefore, traditional arbitrage and many high-frequency trading activities (which sometimes suggest sending thousands of orders *per second*) are definitely not for Python.

Besides that, there is another risk even for *slow* trading strategies that derive from automated memory management. We already know that trading strategies rely on price time series and the amount of processed market data may be quite large. Although both native Python and third-party libraries such as pandas offer data structures that ensure data persistence, it may become problematic to update data on the fly, especially in trading environments with high throughputs.

There are different ways to speed up Python to some extent. There are static compilers such as Cython (`https://cython.org`), which help execute the Python code faster and write C extensions for Python as well. There are runtime translators such as Numba (`https://numba.pydata.org`), which also help execute Python code at speeds comparable to C. It also helps to use `numpy` structures instead of pandas because, at the cost of reduced convenience in some aspects, we have a gain in speed. However, in this book, we won't really focus on this problem because we start with less latency-critical, more simplistic strategies that help us to understand the development of trading apps in general.

To summarize, we can say that the Python ecosystem is an excellent tool for the research and development of trading strategies of any kind. It can also be used for live automated trading if the trading strategy meets the following two criteria:

- It doesn't require large amounts of market data to be received in real time
- It is not sensitive to internal latency (a delay between data reception and order submission)

In this book, we will mostly focus on using Python for research, development, and simulated trading.

Summary

In this chapter, we considered the pros and cons of using Python for algorithmic trading strategy research and development. We considered various options for using native Python data structures to handle market data. We learned about the various ecosystems, third-party libraries, and environments that speed up the development process. We also learned about the most important phases of development and the essential procedures that aim to make sure that the strategy has the potential to make money in live markets.

However, as with any project in any domain, before we can proceed to actual coding, we should get acquainted with the subject. In our case, it is the market itself, its basic elements, structure, and the organization that we will consider in order to see how it operates and what we should take into account to build robust trading applications. This is what we are going to do in the very next chapter.

3

FX Market Overview from a Developer's Standpoint

The FX market has long been very attractive for developers, mostly because there's a lot of free stuff associated with this market, such as market data, trading software, and various third-party solutions. However, the quality of freely available solutions is frequently so low that it's in fact not possible to use them for any serious trading.

The main problem with trading in the FX markets is their strong fragmentation. Historically, FX was an interbank market with no dedicated center. So, trading venues offer not only different trading platforms but also different market data, different types of orders, and different access to liquidity. This fragmentation may be quite confusing, so it's essential to obtain a sufficient level of understanding in order to avoid making mistakes, which at times can be quite painful.

In this chapter, we will look at this market from a developer's standpoint to discover some important – and overlooked – features that may be critical for the overall success of any project in FX algo trading. We will start with the organization of this market and see the obstacles it creates for the developer. We will learn about the essential types of market participants, why the price moves at all, and whether a particular movement is something we can make money with. We will also consider various ways to access this market, their pros and cons for various practical trading applications, and estimate how expensive it may be.

All this knowledge is absolutely essential for sustained success in FX algo trading. This market is one of the most rapidly changing markets. Without understanding how these changes may affect the performance of your trading strategies, it will be difficult to survive this market from a long-term perspective. In this chapter, we will cover the following topics:

- Trading venues – where money meets… other money
- Trade mechanics – again, some terminology
- Market makers – comfortable, sophisticated, expensive

- Liquidity providers – the whales that support this planet

- ECN – looks like a fair game, but is it?

- Aggregation – in search of the best price

- Trading the FX market – what and how

- Why do I need all this?

Trading venues – where money meets... other money

First, let me note that despite the overall colloquial language used in this book, I am always trying to stick to the traditional academic approach that follows the same paradigm: definition | logical conclusions | theory | experiment | proof. Without proper definitions, especially when we talk about the foundation of the subject domain, we won't be able to make logical conclusions, suggest a theory, or test and finally prove a theory – which in our case, means making money. In even simpler words, without a full understanding of the subject, we are unable to suggest appropriate methods to use it.

So, as we mentioned in *Chapter 1*, financial markets facilitate buying and selling assets at special marketplaces called **trading venues**. A bit too vague to be useful, right? Well, let's go into specifics.

Organizing chaos – types of trading venues

A trading venue in the financial world is a place where buyers meet sellers – both physically and electronically. There are different kinds of trading venues, each having its advantages and disadvantages and requiring a special approach to trade.

A formal classification of today's trading venues is based on a number of criteria including the regulatory environment, types of market participants, methods of dissemination of market information among them, and many, many more. Therefore, such a classification is very complex and definitely lies way beyond the scope of this book.

The good news is that not all of these criteria are important for us as developers of buy-side trading applications. We will try to suggest a few informal criteria looking at this subject domain with the eyes of a developer.

From the structural standpoint, the key difference between trading venues is the way the market price is determined. To better understand it, let's again consider our example of a farmer's market.

Auction (open outcry)

Buyers and farmers stand in a crowd, crying out loudly about quantities they would like to buy or sell along with their prices. As soon as two parties find each other, a contract is made.

This is exactly how trading had been performed for many centuries and even thousands of years. In the financial world, such a marketplace is called an **exchange**, and the market square where buyers and sellers squawk their prices is called a **pit**. Although this method looks fair, it has one global intrinsic limitation: the marketplace cannot physically accommodate all those willing to trade. So, traders soon became elite with unlimited access to liquidity and began acting on behalf of others for a commission. Of course, such a privileged position asked for misbehavior and many traders could not resist the temptation to trade against their clients, thus doubling their profits – which in turn caused changes in regulations and severe punishments. Although very interesting, this is another story.

Pit trading in its natural form has almost died out completely in the last 15 years. Electronic trading made access to markets far more democratic and available to virtually anyone (with important limitations and restrictions – as always), so pit traders are no longer needed.

Nevertheless, the *structure* of such a market, where *price discovery* is performed by direct communication between multiple parties in an *auction*, is still very popular. Modern trading venues operate electronically but use the same paradigm.

We can see that there are two ways a buy-side order can be placed in such a market. We can just cry out, *"I buy!"* or *"I sell!"* and such an order will be executed at whatever price comes first. Such an order is called a **market order** (see *Chapter 10, Types of Orders and Their Simulation in Python*) and if a market order is sent to the market, we say that we buy or sell **at market**.

Alternatively, we can cry, *"I buy at $100 or cheaper!"* or *"I sell at $200 or higher!"* and then such an order will be executed only when there's a seller or a buyer for such an order respectively. Such an order is called a **limit order** (again, see *Chapter 10, Types of Orders and Their Simulation in Python*, for details), and sending such an order to the market is called buying or selling **at a certain price**.

> **Note**
> Although a limit order helps limit the price (to avoid buying too high or selling too low), it is not guaranteed that such an order will be executed at all: there may be no buyers who would like to buy from you or no sellers to sell to you at your desired price.

As with any auction, the price of the traded asset can jump or fall very quickly. Thus, for us as algo trading developers, it's important to remember that in such a market it would be a good idea to follow some useful guidelines:

- Never buy at market without checking the supply first. Such an action would mean *"I am ready to buy this at whatever price will be"* and you will be filled at the worst possible price.

- Never sell at market at all. Always specify the price you're ready to sell at. It is essential to send your sell orders in advance, posting the price you're ready to sell.

Exchange and order book

Buyers and farmers arrive at the market, but do not enter it. Instead, they are welcomed by an officer who records their bids (orders to buy) and offers (orders to sell) in a book. If a new buyer comes in with a bid at $10 but there is already another order at $10 in the officer's book, then this newcomer's order is placed in the queue and will be filled only after the previous order has been executed.

Similarly, farmers do not show off their goods on shelves; instead, the same officer records their offers (the prices at which they would like to sell goods). Similar to buyers, if a new farmer comes in with an offer to sell at $11 and there is already another farmer willing to sell at $11, then the newcomer's order is recorded in the book after the already existing order and will be executed only after the preceding order has been filled.

As long as buyers come in with prices lower than offered and farmers do not want to sell at a lower price, no contract is made and no trade happens.

So, in such a market, the only way for a trade to happen is as follows:

- A buyer agrees to buy at a higher price
- A farmer agrees to sell at a lower price

Although it looks a bit awkward from a common sense standpoint, such an organization of the market has a clear advantage: all buyers and sellers are served on a **first in – first out** (**FIFO**) basis and have equal opportunities.

The marketplace which works this way is also called an exchange and the officer who registers bids and asks is today replaced by computers and is normally called **matching engine**. The book into which bids and offers are recorded is called the **order book**. The information about orders in the book is called **depth of market** or **DOM**.

> **Note**
> Open outcry and order book trading can co-exist at the same exchange and for the same market. For example, stock trading sessions start with an opening auction and then continue with trading through the order book.

The difference between the highest bid and the lowest offer price is called the **spread**. When someone concludes a deal, it is called **crossing the spread**.

From a programmer's standpoint, we have a two-dimensional structure where the price is along the vertical axis and orders are along the horizontal one. As new orders come in, they are sent to the respective FIFO queue on each price level and are called **limit orders**. *Figure 3.1* presents a schematic view of such a structure, where each block in a horizontal lane means the number of contracts sent to the order book as the limit order size:

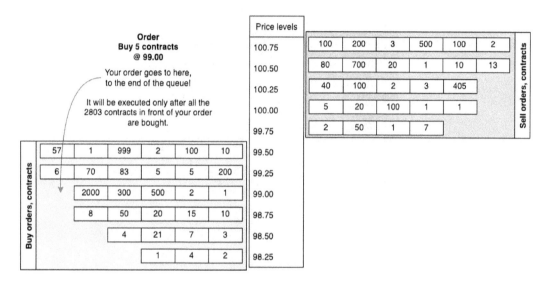

Figure 3.1 – The two-dimensional nature of the order book

> **Important note**
> If you send an order and there are 10 more orders already in the book, your order is going to be filled only after all 10 preceding orders have been filled.

This is why *a lot* of trading strategies that use limit orders work well only *on paper*, that is, they rely on guaranteed execution of all generated orders, while in reality only 40-50% of these orders are indeed executed. We will look into this and other problems in detail in *Chapter 10, Types of Orders and Their Simulation in Python. Figure 3.2* shows a typical DOM for one of the exchange-traded assets:

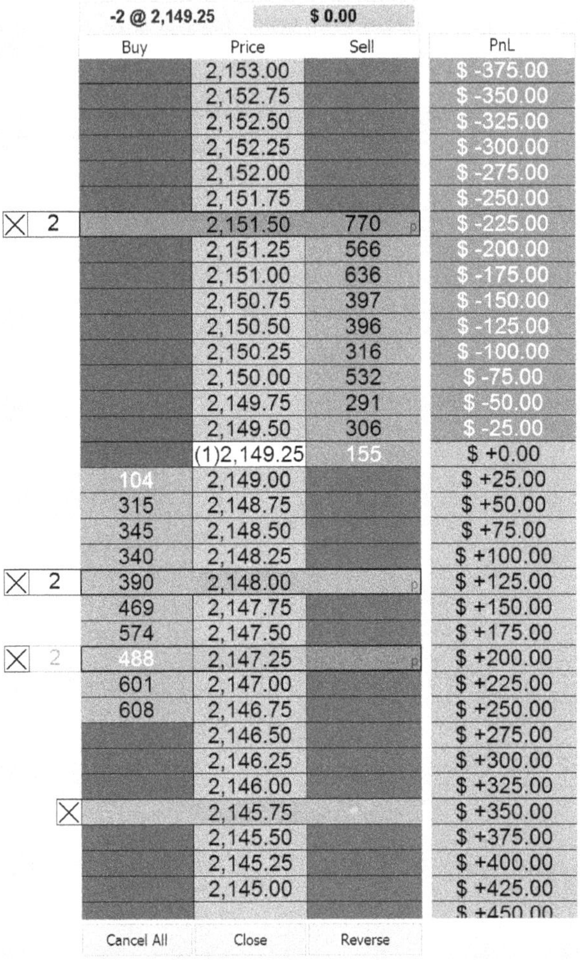

-2 @ 2,149.25		$ 0.00			
	Buy	Price	Sell		PnL
		2,153.00			$ -375.00
		2,152.75			$ -350.00
		2,152.50			$ -325.00
		2,152.25			$ -300.00
		2,152.00			$ -275.00
		2,151.75			$ -250.00
☒ 2		2,151.50	770		$ -225.00
		2,151.25	566		$ -200.00
		2,151.00	636		$ -175.00
		2,150.75	397		$ -150.00
		2,150.50	396		$ -125.00
		2,150.25	316		$ -100.00
		2,150.00	532		$ -75.00
		2,149.75	291		$ -50.00
		2,149.50	306		$ -25.00
		(1)2,149.25	155		$ +0.00
	104	2,149.00			$ +25.00
	315	2,148.75			$ +50.00
	345	2,148.50			$ +75.00
	340	2,148.25			$ +100.00
☒ 2	390	2,148.00			$ +125.00
	469	2,147.75			$ +150.00
	574	2,147.50			$ +175.00
☒ 2	488	2,147.25			$ +200.00
	601	2,147.00			$ +225.00
	608	2,146.75			$ +250.00
		2,146.50			$ +275.00
		2,146.25			$ +300.00
		2,146.00			$ +325.00
☒		2,145.75			$ +350.00
		2,145.50			$ +375.00
		2,145.25			$ +400.00
		2,145.00			$ +425.00
					$ +450.00
	Cancel All	Close	Reverse		

Figure 3.2 – DOM screen shows consolidated liquidity on each
price level (level 2 data) – source: MultiCharts

This window shows the consolidated liquidity instead of individual orders: the sizes of all orders for a particular price level are summed and the sum is displayed to the left or to the right of the price axis.

> **Important note**
>
> Level 2 data normally does not contain information about individual orders, so you never know whether 1,000 contracts means a single order from a solid large-volume trader or 1,000 orders by 1 contract sent by retail traders.

Exchanges are de-facto industry standard trading venues for equities (stocks, exchange-traded funds, and so on), commodities, and some derivatives. In the FX world, mostly derivatives, such as currency futures, are traded at exchanges. Most of the cash, swaps, and forward contracts are traded **over the counter (OTC)**.

OTC markets

Farmers arrive at the market but do not reveal their goods at all. Buyers walk between them and ask for the price. The farmer looks at the buyer and decides what price to offer based on the buyer's appearance.

This scenario may sound truly ridiculous, but it gives a very good first impression of how an OTC market works.

As we saw previously, in the case of an exchange-traded market, all market participants at any moment know the *three key prices*:

- Best bid

- Best ask

- Last trade

These prices are identical for everyone and the difference between professional and non-professional market participants is mostly in the latency of the data feed and some data compression (see *Chapter 1, Developing Trading Strategies - Why They Are Different*, for the discussion on market data and related issues). So, in exchange-traded markets, these three prices are commonly called **market price**.

The term *OTC* means in the financial world that the contract can be made at virtually any price as long as this price satisfies the buyer and the seller – regardless of whatever price at which the previous contract was made.

In essence, this renders the very concept of market price meaningless to a considerable extent because not all of these prices are reported and made publicly available. Therefore, in OTC markets there is no such thing as a public quotation (as is the case with exchange-traded markets) but instead, they use *indicative price*, which is an *approximate* representation of the last traded price or a number of last traded prices.

At this point, I think it will be natural for you to ask, *"wow, but who uses these markets and why?"* The answer is very simple and can be found in the structure of the exchange-traded market.

As you hopefully remember from the previous section, any exchange-traded market is based on the order book. The number of orders in the order book forms liquidity in this market.

Now, imagine a situation when a really large market participant (such as a hedge fund, a mutual fund, an investment bank, and so on) comes in with a desire to buy a really large amount of an asset and the amount *exceeds the existing liquidity*. Such an action would swipe the entire order book by moving the last trade price very far from the previous readings in a moment and even worse – leaving one side of the order book totally empty. Of course, this is a scenario that all market participants and the exchange itself would like to avoid.

So, here comes the OTC market. If you are a bank dealer, you can find the best price for your large order over your own network of contacts and do it privately, without too much fanfare about it.

Another important feature of OTC markets is that they are far less regulated than regular, exchange-traded markets. There were attempts to add regulation to these markets, the most remarkable probably being MiFID and MiFID II, but still, OTC markets are far more *relaxed*. If you are interested in learning more about market regulations and how they impact pricing, liquidity, and overall trading, I would recommend starting with `https://tokenist.com/investing/guide-to-forex-regulations-in-the-us/` where the basics are explained. I would also recommend reading this interview with Phil Lloyd, head of trading and sales delivery at NatWest (`https://www.natwest.com/corporates/insights/regulation/regulation-and-market-structure-what-to-look-out-for-in-2021.html`), who provides very interesting insights on global challenges, changes in regulations, and their relationships with the market.

Understanding the structure of OTC markets leads us to a number of very important conclusions.

First, OTC markets are ideal for large-volume trades. If you are a small retail trader then trading at an OTC market would probably be problematic because of the arbitrary pricing – and you can be sure that small traders always get the worst possible execution for their orders.

Second, you cannot really know at which price your order will be executed if you send a market order (an order to buy *right now*, regardless of the price). You won't ever be able to argue about the price at which your trade was made.

> **Note**
>
> As the immediate corollary from the aforementioned, you should always check the actual price at which your order was executed in your code and subtract a certain amount from the theoretical returns of your model while doing tests. This will make the theoretical results at least a tiny bit closer to reality.

The third, and probably the most counterintuitive conclusion is the fact that in an OTC market *there can be multiple different prices for the same financial instrument*. It is normal that each liquidity provider, market maker, bank, fund, and any other market participant in such a market offers their own price for the same product and that these prices co-exist at the very same moment in time.

This market fragmentation can be exploited by **arbitrage strategies**: strategies that look for situations where the same instrument is quoted differently at different trading venues. They make money by simultaneously buying and selling the same instrument at different trading venues in cases where the price difference is sufficient.

> **Note**
>
> Arbitrage strategies can be developed and tested using Python but they cannot actually be run using it because arbitrage opportunities typically last for milliseconds. Production code for arbitrage strategies is normally written in C or C++, or by using Numba or Cython (see *Chapter 2, Using Python for Trading Strategies*).

Fourth, you can never, ever offer your own price in this market – unlike an exchange-traded market, where any order, even one contract received from a retail trader, goes into the *same order book*, which is identical for everyone. You can only accept the price offered by other market participants who have permission to post prices into this market. These market participants are called **liquidity providers** or **market makers** (although it's important to note that these are not synonyms) and they are commonly known as **price givers**, while retail traders (or any other trader who only accepts offered prices) are known as **price takers**.

Finally, the worst news for us, the FX traders, is that about 90% of the FX market is traded OTC. So, we have to live with it and find the right solutions to survive in this quite unfriendly environment.

Liquidity and order limitations

A trading venue in the financial world is not only a place where buyers meet sellers but they also trade under the supervision of the venue's management. Thus, a traditional farmers' market is not a financial trading venue in this regard, whereas a stock exchange definitely is. The key difference is that trading at a trading venue is always supervised or moderated. For example, if someone comes into a grocery market and offers to buy whatever produce the sellers have at the moment, most likely, the farmers will sell the produce and the market will close till next Sunday. If anything similar happens in the financial world, it would be a real disaster. So, the trading venue always moderates incoming orders, and if the requested trading size is too big, the order will be rejected (or, to be more precise, considered a **block order** and treated in a special way – see *Chapter 10, Types of Orders and Their Simulation in Python*).

Another possible issue with order execution is *partial fill*. This happens when the liquidity in the order book is not sufficient to fill the entire order, so only part of the order is filled. Normally, you can explicitly specify the order type which decides whether the order is to be rejected or partially filled if the liquidity is not sufficient. In either case, you have to add an order execution control module to your trading application that handles, rejects, and partially fills orders.

Getting your order filled at a non-desired price is probably the last thing you may want to happen, and still, it is quite possible if you use market orders (remember, a market order means *"I want to buy/sell now, regardless of the price"*). Now, you understand the reasons why an order may be filled at an *unexpected* price – those same liquidity issues. So, in production, it is reasonable to consider using limit orders instead of market orders even if the strategy assumes buying and selling at market.

Ordering will be discussed in detail in *Chapter 10, Types of Orders and Their Simulation in Python*.

Now that we've got more or less familiar with the most general types of trading venues, it's time we familiarized ourselves with their market participants. This will give us a better understanding of how trades are made and which risks to expect and avoid in the market.

But before we proceed to market participants, let's learn some new terms.

Trade mechanics – again, some terminology

A trade is made when two parties meet and agree to buy or sell from each other. These parties are called **counterparties**.

If I buy 1 million euros for the equivalent in US dollars and the exchange rate is 1.1, then I paid 1.1 million US dollars to have *a position* of 1 million EURUSD. I am going to have this position until I sell back this amount of euros for the equivalent amount of US dollars and, therefore, *liquidate* my position and become *market neutral* again until I open a new position.

If I improve the asking price by sending an offer that is lower than the previous best offer, then I *provide liquidity* to the market.

If I simultaneously improve ask *and* bid, and other traders become counterparties for both, then I *make the market*. Making the market means earning the spread (the difference between bid and offer) while remaining market neutral. The market participant whose main business is making the market is called a **market maker**.

As opposed to making the market or being a *price giver*, traders who take the other side of the trade are *price takers*. Price takers can only buy or sell at the prices offered by price givers, and unlike price givers, price takers *always pay the spread*.

> **Important**
>
> If a price taker opens any position using a market order, the very moment the position is opened, its running profit is already in the negative zone.

This happens because, in most markets, offer prices are always greater than bid prices, and price takers can only buy at the offer price and sell at the bid price. Therefore, if you bought an asset, this means you paid the offer price. If you want to immediately liquidate your position, you can do that only at the bid price. If the market price hasn't changed since the moment you entered the market, you will lose the difference between the bid and ask prices – which is the spread. That's why we say that price takers always pay the spread to price givers, who in turn, earn the spread.

If I buy an asset then I have a *long* position. This term came from stock trading and means that you bought something and now hold it (normally, investors hold shares for a long time). If I sell an asset, and this sale was not liquidation of a previously opened long position, then I have a *short* position. Again, this term has the same origin and means that you sold something without previously having it.

You may wonder how it's possible to sell something that you don't own. Well, in financial markets it's really easy. If we talk about equities trading then most brokers have an *inventory* of equities and traders can borrow from this inventory to sell. If the price of the asset sold this way goes down further, then the trader liquidates the position, returns the asset to the broker, and pockets some profit. If the price of the asset goes up then… well, the trader liquidates the position anyway, returns the asset to the broker, and pays the difference – which means pocketing a loss this time.

If I have a position, then my profit (or loss) is calculated as the difference between the price at which the position is liquidated and the price at which I bought it. If I opened a long position and the liquidation price is greater than the opening price then I made a profit; if it is lower then I suffer a loss. Symmetrically, for short positions: if the liquidation price is lower than the opening price then I made a profit, and vice versa.

As long as I have an open position, my *potential* profit or loss can be recalculated at any moment, even if the position is not liquidated yet. This potential profit or loss is called **running profit or loss** (**running PnL** or **P/L**).

To be able to send orders to the market, I either have to be a member of an exchange with direct access to the order book (which is quite expensive) or use the services of a third party that takes my orders and brings them to the market. Such a third party is called a **broker**.

> **Important note**
> There is a lot of confusion between brokers and market makers in FX trading. Read the following sections carefully as we are going to clarify this confusion once and for all.

If I have $100 and the rate of the euro versus the US dollar is 1.1, then I can buy approximately €91. But if the broker provides me with a **credit line**, then I can buy from €3,000 to €9,000, or even more with just my $100. This credit line is called a **margin** and the ratio of how much I could buy without a margin to how much I can buy with a margin is called the **leverage**. Normally, the leverage in the FX market is up to 30:1 for non-professionals and 100:1 for professional traders.

If I opened a position on a margin and the market price moved against me to the extent that I have nothing in my trading account, then I would have entered a situation called a **margin call**. Historically, this meant that the broker would call the client asking to add funds to the account to maintain the position. Such a practice is difficult to find today, at least among retail brokers. Today, brokers prefer to just force close the positions that drive the client's account into the negative zone because otherwise, it may cause problems not only for the client but also for the broker.

If I open a position on margin then the size of my position is called the **notional amount**. This means that I don't actually possess €9,000 if I opened a long position in EURUSD with the $100 in my account and a leverage of 100:1. I have a notional position of €9,000, which I would have to liquidate before any *real* money condenses in (or thaws from) the trading account.

If I buy an asset directly, then it is an **outright** asset. If I buy a financial instrument that gives me the right or obliges me to buy or sell the asset in the future, then it is a **derivative** asset. In fact, derivatives can be much more sophisticated than this but they are mostly available to only professional market participants. A discussion on derivatives is way beyond the scope of this book.

If I buy an *obligation to buy or sell the asset in the future at a certain price on a certain date,* then I am buying a **future contract**, or simply a **future**. The date is called an **expiration date** or simply an **expiration**. For example, the current price of the asset is $10 but I may buy a future that guarantees that its seller will sell me the same asset at $9 in a month, a quarter, or any other time span. Then, this month, quarter, or other time span is the expiration term of this future contract. In the case that the price of the asset itself is greater than $9 by its expiration, then I make money: the seller of the future is obliged to sell me the asset at $9 and I can immediately resell it at a higher price. If the price of the asset by the expiration is lower than $9, then I lost money as I now have the obligation to buy the asset at $9 anyway and I can do whatever I want with it (most likely sell and take a loss).

If I buy the *right to buy or sell the asset in the future at a certain price*, then I am buying an **option**. Options trading is quite a complex subject and is not considered in this book.

That is enough on terminology. Now that we know all we need to learn about the key market participants, we need to know what they do and how we can actually participate in this market as well.

Market makers – comfortable, sophisticated, expensive

The term *market makers* actually has two different meanings, although they lie quite close to each other.

In cases where both buyers and sellers need to meet each other at a single *marketplace* – which is an exchange in most cases, as we saw earlier – such a market is called a **two-sided market**. In two-sided markets, market makers provide liquidity to the market and this activity will be considered in the *Liquidity providers – the whales that support this planet* section.

In OTC markets, the situation is different. In these markets, only dedicated market participants can publish their bids or offers, and in some cases, they are not published at all. So, finding a counterparty for your trade could potentially be even more complex than in a two-sided market, and given that the quoting is not public, you can get your orders executed at really surprising prices (and of course, it's not going to be a pleasant surprise).

So, at this point, enter the market makers. In OTC markets, market makers act both as liquidity providers and counterparties for their own clients.

What does this mean?

Counterparties that provide liquidity

If you come to an exchange, then your orders are visible to all other market participants and anyone can take the other side of the order. Say, you want to buy just one contract of a currency future – then you can actually buy it from a retail trader and from a large bank (but, most likely, you will never know who was the seller). But if you trade with a market maker, then it is this very market maker – and no one else – who will be the counterparty for all your orders. Only this market maker will always buy from you and sell to you.

It means that a market maker is a professional market participant who *quotes the market for their clients*. These quotes are different for different clients and mostly depend on the trading volume of the client and their order size.

How do market makers make money?

Market makers are rewarded by earning the *spread* (the difference between the bid and the ask), and in this regard, their business is very similar to that of a liquidity provider. Market makers always sell at a price that is greater than the price at which they are ready to buy. So in cases where there are multiple clients with this market marker that generate a constant **order flow** (stream of orders to buy and sell at virtually the same time), then our market maker buys and sells simultaneously, pocketing the difference between bids and asks.

As you can see, the source of profits for market makers is quite different from that of their clients. Market makers as *price givers* (see the *OTC markets* section) remain *market neutral,* while their clients open and close *positions* in the market due to situations when the clients have bought something but haven't sold it yet.

However, the market maker from which I bought and then sold my position to has remained market neutral while I had a position because they have multiple clients and, most likely, at the very same moment when I was buying 1 million EURUSD from the market maker, another client was selling 1 million EURUSD to them. So, the market maker earned the spread and I and another unknown trader went away with two positions: I had a long position and the unknown trader had a short position.

It looks like a free lunch (for market makers, of course) and an unfair advantage (again, for market makers), but in reality, this is just another risky business – as everything in the world of trading is. Imagine a situation where someone bought from a market maker, but no one sold. Now, imagine that this happens once and then happens very quickly again. Such a scenario can easily develop when most traders think the price is going to move in a certain direction and they begin buying or selling massively. For the market maker, it means that they no longer earn the spread. Even worse, in such a situation, the market maker holds an open position in the market – instead of being market neutral – and becomes a trader with their PnL now depending on the price movement! Moreover, this position immediately creates a floating loss for the market maker (floating means that the position is not liquidated yet, so the loss may decrease or further increase with each new tick). Of course, market makers don't like having positions and, therefore, they protect themselves.

Market risk and how market makers mitigate it

There are two essential options for a market maker to mitigate their market risks.

First, market makers can hedge their net position elsewhere. To better understand it, let's consider an example.

On average, during the so-called normal market hours, the amount of open long and short positions is more or less the same. As we already know, there's not much publicly available data from OTC markets in general and the FX market in particular, but even from public sources, we can see that this statement is very close to reality. For example, FXSSI has nice tools which visualize traders' sentiment, the ratios of open long and short positions, and snapshots of the depth of the market. You can find these tools at `https://fxssi.com/tools/` and can check them out yourself. Pay particular attention to the open position ratios (`https://fxssi.com/tools/ratios`). These charts report positions from a number of trading venues and it is clearly seen that the larger the client base of a trading venue, the more linear the chart of the ratio of the open positions. This essentially means that the ratio doesn't change significantly over time and that newly opened long positions are in balance with newly opened short ones.

If we sum up all long positions and subtract from this the amount of all short positions currently opened with this market maker, then we get the so-called **net position** of this market maker. Under normal market conditions, and given the market maker has a sufficient number of clients, this net position is always close to zero.

If there's panic in the market, or if due to whatever reason most traders begin to open more long positions than short (or vice versa), or just a single but very large trader opens a very large position, then the market maker's net position is substantially greater than zero. In this case, the market maker opens another position that equals their own net position, but in the opposite direction. Say the market maker has a client's net position of 1 million long, then the market maker opens a position of 1 million short. In this case, the market maker remains market neutral.

You may wonder how a market maker can open a position themselves. This is possible because OTC markets are very fragmented and there are many large and small market participants who may or may not be directly connected. For example, a market maker can easily access liquidity provided by large banks and, therefore, hedge their net positions there, but their clients, retail traders, are really unlikely to access the same.

The second thing market makers can do to protect themselves is to increase the spread. As you'll remember, in an OTC market, the spread is not determined by all market participants as there's no such thing as a centralized exchange and a single order book. Instead, any price giver can offer their own price, and market makers are no exception. Normally, a market maker has access to better bid and ask prices than what they offer to their clients. In this sense, market makers act as retailers, buying wholesale liquidity at lower prices and re-selling it to retail at higher prices.

Of course, wide spreads are not good for traders in general. However, there are several reasons that we will discuss closer to the end of this section that may make us consider wider spreads as extra costs of trading that we pay to get some benefits.

Now, we have come to the very point that causes a lot of criticism from traders.

The point is that in an OTC market, where price discovery is not uniform and prices of the same asset differ from one trading venue to another, one price giver to another, and especially in weakly regulated OTC markets, it is quite possible for a market maker to play tricks against their own clients.

This behavior (or, rather, misbehavior) was especially widespread in the early 2000s when forex was only becoming more and more popular. A lot of market makers who called themselves *brokers* appeared, offering trading at ridiculous leverage such as 200:1, 500:1, and even 1000:1, promising to *open client positions in real forex* and accepting negligibly small accounts of $100, $10, and even $1. The main source of income for those market makers was not the spread but rather the accounts of their clients because, under such extremely risky conditions, more than 80% of their clients completely lost their money in less than a month.

Obviously, a consistently winning client was a disaster for such a market maker. Any position liquidated with a profit was a direct loss for such a business. Therefore, quite often, market makers of this sort started playing against their own clients by giving them worse quotes and even rejecting their orders without any serious reason. Their only goal was to make trading for a successful trader so uncomfortable that they would prefer to close the account and try their luck elsewhere.

Is this unfair and nasty behavior?

Of course.

Is trading with market makers the only way for retail and institutional traders to trade on the FX market?

No, there are alternatives and we are going to discuss them later in this chapter.

But what is the reason to trade with market makers, then?

Well, there is more than one reason and all of them are quite solid.

Reasons to trade with market makers

First, regulations have improved since the early days of retail FX trading, and today such (mis)behavior is almost not possible for a regulated market maker.

Moreover, regulations require that market makers explicitly call themselves market makers and brokers explicitly call themselves brokers. This puts an end to almost two decades of confusion between the two, which cost the reputations of many fair businesses and the FX market itself, at least in the eyes of retail traders.

Second, regulated market makers are required by regulators to maintain liquidity and quote the market virtually at any moment, even if there's panic in the market. This means that you can open or liquidate a position any time you want and this is quite the opposite of how you can open or close positions at an exchange. Advanced traders can even take advantage of this, placing trades before or after important economical news is released and liquidity quickly evaporates from the market and prices may differ from one trading venue to another very significantly – which opens excellent opportunities for arbitrage trading. We will consider arbitrage in various forms in *Chapter 9, Trading Strategies and their Core Elements*.

To be able to survive even the most disastrous price movements, regulators require that market makers have sufficient capital. The now famous **currency crash** when the Swiss franc appreciated almost twice against the euro in a few minutes in 2015 clearly showed which market makers met the regulatory requirements: they are still in business while others were swept away. If you are interested in learning more about what happened on January 15, 2015, I'd recommend reading this article (`https://fbs.com/analytics/news/5-years-aninversary-of-the-notorious-eurchf-usdchf-crash-7595`) that focuses more on the macro-economical side of the event, or this article (`https://fxssi.com/swiss-franc-15-january-2015`) that looks at the sequence of events from a more technical standpoint.

Third, market makers are excellent for large-volume traders. If you need to fill orders that exceed typical liquidity presently in the order book, you have only two options: to split your order into parts and fill them one by one (without any guarantee that the price remains the same during the process) or ask your market maker for a quote and fill the entire amount in a single chunk. Quite an advantage, isn't it?

Fourth, market makers often offer products that are really hard to find in any two-sided market. A good example could be binary options (contracts with *all-or-nothing* outcomes depending on whether a certain event happens or not, quite similar to betting) or structured products (for example, a mix of fixed income, currency, and equities traded as one single contract).

Lastly, market makers can offer derivatives that are priced very closely to the underlying asset but are not technically considered as the asset itself. One of the most well-known derivatives is **contracts for difference (CFDs)** — a contract that you make with the market maker and according to which the market maker is obliged to pay you the difference if you purchased the contract and the price of the underlying asset went higher (or if you sold the contract and the price of the asset went lower). So, a CFD typically works as a proxy for the asset. The reason for using CFDs instead of the underlying asset is that in certain jurisdictions, any income from CFD trading is not taxed at all. Isn't it a good reason to consider trading with a reputable regulated market maker?

Of course, market makers are not the only important market participants in the FX market. Let's get to know another no less important type of market participant.

Liquidity providers – the whales that support this planet

In the previous section, we already noted that some activities of market makers are similar to those of **liquidity providers** (**LPs**). An LP is a market participant whose business is to earn the spread by providing liquidity to the market, that is, always maintaining orders to buy or sell on both sides of the order book at the same time. Therefore, as in the case of market makers, LPs act as price givers earning the spread.

In two-sided exchange-traded markets, it's hard to tell the difference between a market maker and a liquidity provider. However, in OTC markets it becomes fundamental.

In an OTC market, a market maker is an entity that has its own clients and quotes the market for them. A liquidity provider normally does have clients which trade directly with them, regardless of whether it's a small retail client or a large fund. LPs only provide liquidity to an order book – or multiple order books – as OTC markets are very fragmented and there are multiple trading venues for the same financial instrument (see the *OTC markets* section). So, a typical LP's clients are banks, ECNs, and brokers.

Many traders think that LPs are *parasites* of the market and that without them, pricing would be more transparent, the execution of their orders would be better, and eventually, they would have made more money (or, rather, would make money instead of losing it). This is a common delusion and we will explore why.

Do you remember the typical order book that we saw in the *Exchange and order book* section? It clearly shows the liquidity currently present in the market. In that particular example, each price level lists a few hundred orders, which is in fact not much for a large market. Now, what happens if a large order, say, to buy a couple of thousand contracts, hits the market?

Such an order will immediately swipe the order book, buying out all offers first from the best ask price level, then the next price level, then the next, and the next, pushing the price up, higher and higher. All this would happen in a fraction of a millisecond so other market participants wouldn't have time to react.

On the contrary, if there is sufficient liquidity in the order book then price movements become more moderate as it becomes more difficult to push the price up or down by any significant distance.

> **Note**
>
> So LPs play a very important role in OTC markets: they facilitate trading in large volume – and not only to large traders but for any buy-side traders, including retail.

At the same time, LPs make the life of speculators more difficult because the greater the liquidity in the market, the smaller the price movements, and the more difficult it is to profit from buy-side speculations based on the ancient principle, *buy low, sell high*.

Every speculative trader must understand that markets were not invented for speculation. The purpose of any financial market is to facilitate the exchange of goods or money and to find the best price for them. The fact that it is possible to make money by speculation is only a side effect and not the purpose of the market itself.

Liquidity and volatility – how one transforms into another

As the number of LPs grows, the market price becomes less and less **volatile**. Volatility is one of the key metrics of both the market price and the returns of a trading strategy. In simple terms, volatility means ease of price movement: greater volatility means that the price is expected to jump up and down at a greater distance within the same period of time, while lower volatility means that the price is **not** expected to move to any significant distance within the same period of time. There are many methodologies to measure volatility and the subject itself is quite complex and multifaceted (there is even a special term **volatility trading**) but this lies beyond the scope of this book. For now, it is sufficient to remember that volatility means how easily a price can move in any direction.

We can illustrate volatility by calculating the difference between the highest price and the lowest price for a fixed period of time and plotting it as a histogram. *Figure 3.3* shows such a plot for the euro versus the US dollar, sampled at one-minute intervals:

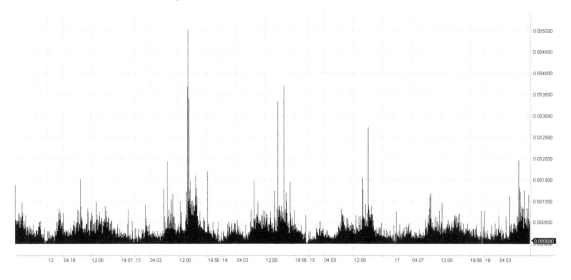

Figure 3.3 – A simple representation of intraday volatility (chart by MultiCharts)

In this illustration, we can clearly see that **intraday** volatility (the one measured for sampling rate less than 24 hours) in this market is cyclic and that it is always lower during nighttime. This is quite natural as most of the large market participants trade during normal business hours.

This illustration, however, does not give us an idea about how LPs affect volatility. In order to see this effect, we need to look at a much bigger picture. Let's plot the same representation of volatility for daily time intervals and look into its history back to the beginning of the 21st century. *Figure 3.4* shows such a volatility chart for the euro versus the US dollar:

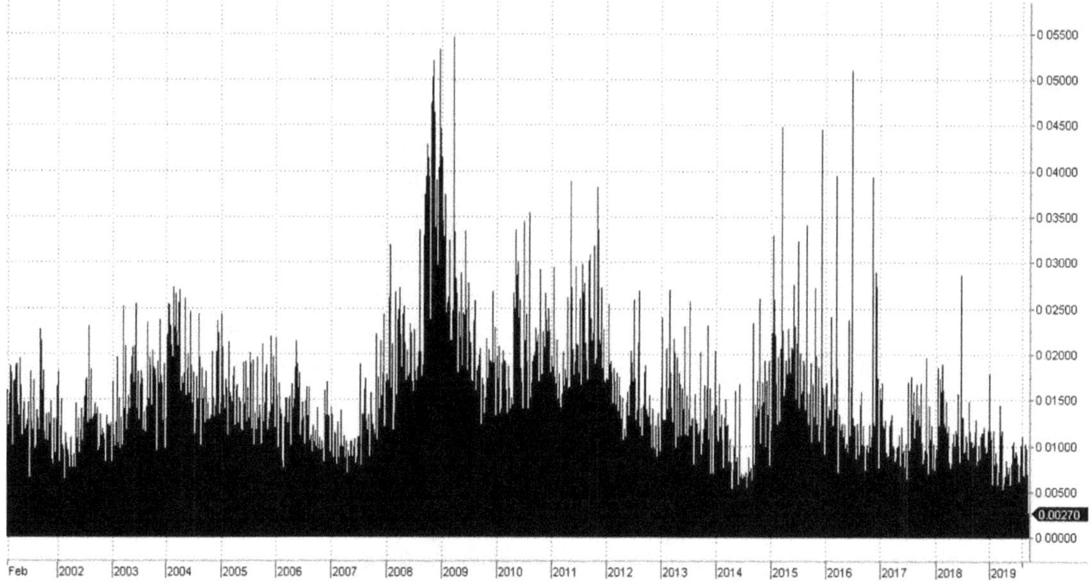

Figure 3.4 – Daily volatility, EURUSD (chart by MultiCharts)

In this illustration, we can see multi-year cycles that start with a financial crisis (clearly seen as an increase in daily volatility) and the following continuous decline in volatility that lasts for 4-5 years.

One of the possible explanations for this phenomenon is that during crisis time, LPs and market makers are the first to suffer from a sharp increase in demand or supply as they are obliged to maintain liquidity in the market. So, after the initial series of big losses for the sell side and margin calls among the buy side, LPs review their risk metrics and start to withdraw liquidity from the market. We already know that when liquidity goes down volatility goes up; this is what we, the traders, observe as sharp price movements and the rest of the world calls a *crisis* or a *catastrophe*.

So, all in all, LPs and market makers do a very important job of keeping the market together and ensuring its efficiency – the ability to buy or sell any quantity of the asset at any time.

We have gotten acquainted with the two most important sell-side market participants and we already know that there are many buy-side market participants including ourselves. But how do we all find each other? Where are all our orders sent to and how are they matched?

ECN – looks like a fair game, but is it?

When I speak about the structure of OTC markets, especially the fact that prices in them are offered by just select market participants and can vary significantly for different buy-side clients, many traders say, *"This is not fair! Why won't FX work in the same manner as other regulated markets with centralized exchanges where anyone can improve the price?"*

There is no single and simple answer to this question.

First, the FX market trades money for money and not any asset for money. Its original purpose was to facilitate currency exchange rather than speculative trading with various financial instruments. And (fortunately!) we don't have to go to an exchange to just get some British pounds for euros or Indian rupees for US dollars. Therefore, OTC trades are quite natural for this purpose and a currency exchange shop is an excellent example of trading OTC.

Second, the FX market consists of multiple financial instruments that are quite flexible in their specifications. For example, cash constitutes only a small fraction of this market, while forward contracts make up to 50% of its daily turnover. These forward contracts can be made directly between banks and other market participants without any need for an exchange. We will look into the FX instruments a bit later in this chapter, in the *FX instruments* section.

However, as time went on and markets became more and more computerized, traders thought such a market design was not fair enough. Many professional buy-side traders along with market makers, LPs, and brokers thought the same. Buy-side traders sought better, more efficient ways to find the best price in the market rather than just calling multiple banks on the phone and talking to desk dealers. Sell-side traders were keen on providing the best bid and ask prices because this increases the chance to make money earning the spread.

This is of course true not only for the FX market but for any market: the battle for the best execution has a long history. In 1969, the first electronic network that allowed placing bids and asks by qualified market participants was introduced. It was a revolutionary improvement that allowed negotiating prices and finding the best bid and best ask much quicker than before. The **Securities and Exchanges Commission (SEC)** acknowledged this network and named it an **electronic communication network (ECN)**. In 1975, the SEC adopted amendments to the Securities Act (the main legal document that regulates securities trading in the US), which opened doors to the explosive growth of ECNs and electronic trading.

So, what is an ECN anyway?

The organization of ECNs

If you connect to an ECN and retrieve market data from there, you will see something really similar to the depth of market data received from an exchange. You will see multiple price levels and liquidity on each price level. Depending on your subscription, you may be able to see just the top level, top 5 levels, top 10 levels, or the entire order book. You can wait for the price that is required by your trading strategy and send an order to buy or sell – pretty much like you do that at an exchange.

So, can we say that ECN is an *exchange*?

No, it is not.

The key difference between an ECN and an exchange is the availability of its order book. At an exchange, its order book is available for *any* order from *any* market participant. Anyone can send an order of any size and it will get into the single, universal order book. With an ECN, *only qualified market participants* can send their bids and asks to the order book. In the case of the FX market, these are mostly banks, LPs, market makers, and other professional sell-side market participants. Simply put, most likely, you will not be able to send your own bid or ask for the order book at an ECN.

At this point, we should revisit the description of the trade mechanics as it's going on at an exchange. If you send a limit order – that is, an order to buy or sell an asset at a price that is respectively lower or higher than the current last price – then your order enters the order book at the respective price level and is added to the end of the queue (see the *Exchange and order book* section). Anyone in the market can see this order as the liquidity at this price level will have increased.

However, if you do the same at an ECN, the order book does not change visually. Instead, your order is kept by the ECN matching engine and is executed only when the last price approaches this order. No one, including yourself, will see your order in the order book and you do not have the ability to improve the best bid and the best ask. Only qualified ECN members can improve the best bid and ask.

ECN – not all market participants were created equal

So, going back to the discussion of market *fairness* at the beginning of this section, can we now say that an ECN is a *fair* market? Well, if compared to an exchange – probably not. But it solves the main problem of OTC markets: it facilitates price discovery among multiple sell-side market participants, adding competition between them, and thus improving the best bid/ask for the sell side.

Trading with an ECN was originally available only to professional market participants, but for over a decade, it has been available virtually to anyone. All you need is to find a broker who supports the **Straight-Through Processing** (**STP**) business model. STP means that the broker does not act as a market maker for their clients, they only route client orders to an ECN.

Let's recap trading with an ECN once again. LPs and market makers send in their bids and offers and buy-side traders consume this liquidity.

Now, let's perform the same imaginary experiment – a stress test for such a structure as we did with the exchange order book. Let's imagine that a large volume buy-side trader comes in with an order to buy or sell more than presently exists in the order book.

In most cases, such an order will swipe the entire liquidity in the order book leaving one of its sides empty for a few moments – a situation that is less than acceptable for LPs. So, if a trader does it only once then there will most likely be no reaction – LPs will rebalance their order books and liquidity reappears in the market. But if this trader repeats this action, then such an activity is considered

predatory, and the order flow generated by the trader is called **toxic**. A wide range of sanctions may follow, from just a call from the broker to a permanent ban at the ECN.

You may think that this issue is not relevant to small-volume traders, such as retail, but in fact, it is.

Let's revise the definition of the toxic order flow: it is a sequence of orders that systematically and consistently tries to swipe the order book, that is, consume the entire liquidity on either side (bid or ask).

During normal business hours, it is indeed hard to achieve with small order sizes. But do not forget that not all LPs work 24 hours a day. Moreover, there are moments, and even spans of time that last for minutes, when liquidity at the ECN is really close to zero (see an explanation of bank settlement and associated issues in the *FX instruments* section in this chapter). If even a small retail trader sends a small order at such a moment, it would drain the thin order book completely, leading to the execution of this order at an absurd price and a phone call from the broker or the exchange with unpleasant questions about the trader's behavior.

> **Note**
> If you trade with an ECN, always check the liquidity in the order book before sending any order to avoid really unpleasant situations.

Today, trading at an ECN ensures the second most efficient price discovery process. But what is the most efficient then, you may wonder. Well, we are now going to discuss *aggregation*.

Aggregation – in search of the best price

Do you remember that any OTC market in general, and the FX in particular, is highly fragmented? There are multiple market participants offering different prices for the same asset at the same moment in time.

This is true for any market participant and any trading venue, and ECNs are no exception. If ECNs were closed systems without any links to the outer world, then the price could potentially be very different from prices in the rest of the FX market. Indeed, if we have there an exchange-like trading venue then even though bids and asks are posted by only a small group of qualified members, the price will be determined by supply and demand, quite like in any other market. This means that price takers will be those who drive the price up or take it down. In a closed system, the price is determined only by members of this system.

It may seem that theoretically nothing prevents the price of the same euro versus the US dollar to be 1 at one ECN, 2 at another, and 10 at the third – as long as members of the third ECN think the euro should cost that much!

However – and luckily – this is not true. If each ECN traded a **separate** asset such as a unique currency, then indeed its price would be determined only by the supply and demand at this very ECN. But as long as they all trade the same asset, like in our example, someone could buy the same euro at 1 dollar at one ECN and sell it for 10 dollars at another. Be sure that these smart traders are always present in any market. They are called **arbitrageurs** and their trading strategy is called **arbitrage**.

Besides that, ECNs are not closed systems. All LPs participate in multiple ECNs and other liquidity pools; many of them run their own dealing desks or act as market makers for their clients. Moreover, an ECN can also act as an LP to another ECN!

So, instead of a centralized market, we can again see a very fragmented, very complex network where market participants are linked to each other and to other groups, then these groups are also linked, and so on, and so on. Both buy-side traders (arbitrageurs) and sell-side market participants (LPs and market makers) make the price across the entire FX market far more uniform than in our simplified example previously.

Although we no longer expect as dramatic a difference in price as 1,000% from one trading venue to another, due to the intrinsic fragmentation of the FX market, prices are still slightly different here and there. For example, that same euro can be quoted at 1.13458 at one ECN and 1.13459 at another, and at the same time a market maker can quote it at 1.13461 and a bank at 1.13456. The difference is very tiny and running classical arbitrage as described is very difficult in the today's FX market. However, we can look at this price diversity from another angle: what if we could find the absolute best price in the market by checking all available prices?

This is the core idea of **price aggregation**. An aggregator is not a trading venue as such because it doesn't have its own order book and LPs. Instead, an aggregator scans trading venues in search of the absolute best bid and offer and then routes orders to the respective venue.

Due to the nature of aggregation, it is normal that for a brief moment, typically milliseconds or shorter, the best bid price would be **greater** than the best ask. Think about it! A price at which you could buy is lower than the price at which you could sell! No wonder aggregators very quickly became the favorite trading venues for arbitrage traders – and not only for them. Indeed, price aggregation is the way to get the best execution in a fragmented OTC market.

Unfortunately, today aggregators are available only to professional market participants, such as banks and brokers. So, ECN trading remains the most efficient among what is available to a wider audience.

Trading the FX market – what and how

We have talked quite a lot about **where** it is possible to trade but wait! We totally forgot to discuss **what** is possible to trade and **how** it is possible to place trades. Let's fill this gap immediately.

FX instruments

You probably heard that the FX market is the largest market in the world, with a daily turnover of over 2 trillion dollars. But have you ever wondered what instruments are traded in such enormous quantities? Do you imagine piles of cash or gold coins? Maybe instant transfers of money from one bank account to another?

No, of course, this is not the way this market operates. When we say *forex* we generally mean trading obligations to deliver one currency for another currency.

If I come to a currency exchange shop and exchange €100 for the equivalent amount of British pounds, then such a transaction is done immediately. My obligations to deliver the euro as the seller and the shop's obligations to deliver the British pounds to me as the buyer is fulfilled at the moment we make a deal.

However, if I wanted to exchange 1 million euros for the respective amount of British pounds, I would rather call my bank and ask for the price. The bank would be happy to make a special offer as the amount to exchange is quite attractive. This offered price would be way better than anything a cash exchange shop could offer.

Start getting the point? That's how multiple prices for the same asset may exist in an OTC market.

I may go even further and check prices with various financial institutions, especially those specializing in currency exchange and international money transfers – and, most likely, I would find the best offer at which I agree to place my trade.

But the price I am offered by the financial institution is by far not the best possible offer on the market. They will then go to the *big* forex and place their offer to sell the euros for British pounds at a price that is higher than the one they purchased the euros from me.

This may look simple and straightforward but it's not.

The problem is that I get a deal now but it's quite possible that it will take time for my money to get transferred from my bank account to the chosen financial institution that performs the exchange. The exchange rate is already fixed with me. So, for this financial institution, it is critical to be able to hedge their position or liquidate it the very moment they get a deal with me, and not at a later time as the market price may be quite different and they may suffer a loss from such an operation.

So, the financial institution places its offer in a so-called forwards market. A forward contract is an obligation to deliver physical goods (or, in the case of currency markets, a currency) on a certain date at the price fixed at the moment the contract is made. For example, that same financial institution can sell a forward contract that means, *"we will fix the exchange rate of the euro versus the British pound at 0.85 now but I will deliver you the euros later."*

During a business day, a financial institution can make lots of forward contracts with various counterparties. To understand how much they owe to whom and how much others are due to them, there is a special process called **settlement**. This is the procedure of netting all mutual obligations of all market participants and figuring out their daily profits and losses.

> **Note**
>
> For most currency pairs that involve the US dollar, the settlement time is 5 P.M. New York time. It is extremely important to take special care trading around this time because there is almost no liquidity in the market. It's always best to avoid trading at all 15 minutes before the settlement and 15-30 minutes after the settlement.

There are various forward contracts among which the heavily-traded contracts are the following:

- **Today (TOD)** – a forward contract with the delivery date on the same business day, or *T*

- **Tomorrow (TOM)** – a forward contract with the delivery date on the next business day, or *T+1*

- **SPOT** – a forward contract with the delivery date in 2 business days, or *T+2*

As of 2022, the overall daily turnover in all the FX markets is at about $6.6 trillion. SPOT is the largest part of the average daily turnover in forwards, with a value of about $2 trillion. Other forward contracts contribute another $1 trillion. The remaining $3.6 trillion is mostly taken by **swap contracts** or **swaps**.

Swaps are very interesting financial instruments mostly used by manufacturers and importers/exporters to hedge their currency risks. If I make a swap contract with you this means that I give you a certain amount of euros and you give me a certain amount in British pounds (or any other currency) and we fix the exchange rate. Then, after some time, typically a year or more, we will exchange our currencies back – and what is most important at this point, at the same exchange rate we traded it originally.

So, a currency swap contract assumes a currency risk for each of us because the exchange rate in the forwards market may change quite substantially during the term of our swap agreement. But this risk can be sold for a premium and this is how swap traders can make money.

We are not going to consider this class of financial instruments. If you are interested in learning more about them, I'd recommend starting at `https://www.investopedia.com/terms/c/currencyswap.asp`.

Besides cash, forwards, and swaps markets, there are many derivatives – contracts that may and may not assume physical delivery of the asset. One of the most well-known currency derivatives is currency futures, which are available to trade at **Chicago Mercantile Exchange (CME)**.

> **Note**
>
> The most important markets for retail traders and active speculators are SPOT and currency futures. These are the two markets that we will be discussing further in the book.

Naming conventions

Let's quickly clarify the way the currencies market uses the names of its instruments.

International standards (ISO 4217 to be precise) assume that each currency has a numeric three-digit code and a three-letter alphabetic code. Thus, the numeric code for the euro is 978 and the alphabetic code is EUR.

Forex is a special market because we don't buy goods for money, we buy and sell money for money. Therefore, any instrument in this market is a currency pair and its respective code (which is often called a ticker) consists of two alphabetical currency codes.

The first currency in a pair is the one that is quoted and the second currency is the one in which it is quoted. In other words, the first currency acts as an asset and the second acts as the measuring unit. For example, EURUSD means how many US dollars there are in 1 euro, USDJPY means how many Japanese yen there are in 1 US dollar, and so on.

> **Note**
> Be extremely careful with FX tickers! Always remember what you buy and what you sell as it's very easy to confuse.

Prices in the FX market are quoted in fractional amounts. For example, if EURUSD is quoted at 1.0345, it means that I will get 10,345 US dollars if I sell 10,000 euros, and a quote of 113.78 USDJPY means that I will pay 11,378 Japanese yen to get 100 US dollars. It's very easy to calculate if you multiply the rate by the respective power of 10 to get rid of fractions.

For many decades, there were mostly four-digit and two-digit prices in the FX market, such as those in the preceding example. The minimal price fluctuation – which is the minimal change in the fourth or second digit – is called a **price interest point** (**pip**).

However, a few years ago they got an extra digit. So instead of four-digit prices such as 1.2345 we now have 5-digit prices such as 1.23456, and similarly three digits instead of two digits.

> **Note**
> Although now most of the prices use five-digit or three-digit notation, the pip is still considered to be in the fourth or second digit respectively. So, the extra digit is called fractional pip or fractional price.

One of the possible explanations as to why this extra digit was added could be the fact that the FX market has been evolving rapidly and a lot of LPs literally flooded it with money. Do you remember our discussion on volatility and its relationship with liquidity in the *Liquidity and volatility: how one transforms into another* section? Well, the greater the liquidity, the lower the volatility, and at some point, if we continue using the old 4-digit prices then the spread (the difference between the bid and ask) is zero. In turn, this means that the sell-side market participants no longer can earn on liquidity provision. So, introducing more granular price levels was the only reasonable solution to the problem of excessive liquidity.

So, the introduction of more granular prices is a reliable indicator of growing liquidity in the market. Is it good or bad?

At first glance, it's definitely good news: the greater the liquidity, the easier it is to make contracts and, therefore, traders get a better execution for their orders. However, if every buyer and seller can immediately satisfy their needs, the price stops moving anywhere. So, highly liquid markets are attractive for the sell side, but for buy-side speculators, it becomes more and more difficult to make money using directional trading strategies.

To give you an idea about how liquidity can affect the performance of buy-side speculators: in 2001-2004, it was possible to use a quite simplistic trend following trading strategies and it was considered normal if such a strategy made about 10 pips per trade, on average. Today, following the trend almost completely ceased to work in the FX majors and the average profit per trade fell down to 1 pip. This is the price traders pay for the ability to fill their orders more efficiently.

How do I place a trade?

Alright, now that we know what we can trade, it's time to figure out how we can do that.

In the case of cash exchange, it's more or less clear: I can go to an exchange shop or go to a bank. But don't forget that, in this case, I will have to get one price and this price will most likely be very far from the best in the market.

So, if I want to benefit from a market where liquidity is huge and prices are really competitive, I need to be able to access it somehow. Unless I am a financial institution myself (which is most likely not the case), I have to use the services of various intermediaries that introduce me to the market and provide access to trading venues. These intermediaries are called **brokers**.

A broker is a market participant whose business is to route orders from clients to trading venues while checking them for market risk and, if necessary, providing leverage (see the *Trade mechanics: again some terminology* section).

Again, as in the case of market makers, the very words **forex broker** are associated with something negative for many. No wonder in the early years of retail FX trading many dishonest businesses called themselves brokers but in reality, they never routed any order anywhere. This is again no surprise, the minimal ticket in the spot FX market in the late 1990s was 1 million base currency, and in the early 2000's it went down to 100,000 – 10 times as low but still too big for small retail traders. So those *brokers* offered *mini contracts* and *micro contracts*, which of course never left this broker's closed system.

So, in the early days of retail, FX trading brokers had only two options in case they wanted to work with small retail accounts:

- Act as market makers for their client

- Do internal netting of clients' positions and hedge the net amount in the *large* market

Unfortunately, many so-called brokers chose the third option – to do nothing and just steal money from their clients. So, we can understand why the mention of forex brokers and the word *forex* in general sometimes causes quite an acute reaction.

However – and fortunately – times changed. Now, most of the surviving brokers are regulated and, at the very least, guarantee the safety of the client accounts. Of course, it is not a guarantee against losses in trading but that's a completely different story.

Besides that, the structure of the FX market has evolved dramatically since the early 2000s. If at the beginning of the century it was populated mostly by banks, then today, the variety of both buy-side and sell-side market participants is very diverse and the number of trading venues available to virtually anyone is quite considerable.

Today, it is really easy to check the broker with the regulator and ask them to provide direct access to a liquidity pool or an ECN –and then trade along with professional market participants in quite a similar manner as if you traded at a centralized regulated exchange.

> **Note**
> When we develop trading applications with Python, I assume that we directly connect to a trading venue such as an ECN, avoiding platforms such as MetaTrader or proprietary trading platforms because they only add unwanted latency to our orders. MetaTrader can be used as a monitoring tool to watch for open positions and check the correctness of order execution.

It's been quite a long chapter and quite a long trip into the world of the FX markets – sometimes clear and straightforward, sometimes weird and spooky. But I am sure there is one question that has long been spinning in your mind while reading all of the aforementioned information.

Why do I need all this?

Well, actually you don't. Of course, you can just quickly download unclear historical price data from an unknown source, develop a model using tools you don't fully understand and optimize it using this data, connect to an unknown broker and start trading. The question is: will this trading be successful? Most likely not.

If you read this chapter carefully, you'll most likely already understand why.

Firstly, when you plan to use certain historical price data for your models you should realize what exactly you are going to use: whether it's last trade, bid, ask, or both, or anything else. You should check if historical data contains correct timestamps and that no tick is dated earlier than the preceding one. You may want to make sure the data you use contains information about trading volume – otherwise, you won't be able to develop a wide range of trading strategies. You should make sure that data is clean and consistent, and that there are no erroneous quotes that will affect the parameters of your strategy during its development.

Secondly, you should carefully choose the right trading venue for your strategy. Does it trade large volumes? Does it trade frequently? Does it attempt to trade in *problematic* periods of time when liquidity in the market is thin? Answers to all these questions will help you make the right choice.

Finally (something which probably should have been first) – you should make absolutely sure that your strategy generates trades that are executable and returns that will cover all trading costs, including the market spread and any commissions that your broker charges you.

So, at this point, I would recommend you read this chapter once again now and that you return to it from time to time in the future to keep your development consistent with the real market.

Summary

In this chapter, we learned about the different ways a market can be organized and operated. We familiarized ourselves with key concepts such as exchange, order book, and liquidity, noted the possible impact of various factors on price behavior, and discovered important intrinsic factors that may negatively affect the performance of a trading strategy. With all this fundamental knowledge in mind, we're ready to move on to study the architecture of a trading application in detail, to see what we should use in order to meet the challenges of the modern FX market. This is what we're going to do in the next chapter.

Part 2:
General Architecture of a Trading Application and A Detailed Study of Its Components

Being familiar with the subject domain is essential for any software development, and *Part 1* introduced the basics of the FX market and the key features typical of trading applications. Now, it's time to outline the architecture of such an application and consider its main components in greater detail.

Part 2 suggests several solutions used to retrieve and handle market data, explains the difference between fundamental and technical analysis, focuses on the meaning of classical **technical analysis** (**TA**) indicators from a market process standpoint, and provides possible implementations of these indicators in Python, in a way compatible with further developments. We will also familiarize ourselves with the basics of simple data visualization, which is typically used to quickly check market data and the correctness of calculations, and generate entry and exit orders.

This part comprises the following chapters:

- *Chapter 4, Trading Application – What's Inside?*
- *Chapter 5, Retrieving and Handling Market Data with Python*
- *Chapter 6, Basics of Fundamental Analysis and Its Possible Use in FX Trading*
- *Chapter 7, Technical Analysis and Its Implementation in Python*
- *Chapter 8, Data Visualization in FX Trading with Python*

4

Trading Application: What's Inside?

Almost any application that implements a trading strategy has a number of more or less standard components. Let's first have a quick look at a somewhat generalized architecture of a typical trading application and then go into greater detail on specific points related to the development of a trading strategy using Python.

In *Chapter 1, Developing Trading Strategies – Why They Are Different*, we saw a very generalized diagram of a typical trading application. Now, we are going to consider its blocks in greater detail. We will learn how to connect our application to data sources and trading venues, how to retrieve data and check its consistency, and consider important points about trading logic and orders.

By the end of this chapter, you will understand how to develop the main components of a trading application that is efficient, maintainable, and scalable, and how to avoid typical serious problems that arise due to incorrect market data processing, mistakes in trading logic, and insufficient understanding of the trade mechanics.

In this chapter, we will cover the following topics:

- Have your app talk to the world – the gloomy world of communication protocols
- Retrieving data – garbage in, garbage out
- Trading logic – this is where a small mistake may cost a fortune
- Risk management – your safety belt
- Ordering interfaces – make sure you are understood correctly

Technical requirements

You will need Python 3.9 or above to run the code in this chapter.

Have your app talk to the world – the gloomy world of communication protocols

Well, actually, in this section, I could just say, *"in the world of FX automated trading every setup is unique, so go ask your broker."* Of course, I am not going to do this but when it comes to connecting your app to a market maker, **electronic communication network** (**ECN**), or any other trading venue, always keep in mind what I said at the beginning of this section.

As you remember from the previous chapter, the FX market is still the most fragmented one from the trading standpoint; so there should be no surprise that its computerized infrastructure is also very fragmented. Even though there's a standard for exchanging financial information, many trading venues use their own dialects, which simply means extra work in cases where you want to use your application with a different broker. At the same time, many trading venues offer their own APIs and protocols not compatible with anything else so developers never lose their jobs and are perpetually adapting their applications.

Having said all that, let's start with something that is generally considered the only industry standard for communication used in trading applications.

FIX – universal but too flexible

In my opinion, despite its hard-to-read syntax, **financial information exchange** (**FIX**) is the best choice to start diving into trading communications because its messages can at least be read by a human – thus, debugging and learning our own mistakes will ensure the steepest learning curve.

Unfortunately, FIX is considered a protocol mostly for professional use and is not available out of the box to any trader from any broker. One of the possible reasons for this discrimination is that FIX allows you to send any instructions and the receiving server checks only syntax but not the meaning of the message. So, potentially, it may damage not only the trader's account but even the market itself. Therefore, most of the biggest market makers, brokers, and banks require professional status from the trader to allow them to use FIX.

However, there's good news: many smaller but ambitious FX brokers today offer a lot of formerly institutional-only services to retail traders. This doesn't mean that the quality of their business is low: they simply need turnover and it's clear that automated trading strategies generate it way better than manual traders. So, in reality, anyone can get access to institutional liquidity from an ECN using FIX.

Besides that, who knows, maybe one day you will find yourself working with a bank or an investment fund, and then even a general understanding of FIX will help you a lot in your further career.

So, what is FIX anyway?

FIX is an attempt to create a really universal standard that could be used in virtually any situation when you need to transfer financial-related information. It is used by banks, brokers, information agencies, and even insurance companies, along with many others. Of course, such a wide variety of use cases assumes a great degree of flexibility to customize FIX the way you need, and this degree of flexibility paradoxically makes FIX less standard than it aimed to be.

For example, some trading venues may require various tags (basic elements of the FIX protocol) as mandatory while others don't. Some trading venues support limit and stop orders, while others acknowledge only market orders. So, it will require some refactoring if you want to port your trading app from one broker to another because FIX doesn't *require* any particular order type to be accepted. The list may continue but, in essence, the problem is that FIX aims to support *any* market but trading venues use only a *subset* of its tags that are relevant to their market, frequently adapting the standard to their needs.

I think that it's best to consider FIX not only as a protocol or API but rather as a special language with a simple syntax that allows you to convey virtually any meaning. You can also consider it as a framework used to build messages rather than applications and the meaning of the message will depend on the context and environment.

Let's look at FIX as a protocol in the first place and consider its layers. It will help you understand the way we work with FIX connections.

Basic connection

On the transport layer, FIX requires a standard socket connection. Again, as I mentioned at the beginning of this section, everything is very individual because various brokers and trading venues may have different requirements for the way clients connect to them. Normally, you must provide the broker or the trading venue with an IP address (or range of addresses) to whitelist and connect using a **Transmission Control Protocol socket** (**TCP socket**). Others may require complex authorization mechanisms and even the mandatory use of a VPN. So, you may want to consult your broker or trading venue for details.

Learning basic low-level networking such as how to establish a socket connection in Python is not the goal of this book, so if you have never done that before I'd recommend starting with an excellent guide from Real Python (`https://realpython.com/python-sockets`), or if you prefer a *dive or swim* approach based on language in action with lots of live examples, you can watch this tutorial from Geeks for Geeks (`https://www.geeksforgeeks.org/socket-programming-python/`). The point is, establishing a socket connection in Python is not rocket science but rather a simple routine procedure.

Tags

Once a socket connection is established, we're ready to send and receive some meaningful information over it. As with many other protocols, FIX is based on messages. A FIX message is a plain text (ASCII) string that in turn consists of blocks (substrings) delimited by a non-printable character 0x01 (SOH) without any special ending characters such as \n or \r. Each block between delimiters follows a simple syntax:

```
TAG=VALUE
```

A **tag** is a number and its value can be any string that cannot contain the 0x01 character for obvious reasons: it will be interpreted as a delimiter. There is one important exception though: in the case that the tag means retrieving data, any value used as data may be an arbitrary sequence of bytes.

For example, 55=EUR/USD represents a currency pair, instrument, or symbol (remember, they are all synonyms). 40=Limit means that the message contains a limit order (see *Chapter 3, FX Market Overview from a Developer's Standpoint*, for an explanation of types of orders).

Since the delimiter character 0x01 is non-printable, many authors use special characters to divide tags in a FIX message visually. I'm sure you'll agree that it is easier to read a string that is structured as follows:

```
8=FIX.4.4|9=73|35=A|34=1092|49=TESTSND|52=20220728-
07:30:59.643|56=TESTTGT|198=0|108=60|10=133
```

Whereas, reading the following string is more difficult:

```
8=FIX.4.49=7335=A34=109249=TESTSND52=20220728-07:30:59.64356=TE
STTGT198=0108=6010=133
```

However, do not ever use any other delimiter than 0x01 in real FIX messages!

Message structure

Any FIX message is composed of the following three logical parts:

- Standard header
- Body
- Standard trailer

The standard header always consists of the following three tags sent in this very order and not any other:

- tag 8 – means that the message begins and it contains the version of the FIX protocol used by both parties
- tag 9 – the message body length
- tag 35 – the message type (for example, request for quote, order, logon, or logout)

The standard trailer always ends with tag 10, whose value is the message checksum. A checksum is a small piece of data that is returned by a hash function – a function that processes all bits of a meaningful block of data and compresses it according to a special algorithm. Checksums are used to make sure that a block of data (a message in our case) was delivered without errors. If you want to learn more about checksums, hash functions, and related matters, I'd recommend starting with an excellent article on Wikipedia (`https://en.wikipedia.org/wiki/Checksum`) that also has references for further reading.

According to the FIX standard, a tag must have only one occurrence per message. Messages with multiple occurrences of the same tag will be rejected by the target computer.

Tags must have a value. In case no value is specified for any tag, the entire message will be rejected as well.

Sessions

Working with FIX is organized in sessions. A session assumes there are two computers involved: the one that sends the message (*sender*, the respective tag is called `SenderCompID`) and the one that receives the message (*target*, the respective tag is called `TargetCompID`). Normally, the session is initiated by a client connecting to a server, for example, a trader connecting to the broker or a bank connecting to an ECN.

A session starts by sending a handshake message from the sender's computer to the target computer. In cases where there is a reply from the target computer, this message initiates the session. This message type (tag 35) is `Logon (A)`. A sample handshake message header will look as follows:

```
8=FIX.4.4|9=XX|35=A
```

In the preceding message, XX stands for the entire message length (see an explanation of tag 9 in the *Message* section).

Now, we have come to the point where my initial thesis (go and ask your broker for details) becomes apparent. The problem is that, apart from these three mandatory tags and the ending tag 10, all other tags in a logon message are optional. This means that I cannot tell you what you should include there; nor can any other author – except for your broker because it is they who decide what should be sent and in which sequence. So, the best way of learning it is by referring to the documentation obtained from the very trading venue to which you want to send your messages.

Any FIX session ends with a `Logout (5)` message, which in its minimal form looks as follows:

```
8=FIX.4.4|9=5|35=5|10=166
```

Constructing messages

At this point, I would like to warn you against making a very common mistake made by many developers of trading strategies. They think that there's only a limited set of FIX messages that their application may generate; therefore, they hardcode them as strings and pick the appropriate one when they need to send an order.

Do not do this! Here are the following reasons why you shouldn't do this:

- First, this approach makes your code non-scalable. In cases where you need to add a new tag for a new order type, you need to re-write the entire application.

- Second, this makes your code non-portable. In cases where you want to use it with another broker, this broker can require a particular set of tags in a logon message or anywhere else, and again – you will have to re-write your app.

- Finally, even though you may think that you remember the meaning of every FIX tag by heart, believe me, this is a dangerous self-delusion!

So, the reasonable way of constructing a FIX message in Python would be to build it block by block using explicit, human-readable names of tags instead of just numbers. We're going to use a native Python dictionary for this purpose:

1. Let's start by forming a basic FIX dictionary that associates tags with their respective names. We will use names as keys and tag numbers as values because this is the way we want to build our messages:

```
fixdict = {}
fixdict["start"]="8"
fixdict["body_len"] = "9"
fixdict["checksum"] = "10"
fixdict["msg_type"] = "35"
```

2. Now, we need a function that binds tags together in a message. Don't forget that messages may differ significantly in the number of included tags so we will want to use one of Python's most powerful features – *arbitrary keyword argument*:

```
def compose_message(fix_dictionary, **kwargs):
    msg = ""
    for arg in kwargs:
        msg += fix_dictionary[arg] + "=" + kwargs[arg] +
"\001"
    return msg
```

Here, we assume that we pass keyword arguments as pairs of <tag_name>=VALUE and then use the dictionary to replace human-readable names with standard FIX tag numbers.

3. Let's test our code with the following instruction:

```
message = compose_message(fixdict, start="FIX.4.4", body_
len="25", msg_type="A", checksum="56")
```

We will get the following result:

```
8=FIX.4.49=2535=A10=56
```

Note that SOH characters are not visible in this output but if we explicitly request the value of the message variable, it will return the following output:

```
In[28]: message
Out[28]: '8=FIX.4.4\x019=25\x013
5=A\x0110=56\x01'
```

Here, the non-printable character is clearly visible.

However, it is not reasonable to pass the standard header manually each time we need to compose the message. So, we need to include it in the function.

With the first tag, 8, it's simple. We can store the value in a special variable and add it at the last stage of the process of composing a message. The first tag always contains only the version of the FIX protocol. But anyway, we should calculate the length of the message body and the checksum and include them (the length and the checksum) in tags 9 and 10, respectively.

Important

Do not confuse the message body with the message itself! Tag 9 means the length of only the message body, that is, between tag 9 and tag 10. In our example, the message body length is 5 (not 4 because the body consists of characters 3, 5, =, A, and one non-printable 0x01).

The easiest way of implementing the calculation of the body length is restricting provision tags in **kwargs to just the message body. This can be done in a variety of ways:

1. Let's start by using a list that we will call fix_exceptions:

    ```
    fix_exceptions = ["8", "9", "10"]
    ```

2. We will then add tags to our composing message only when they are not in the list of exceptions:

    ```
    if fix_dictionary[arg] not in fix_exceptions:
    ```

3. Now, the new version of our message-composing function will look like this:

    ```
    def compose_message(fix_dictionary, fix_exceptions,
    **kwargs):
        msg = ""
        for arg in kwargs:
            if fix_dictionary[arg] not in fix_exceptions:
                msg += fix_dictionary[arg] + "=" +
    ```

```
          kwargs[arg] + "\001"
      return msg
```

If we test it using the preceding parameters, we will get the following output:

```
35=A
```

Tags 8, 9, and 10 are now ignored because they are in the list of exceptions. Since tags related to the standard header and standard trailer are ignored, whatever is not ignored remains in the message body.

4. Great, we can now calculate its length and add it to the message:

```
msg = fix_dictionary["body_len"] + "=" + str(len(msg)) +
msg
```

5. Now, let's add tag 8:

```
msg = fix_dictionary["start"] + "FIX.4.4"
```

6. Finally, in the following code we sum all ASCII codes of all characters in the string, then divide this sum by 256 and take the remainder (we will use the `reduce` function here, which is part of `functools`, so should be imported as `from functools import reduce`):

```
checksum = reduce(lambda x, y: x + y, list(map(ord, msg))
% 256)
```

We will then add it to the message:

```
msg += fix_dictionary["checksum"] + "=" + str(checksum)
```

Let's now see the entire upgraded code:

```
from functools import reduce

fixdict = {}
fixdict["start"]="8"
fixdict["body_len"] = "9"
fixdict["checksum"] = "10"
fixdict["msg_type"] = "35"

exceptions = ["8", "9", "10"]

def compose_message(fix_dictionary, fix_exceptions,
**kwargs):
    msg = ""
```

```
     for arg in kwargs:
          if fix_dictionary[arg] not in fix_exceptions:
               msg += fix_dictionary[arg] + "=" +
kwargs[arg] + "\001"
     msg = fix_dictionary["body_len"] + "=" +
str(len(msg)) + msg
     msg = fix_dictionary["start"] + "=" + "FIX.4.4" + msg


     checksum = reduce(lambda x, y: x + y, list(map(ord,
msg))) % 256
     msg += fix_dictionary["checksum"] + "=" +
str(checksum)
     return msg
```

Now, let's test it with the following input:

```
message = compose_message(fixdict, exceptions,
start="wrong version", body_len="10000", msg_type="A",
checksum="78909")
```

We will still get the correct output:

```
8=FIX.4.49=535=A10=178
```

Note that all tags found in the list of exceptions are ignored and their ridiculous values are not included in the message – which is great because otherwise such a message will be rejected (in the best case). Moreover, now we can safely omit all tags but the body when we call the following function, which will give us exactly the same result as before:

```
message = compose_message(fixdict, exceptions, msg_type="5")
```

What to do next

If you work with FIX, you definitely need a reference that has a comprehensive dictionary of all tags with explanations of their meaning. One of the best resources is OnixS (they develop SDKs for direct market access, so no wonder FIX plays the central role in their products), which can be found at https://www.onixs.biz/fix-dictionary.html. If you plan to work with FIX professionally, I definitely recommend visiting the official website of the FIX community at https://www.fixtrading.org and checking the *Standards* section, where you can find information on technical standards, specifications, and a link to FIX GitHub.

When it comes to professional utilization of FIX, the most important and de facto industry-standard solution is QuickFIX (https://quickfixengine.org). It features implementations of the FIX protocol for many languages, including Python, and simplifies the development of messaging and data retrieval for trading applications by relieving the developer of the burden of low-level composing FIX messages.

There are also several ready-made FIX implementations for Python, of which Simplefix (`https://pypi.org/project/simplefix/`) is probably the most straightforward. It doesn't implement a socket connection or any other transport layer functionality, nor does it support logging or ensure message persistence. It only serves as a convenient wrapper for encoding and decoding FIX messages with easy-to-read functions.

It's also worth mentioning another protocol built on top of FIX. It is called **FAST**, which stands for **FIX Adapted for STreaming**. In simple terms, this protocol is designed to facilitate fast and a large volume of messaging without generating excessive processing overhead or latency. If you're interested in learning more about FAST, I'd recommend starting with the official documentation (`https://www.fixtrading.org/standards/fast/`) and also having a look at a FIX Fast tutorial at `https://jettekfix.com/education/fix-fast-tutorial/`.

Now that you know how to compose FIX messages, you just need to fill them with meaning. That is, you need to add any trading logic that is most likely based on market data, generate orders, transform them into FIX messages, and send them to the broker, an ECN, or elsewhere. You also need to be able to receive and understand replies to your messages. For example, your broker may respond with `8=8` in the message body, which means that your order is successfully filled (message type 8 means order execution report and value 8 means *order filled*). The broker may send you back `8=5` which will mean that your order is rejected and your code should be able to handle situations of this kind.

What if your broker doesn't support FIX or doesn't provide non-professional traders with access to it? At this point, we, unfortunately, return to my statement at the very beginning of this chapter, *"in the world of FX automated trading, every setup is unique so go ask your broker."* As we saw previously, even in a highly standardized FIX protocol, there is still a certain degree of flexibility so it's always best to read the documentation provided by the very trading venue to which you plan to send orders. With proprietary protocols, it's even worse because there is no standard and every broker offers their own API designed the way they think is best.

However, the most important thing for you to conclude from this section is that any protocol, any API, and any framework only serves to deliver a certain message, in most cases a trading order, and to receive the reply. If you design your trading application so that you have independent interfaces between data processing, trading logic, risk management, and ordering modules, you will be able to switch from one protocol to another without rewriting the entire application – and this is what we're going to learn more about in this book.

Now that we are more familiar with the means of exchanging information between your application and a trading venue, it's time to learn *what* we can send and retrieve from there. Let's start with market data.

Retrieving data – garbage in, garbage out

The FIX protocol is universal by design and thus can be used not only for ordering but also for data retrieval. However, in most cases, it is not actually used for market data transfer; instead, trading venues provide their own proprietary APIs to retrieve data from there.

As always, in this *gloomy world* of communication protocols, everything is individual and each trading venue offers its own API. However, in general, all broker APIs are implemented as REST or Websockets. The former is convenient for occasional requests for quotes, while the latter is best for continuous subscriptions that allow receiving real-time market data.

The following examples I provide are taken from the API of LMAX, one of the key ECNs in the FX market. They are not only great because of their openness to any client, big or small, but also because they are one of the very few trading venues that publicly disseminate real-time market data – and they do it completely free of charge.

Before you start working with FX market data you should understand and always remember one important thing:

Data in demo environments is always different from that in a live environment.

This means that if you receive public data or open a demo account with an ECN to receive market data from there, you should be ready to see quotes that are slightly different from the *real* market. The good news is that this difference is not significant; in our particular example with LMAX, it is normally 0.1 to 0.5 pips with a probable slight increase in difference closer to the New York bank settlement time (5 P.M. New York time – see the *Trading the FX market: what and how* section in *Chapter 3, FX Market Overview from a Developer's Standpoint*). So, even this publicly available data is good for most development and even for live trading.

In cases where you need only a quote here and a quote there from time to time, then mostly LMAX's REST API is the way to go for you.

As with any regular REST API, it supports a few endpoints that allow retrieving market price data both as the last trade price and as the top of the order book. It also supports retrieving information about all instruments (symbols) supported by the LMAX demo server.

In order to retrieve such a list, let's execute the following:

```
curl -i -X GET "https://public-data-api.london-demo.lmax.com/
v1/instruments"
```

The response will deliver us a JSON with the list of available instruments:

```
[{"instrument_id":"eur-usd","symbol":"EUR/USD","security_
id":"4001","currency":"USD","unit_of_measure":"EUR","asset_
class":"CURRENCY","quantity_increment":"1000.0000","price_
increment":"0.000010","ticker_enabled":true},...]
```

I removed the remainder of the JSON to keep it compact but the rest is just repetitions of similar records for other instruments. Let's parse this answer to understand its components:

- `instrument_id`: This is the name of the FX instrument supported by the LMAX demo server in the correct notation (note that no slashes / are allowed in the names, so they are replaced with a dash -).

- `asset_class`: Most of the instruments traded at this ECN are currencies but there are also **contracts for difference (CFDs)** on metals and energies, so be careful.

- `quantity_increment`: This is the minimum *quant* of the order size; an increment of 1,000.000 euros means that you can send an order to buy or sell 1,003,000 euros for just 2,000 EURUSD, but not 1,003,300 or 1,100,301 euros.

- `price_increment`: This is the minimum price fluctuation. 0.00001 means that the minimum change can be in the fifth digit to the right of the decimal point and the amount of this change is 1 (so-called **fractional pip**).

- `ticker_enabled`: This means that the symbol is available for ordering.

To retrieve the entire order book information for the particular symbol, we can use the following:

```
curl -i -X GET "https://public-data-api.london-demo.lmax.com/
v1/orderbook/eur-usd"
```

The response will contain the list of bids and asks for the depth allowed by LMAX for demo accounts again in the form of a plain JSON.

If you want to receive continuous data from the ECN, you may want to use WebSockets instead of REST:

1. First, you will need to install WebSockets, which you can do using pip:

   ```
   pip install websocket_client
   ```

   If you use Python with an Anaconda distribution, you can use the following code:

   ```
   conda install -c conda-forge websocket-client
   ```

2. First of all, we need to import the WebSocket module:

   ```
   import websocket
   ```

3. Then, set the URL to which we're going to subscribe:

   ```
   url = "wss://public-data-api.london-demo.lmax.com/v1/
   web-socket"
   ```

4. Then, create the WebSocket and connect it:

```
ws = websocket.WebSocket()
ws.connect(url)
```

5. Then, form the request as a regular JSON:

```
req = '{"type": "SUBSCRIBE","channels": [{"name":
"ORDER_BOOK","instruments": ["eur-usd"]},{"name":
"TICKER","instruments":["usd-jpy"]}]}'
```

6. Send the request:

```
ws.send(req)
```

Watch the response:

```
print(ws.recv())
```

If you did all the steps correctly, you're going to see something like this:

```
{"type":"SUBSCRIPTIONS","channels":[{"name":"ORDER_
BOOK","instruments":["eur-usd"]},{"name":"TICKER","instru
ments":["usd-jpy"]}]}
```

This response means that the subscription has been set up and that the subscribed instruments are the euro for the entire order book and the Japanese yen for the last price data.

As this book is not a tutorial on WebSockets, I recommend reading the very comprehensive tutorial at https://websockets.readthedocs.io/en/stable/intro/index.html if you are not familiar with this kind of network connection.

You can find all supported REST API endpoints and WebSocket requests in the LMAX official documentation at https://docs.lmax.com/public-data-api/.

> **Note**
>
> Please don't forget that the preceding examples are for illustrative purposes only. I would like to keep this book as broker-agnostic as possible so I can't really recommend any particular broker or an ECN. The example with LMAX is provided here only because they have one of the most simple and easy-to-use APIs.

Other brokers and trading venues may have different APIs that are sometimes more complex but the key principles of subscribing to data remain the same.

So, now that we know how to get data from the trading venue, here comes the most important part: **data handling**. All procedures you perform with data in your trading applications must ensure data consistency.

By data consistency in market data, we assume the following:

- If tick A is received prior to tick B, then the timestamp of tick A should precede that of tick B

- If there is a gap in time between two adjacent ticks that is substantially greater than the average, there must be a clear logical explanation for it

- If there is a gap in price between two adjacent ticks that is substantially greater than the average, there must be again a clear logical explanation for it

Let's consider each point in detail in the following sub-sections.

Tick sequence

When you start working with real market data, you will be impressed by the number of ticks with incorrect timestamps. There are several explanations for this phenomenon; the most understandable is probably that the number of ticks (and we remember from *Chapter 1* that a tick is an update in price, either a new bid, a new ask, or a new trade) is so huge that the exchange's or ECN's own servers can't really process all of them in the correct sequence and assign the same timestamps to batches of ticks. There are also other reasons that are more related to the latency between the exchange's servers and trading servers or client computers. Anyway, regardless of the reason, incorrect timestamps are a real problem and before we start working with data, we always have to perform a check and correct the timestamps if there's any inconsistency in them.

There are several techniques that allow fixing the timestamp issue and we will consider them in detail in the very next chapter, which is completely dedicated to processing and storing market data.

Time gaps

Basically, a time gap is a situation when no market data is received for a considerable amount of time. Of course, the question is how to define this *considerable amount*. How much is it? A second? A minute? An hour? If there's no market data update in 5 minutes, does it mean that the connection is lost or that there's simply no activity in the market?

If you receive data as live quotes this problem can be solved relatively easily by adding heartbeat messages to your implementation of market data retrieval.

A *heartbeat message* is somewhat similar to *ping*: a message with dummy content is sent to the server and the server just replies with something that means *"OK, I am still alive and can hear you well."* Such a message is sent automatically at equal intervals and is a simple yet robust method of checking the health of your connection.

If you work with FIX, this protocol natively supports heartbeat (message type 0, tag 35=0). If you work with other APIs – well… as always in this chapter, you should refer to your broker's documentation regarding how they implement heartbeat (and what they expect you to use). If no special heartbeat message is reserved by the broker, you may want to use any neutral request, such as a request for a quote from time to time, and check the response.

The key advantage of using a special heartbeat message is that it works any time the server is up. Even when the market is actually closed and any attempt to receive a market quote fails, heartbeat messages will go through and will be responded to. So, using heartbeat messages is always the preferred way to go.

> **Note**
>
> If your broker or a trading venue does support heartbeat messages, you may want to refrain from using any other type of request just to make sure the connection is alive. In certain cases, such an activity can be a reason for a ban with certain ECNs.

So, with live quotes, the problem of time gaps can be solved relatively easily by adding heartbeat messages. But what do we do in cases where we work with *historical data*, that is, not the data representing what's going on in the market now but data indicating what *was going on* in the market some time ago? In this case, no heartbeat message is recorded into it (at least I am not aware of any single example suggesting otherwise) and if we see two ticks with a pause of 1 hour between them, there is always a question of whether this data is consistent.

Normally, such a consistency check is performed in two stages:

- First, we identify the time gaps. The main problem here is how to decide that the pause between ticks is long enough to become suspicious. We will look into this problem in detail in the next chapter. For now, let's just assume that any pause that is greater than the average plus two sigmas (sigma here stands for standard deviation, we consider it in *Chapter 6, Basics of Fundamental Analysis and its Possible Use in FX Trading*) is considered *suspicious*.

- Next, all *suspicious* pauses are checked against the list of known situations when market data can indeed be paused. We exclude all weekends, pauses before and after the bank settlement, and the opening of the bank day for some currencies, and check the rest against a schedule for known events such as releases of important economic news that also may cause interruptions in market quotes.

If the remaining list of time gap issues is insignificant (let's assume for clarity that it is at least 10 times as small as the original list), then we believe that overall this data is satisfactory to work with. If the amount of unidentified time gaps is still significant, it would be best to refrain from using this data.

Price gaps

A gap in price is a situation where two adjacent ticks have an abnormal difference in price. Of course, like with time gaps, the question is how we define this to be *abnormal*. Here, we can use similar techniques as those we used with time gaps. If the difference in the price of two adjacent ticks is greater than the average plus 2 sigma, then this is a potential price gap.

In cases of price gaps, we frequently use 3 sigmas and more because the goal is not really to catch every situation when the price jumps quickly (in the real market this may happen quite often, at least a few times a day) but to isolate and filter out **non-market prices**.

Maybe you remember the illustration of what non-market price looked like in *Chapter 1*? So, a non-market price is something that lies completely, totally outside of any reasonable range, so we can easily consider 10, 20, and sometimes even 100 sigmas to filter out these erroneous quotes.

You may wonder about the source of these non-market prices. There can be multiple reasons for non-market prices:

- The most common reason is a so-called **fat finger effect**, simply a mistake in the bid or offer sent to the market. Typically, it is 10 times greater or 10 times less than the previous market price because of an extra 0 in the quote or a missing digit. Trades done at these prices are normally reversed in hindsight, but the quotes are recorded in the data stream and stored as historical data.

- Some data providers include data not related to trading; for example, I saw a case where the exchange included transfers to an insurance fund as market price data. Luckily they recorded these *ticks* at zero price – luckily because it is then very easy to filter out.

- In rare cases, there can be glitches in the data provider's database, software, or hardware – erroneous quotes caused by this reason are the hardest to find and filter.

After you have successfully connected to the data source, received data, and filtered it, it's time to do something meaningful with it: that is, analyze the data and make some trading decisions. This is what we're going to consider in the next section.

Trading logic – this is where a small mistake may cost a fortune

Trading logic is obviously the core of the entire trading app. It is the very component that analyzes the market data in search of any pre-defined price-time patterns (sometimes other data such as volume and open interest is included, but this data is typically not available for the spot market) and generates orders. Almost all of the rest of the book will be dedicated to trading logic and various approaches to developing trading algorithms but we can't really move on without considering one very typical mistake that already costs many traders millions, if not billions, of dollars. I mean the **peek ahead** issue.

The phenomenon of peeking ahead is specific to only the development phase of the project when the trading algorithm is optimized or trained using past market data, which is called historical data. As you remember from the previous section, historical data is something pre-recorded either by yourself or a third party such as an exchange, a broker, a data vendor, and so on. This data may contain ticks or may be compressed down to 1-second or 1-minute snapshots. Regardless of data compression, all data in a cleaned-up dataset is sorted by timestamp and there is no situation when any *future* data would go before the *past* data – or vice versa, when any past data would be recorded after any future data. Let's look at the following example to see what this means:

```
1/27/2015,13:30:00,1.12947,1.12959,1.12941,1.12941,230,438,888
,4,7,12
1/27/2015,13:31:00,1.12953,1.12970,1.12951,1.12965,400,240,650
,9,4,14
1/27/2015,13:32:00,1.12944,1.12944,1.12883,1.12883,90,609,749,
2,10,13
1/27/2015,13:33:00,1.12876,1.12907,1.12876,1.12894,589,170,909
,5,4,12
1/27/2015,13:34:00,1.12902,1.12925,1.12902,1.12925,720,400,112
0,9,4,13
```

In this example, the timestamps are in the correct order. This piece of data means that the closing price of the instrument (which can be found in the sixth position of each record) was *first* 1.12941, *then* 1.12965, *then* 1.12883, *then* 1.12894, and *finally* 1.12925.

When we develop and test a trading algorithm, we *simulate* trading by processing past data and making a trading decision based on it. Normally, the simulation engine processes pieces of data from a file, a list, or a pandas DataFrame one by one to simulate what *would have happened* if our algorithm traded *at that time*. So, we *must* make sure that at no point our trading algorithm can receive data *from the future*.

Let's again look at the preceding example. Imagine that we simulated the behavior of our trading algorithm at 13:32. All we and the algorithm may know at this step is that the closing price at that time was 1.12883. We *cannot* know – and the algorithm *cannot* know – that the closing price *would be* 1.12894 one minute later. However, if you store prices in a list (or a pandas DataFrame) it is easy to refer to the *future* price just by its index. So, I could potentially write something such as this (the following example assumes that `current_position` is the pointer which iterates through the dataset and `price_data` is the dataset itself):

```
current_position = x
if price_data[x + 1] > price_data[current_position]:
        order.buy(market)
if price_data[x + 1] < price_data[current_position]:
        order.sell(market)
```

In this code, we assume that the buy and `sell` methods generate buy and sell orders respectively. If we run a simulation using this code, we will have *100% of winning trades*. Not a single one will lose money because we compare a price *from the future* (lines 2 and 4) with the real price that exists *at the moment of simulation*. In our example, it would mean that at 13:32, I *already know what the price will be at 13:33* and compare it to the current price. Well, if I really could know that... Anyway, no one can see the future and you should make sure your algos are no exception.

> **Note**
> Always make sure you refer to prices one by one without peeking ahead. Use queues or refer to timestamps but always avoid referring to data by the index.

Alright, we now know, at least at a surface glance, how to communicate with the market, how to retrieve data and make sure it's consistent, and even how to avoid the greatest mistake that systematic trading strategies developers can make in the trading logic. Now, we should be able to send trading orders and protect ourselves against numerous adverse situations.

Risk management – your safety belt

After your algorithm has generated a trading signal, it should go past risk management. While trading logic answers the question *to trade or not to trade*, risk management answers another question: how much should be put at stake?

In basic terms, risk management involves analysis of the potential maximum adverse excursion per trade, account size, leverage and margin as financial components of risk, and macro-economic factors and political events as external and non-market risk. Just to give you an example, it would be wise to just switch off trading before the Swiss National Bank decision in January 2015 or the presidential elections in the US in 2016.

The topic of risk management is really vast and we will go into detail on this later in *Chapter 10, Types of Orders and Their Simulation in Python*, after we have learned more about types of trading strategies and orders.

Ordering – make sure you are understood correctly

Last, but by far not least, your trading application will have an ordering module. This module performs the following functions:

- It maintains the connection to the execution server keeping it alive.

- It transforms trading signals passed by the risk management module into actual orders – using FIX or any proprietary API.

- It handles all types of responses from the broker or trading venue. These responses range from just *OK* to partial fills and rejects.

- It decides what to do in cases where your order was rejected or filled partially.

- It resubmits orders, full or in parts, in case it is favored by the trading logic.

You may have noticed that one of the responsibilities of the ordering module is maintaining connections – quite like the data handling module. Yes, there's no mistake here, it is absolutely normal that a trading app uses **different** connections for data and for orders. Moreover, it is very frequent when data is obtained from a data vendor and orders are executed at an exchange or obtained from an exchange and executed with a market maker, and so on – in any possible combination. So, the ordering module also maintains the connection because this connection is different and separate.

As with risk management, we will go into the details of ordering along with risk management in *Chapter 10, Types of Orders and Their Simulation in Python*.

Summary

In this chapter, we learned how to connect to a broker or data vendor, retrieve live market data, understand the requirements for the quality of this data, and know all the five core logical blocks of which our future trading application will consist.

In the next chapter, we will move on to discuss the specifics of how we can efficiently handle *historical* market data because this is exactly what is required for the research and development phase.

5

Retrieving and Handling Market Data with Python

If you look at the general logical diagram of a trading application's architecture, which we devised in *Chapter 1, Developing Trading Strategies – Why They Are Different*, you can see that now we're moving from the very first module named `Receive data` to the second one, `Cleanup and filter`, which features the **Store** and **Retrieve** functionality.

In previous chapters, we mentioned many times that any algo trading application is based on market data, and success in algo trading (that is, the ability to make money and not lose it) depends on the quality of the data and its consistency. So, let's proceed to determine which data we really need to collect and how to make sure the collected data is consistent, then decide about the internal format for the trading app, and the way to store, update, retrieve, and delete data (if necessary).

Upon finishing this chapter, you will have a clear understanding of the most efficient ways of handling and processing market data, and, most importantly, you will learn how to keep your trading app universal so that it could be connected to virtually any data source, live or historical, without rewriting all your code.

In this chapter, we will cover the following topics:

- Navigating through data
- Data compression—keeping the amounts to a reasonable minimum
- Working with saved and live data—keeping your app universal

Navigating through data

The problem with data collection starts at the very beginning: every data provider offers its own data, quite often in its own format. Some data providers offer only compressed data or snapshots (see later in this chapter) while others broadcast tick-by-tick data; very few data providers also offer order book (**depth of market** or **DOM**; see *Chapter 3, FX Market Overview from a Developer's Standpoint*) data.

So, first and above all, you should decide on the data granularity: whether your trading algorithm requires tick-by-tick or compressed data, and if you need DOM data or not. At this stage, you may feel lost with these questions, but don't worry—you will get a very clear understanding of your data needs when you've accomplished further chapters of this book.

Let's consider all three cases and see how we can actually handle ticks, snapshots, and DOM market data.

Tick data and snapshots

I would like to reiterate that when we talk about third-party data, formats, and protocols, the ultimate source of the exact information about what is supported and how the third-party documentation is done is your broker.

However, in general, all data providers support two types of market data: tick and snapshots.

Let's quickly recap the terminology:

- A **tick** is a recorded change in any of the three prices of the traded asset: bid, ask (offer), and last

- **Bid** is the price at which market makers, liquidity providers, and other price givers agree to buy—and consequently, this is the price at which price takers can sell

- **Ask** or **offer** is the price at which price givers are ready to sell—and consequently, this is the price at which price takers can buy

- And **last** is the price at which the latest actual trade was made

Let's consider an example. This is sample tick data that you can receive from LMAX (see the previous chapter for more examples of connecting and retrieving data from this **electronic communication network (ECN)**):

```
{
    "type": "TICKER",
    "instrument_id": "eur-usd",
    "timestamp": "2022-07-29T11:10:54.755Z",
    "best_bid": "1.180970",
    "best_ask": "1.181010",
    "trade_id": "0B5WMAAAAAAAAAS",
    "last_quantity": "1000.0000",
    "last_price": "1.180970",
    "session_open": "1.181070",
    "session_low": "1.180590",
    "session_high": "1.181390"
}
```

First, the preceding JSON specifies the type of data. In this example, `type` is `TICKER`, which means that we're dealing with a single tick. It is followed by the instrument name.

> **Important note**
>
> Many data providers use different notations for the same names of instruments. For example, EUR/USD can be represented by `eur-usd`, `EURUSD`, `EUR/USD`, and even `@EURUSD`. So, always check the data provider's documentation, and don't forget to replace the instrument's name in the provider's notation with the internal name used in your application.

For example, if you use the traditional `CCY1/CCY2` notation, then you may want to use the following code, which will transform the `ccy1-ccy2` notation used by LMAX to the traditional one:

```
instrument_id.replace("-", "/").upper()
```

Here, `instrument_id` is the name of the instrument received with a tick from the data provider, `replace()` is the built-in sting method that replaces one character with another, and `upper()` is another built-in method that makes the entire string uppercase.

Next comes the timestamp, and with timestamps comes another degree of uncertainty because data providers use different standards for timestamps. We will discuss timestamps for market data a bit later in this section.

The following fields are self-explanatory:

- `best_bid` and `best_ask` mean the top of the book
- `trade_id` is the ID of the latest trade made at this ECN
- `last_quantity` and `last_price` are the size and price at which this latest trade was made
- `session_open`, `session_low`, and `session_high` mean the first price of the trading session (when the market opens), and the lowest and the highest price from the time the market opened till the time the tick is received

As we can see, most of the fields in a tick are self-explanatory and easy to use, but there's one important exception: `timestamp`.

Timestamps – be careful comparing apples to apples!

In the previous section, when we were analyzing the structure of a tick, we noted that it contained a timestamp and that this timestamp may become another source of headache for the developer. This happens because every data provider thinks they're using the most convenient data format. As always, refer to the provider's documentation and refer to any tutorial on working with timestamps. If you're not familiar with timestamps and their standards, I'd recommend starting with an excellent tutorial on working with timestamps in Python by Avinash Navlani on *Dataquest* (https://www. dataquest.io/blog/python-datetime-tutorial).

Anyway, to keep things simple, a timestamp is a string formatted to one of the standards, and this formatting is normally done by whitespaces, special characters, or regular characters. In the LMAX example in the previous section, the date part is separated from the time part by the letter T, and the entire timestamp is ended with the letter Z.

Python provides a datetime library that covers flexible handling of timestamps. This library introduces the eponymous datetime object, which has multiple methods to convert strings into timestamps and vice versa. In the upcoming example, we're going to use strptime() to convert the timestamp from a string to a native datetime object.

By using strptime() and other methods, all you need is to specify the format of the input timestamp using correct specifiers (see the Python documentation at https://docs.python.org/2/ library/datetime.html#strftime-and-strptime-behavior for a complete list of specifiers).

So, let's convert the timestamp from our LMAX example into a native datetime object. First, we import datetime from the datetime library (yes—it does look ridiculous, but what to do?) and then make the conversion:

```
from datetime import datetime
ts_str1 = '2022-07-29T11:10:54.755Z'
ts1 = datetime.strptime(ts_str1, '%Y-%m-%dT%H:%M:%S.%fZ')
```

Here, we assume that ts_str1 is the timestamp already extracted from the tick received from LMAX as XML (JSON). If we run this code and check the value of ts1, then we will see the following:

```
In [21]: ts1
Out[21]: datetime.datetime(2022, 7, 29, 11, 10, 54, 755000)
```

This means that the conversion was made correctly, and now we can access any component of the timestamp separately. For example, ts1.day returns 29 (the day of the month), and ts1. microsecond returns 755000, which is actually 755 milliseconds.

The real advantage of using datetime objects is that they can be sorted like numbers. For example, if we receive a new timestamp that is just 1 millisecond past the original one (ts_str2 = '2022-07-29T11:10:54.756Z') and convert it into a new datetime object (ts2 = datetime.strptime(ts_str2, '%Y-%m-%dT%H:%M:%S.%fZ')), then we can easily compare two timestamps, as follows:

```
In [27]: ts1 > ts2
Out[27]: False
```

Subsequently, we can sort them in ascending or descending order.

> **Important note**
>
> Never use strings as IDs of timestamps for market data time series. You won't be able to easily sort data by the exact time it's arrived, and thus handling data will be extremely inefficient. Use native `datetime` or pandas timestamps (see the next section).

Storing and retrieving tick data

There are three main approaches to storing and processing tick data in Python:

- Using high-level objects
- Using low-level objects
- Using pandas

High-level objects are normally created for storing considerable amounts of data or processing the entire historical data (see *Chapter 2, Using Python for Trading Strategies*). In this case, we create a single object whose properties include lists (in case we're going to store data samples one by one and refer to them by index) or dictionaries (in case we use timestamps to refer to a data sample).

Using dictionaries allows for quick and easy handling of data by timestamp, so this is the preferred method of storing market data. Let's see an example:

1. Let's begin with creating a general class:

   ```
   class data:
       def __init__ (self):
           self.series = {}
   ```

   This `main` dictionary will store all data samples with timestamps used as keywords.

2. Now, let's add a method that adds a new data sample to the `main` dictionary:

   ```
   def add(self, sample):
           ts = datetime.strptime(sample["timestamp"],
   '%Y-%m-%dT%H:%M:%S.%fZ')
           self.series[ts] = sample
   ```

   Here, we assume that the data sample comes in a form similar to that used by LMAX—that is, JSON, which contains a timestamp in *ISO 8601* format. Since the JSON (or XML in general) is basically the same as native Python dictionaries, we add a dictionary to the dictionary. Now, referring to `self.series` by the timestamp as the keyword will return another dictionary that contains the data sample itself. This is what we referred to as *low-level objects* at the beginning of this section.

> **Important note**
>
> We can refer to ticks by timestamp only in case the data feed doesn't send ticks with identical timestamps. This is mostly the case with direct feeds from trading venues. The suggested code will always rewrite the contents of a tick with the last received value with the same timestamp, so if you really need to keep all ticks stored, consider adding **unique IDs (UIDs)** to them. The public LMAX data feeds that we're using throughout the book for development and testing purposes never send ticks with identical timestamps.

3. So, now, let's add a basic function that finds a data sample by its timestamp:

```
def get(self, ts, key):
        return self.series[ts][key]
```

Note that two keywords ([ts] and [key]) are used here, one immediately after another. This is exactly because of the data structure just explained: we have dictionaries in a dictionary, so the first keyword [ts] retrieves the data sample dictionary, and the second one— [key] — actually returns the value.

It is important to note here that such a method of retrieving ticks by their timestamps assumes that we know the exact timestamp with milliseconds precision. If we are unsure about it or want to extract a few ticks that came—for example—in 1 second or even 1 minute, we can use the following code, which will return a list of ticks whose timestamps start with the same time (actually, we look for a substring in the timestamp key):

```
result = [(key, value) for key, value in self.series.
items() if key.startswith("2022-07-29T11:10:54")]
return result
```

4. OK—let's give our code a try. Let's use the same example as before—create a new data series object, add a sample to it, and read the trade_id value:

```
sample = {
    "type": "TICKER",
    "instrument_id": "eur-usd",
    "timestamp": "2022-07-29T11:10:54.755Z",
    "best_bid": "1.180970",
    "best_ask": "1.181010",
    "trade_id": "0B5WMAAAAAAAAAAS",
    "last_quantity": "1000.0000",
    "last_price": "1.180970",
```

```
        "session_open": "1.181070",
        "session_low": "1.180590",
        "session_high": "1.181390"
    }
series = data()
series.add(sample)
timestamp = datetime.strptime(sample["timestamp"],
'%Y-%m-%dT%H:%M:%S.%fZ')
print(series.get(timestamp, "trade_id"))
```

If we run this code (not forgetting to add `from datetime import datetime` at the very beginning), we will get `0B5WMAAAAAAAAAAS`, which is indeed the trade ID of the stored tick data sample.

This way, we can easily implement creating, adding, and reading data from our storage without using any database. Of course, this approach will somewhat limit the capabilities of retrieving and aggregating data by other keys—for example, retrieving all ticks with the same price or with a trade quantity that lies in a certain range.

> **Remember**
>
> Ignoring or messing with the data, especially the order in which ticks or bars are received, will most likely lead you to develop a strategy which will work only on this damaged data, and won't work with real market data.

So, for most practical trading applications, it is even better not to be able to get data by any other keyword except for the timestamp. However, if you're into some kind of academic research and do need special modes of data retrieval, there's good news for you: pandas will allow you to do even this (we will have a surface look at pandas in *Chapter 8, Data Visualization in FX Trading with Python*).

An alternative way to store tick market data would be in a list, not a dictionary. This way, we could forget about timestamps and read data samples one by one, using an index—which is especially useful when running backtests using historical data.

However, there's one significant problem with storing market data in lists. In case you need to add any data sample *in the past*, you will have to scan the list to find the correct place where to insert the new sample, and this operation is quite time-consuming. So, using dictionaries with timestamps as keywords is always preferable.

You may argue that inserting a sample *in the past* sounds ridiculous and is hardly required. Well, just go on reading this chapter, and in the section dedicated to cleaning up the market data, you will see how in demand such a capability may be.

Order book (depth of market)

Some data providers (not many, actually) are kind enough to provide not only top of book (the best bid and ask prices), but also some depth of market (see the *Exchange and order book* section of *Chapter 3*, *FX Market Overview from a Developer's Standpoint*). In general, receiving order book data is not much different from receiving ticker data. The only difference is that ticker data contains a single value for each bid, ask, and last price, whereas order book data contains multiple values for bids and asks and does not contain any last value.

Storing and retrieving order book data

If we look at the example provided by LMAX in its API documentation, we can see that the JSON representing the order book information can be interpreted by Python as follows:

- **Highest level**: A dictionary similar to that of ticker data, but without last trade and session information

- **Lower level**: A list of bids and asks, sorted by price in descending and ascending order, respectively

- **Lowest level**: Another dictionary that contains the actual price and quantity for each bid and ask:

```
{
    "type": "ORDER_BOOK",
    "instrument_id": "eur-usd",
    "timestamp": "2022-07-29T11:10:54.755Z",
    "status": "OPEN",
    "bids":
      [
          {
              "price": "1.181060",
              "quantity": "500000.0000"
          },
          {
              "price": "1.181050",
              "quantity": "200000.0000"
          }
      ],
      "asks": [
          {
              "price": "1.181100",
              "quantity": "250000.0000"
```

```
        },
        {
                "price": "1.181110",
                "quantity": "350000.0000"
        }
    ]
}
```

Therefore, we can use exactly the same code as we originally used for storing, adding, and reading tick data. We will only need to add another level of indexes and keywords to access actual values. For example, if we add the preceding sample, then we can retrieve the best bid price by the timestamp using the following code:

```
best_bid = series.get(timestamp, "bids")[0]["price"]
```

The beginning of this line is identical to that of the example with ticker data from the previous section, then follows the index [0], which is used to retrieve the best bid (as both bids and asks are sorted, the first element in the list always contains the best bid or ask), and finally, another keyword—price, used to retrieve the price information out of the price/volume pair.

Now, we can retrieve tick data, but remember that it may occupy too much space in memory or on disk. So, it would be nice to use only the required amount of data for a specific trading strategy. That's why we proceed with data compression.

Data compression – keeping the amounts to a reasonable minimum

In the previous section, we already considered one of the most popular data compression techniques used by data providers: snapshots. The difference is that a tick represents a single event (such as a new trade or a change in bid or ask) and a single price value, but a snapshot instead discards information about individual ticks and replaces it with the following prices per period:

- Price of the first tick of the period (or **open**)
- Maximum price for the period (or **high**)
- Minimum price for the period (or **low**)
- Price of the last tick of the period (or **close**)

For example, if the period is 1 minute and during this minute 100 trades were placed, then the snapshot will replace 100 ticks (or 100 prices) with just 4 prices.

The resulting snapshots are called bars when plotted on charts. Very frequently, traders and developers use *bars* instead of *snapshots*. Graphically, a bar is typically presented as a vertical line with two dashes. As you can see in the following diagram, the one pointing to the left means the opening (first) price of the interval represented by this bar, and the one pointing to the right means the last (closing) price of the same interval, while the top and bottom of the vertical line represent the maximum and the minimum prices of the interval, respectively. These bars are called **Open-High-Low-Close bars** or **OHLC bars**:

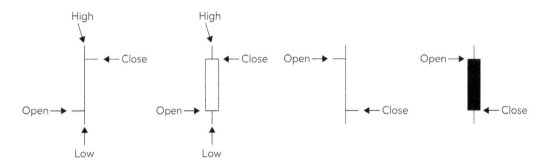

Figure 5.1 – Bars and Japanese candlesticks as a visual representation of data compression

In case the left dash is lower than the right one, we say that the bar *closes up* or the price movement was upward during that period of time (during that bar). If the right dash is lower than the left one, we say that the bar *closes down* or the price movement was downward.

There is another way of presenting bars, which is known as **Japanese candlesticks**. They don't have dashes to the left and to the right, but instead the range between the open and close prices is drawn as a rectangle. And to show whether the opening price was greater or less than the closing one, we use color coding: white or green normally means that the bar closes up (that the closing price was greater than the opening one), and black or red means that the bar closes down.

Then, is data compression good or bad?

Of course, the answer depends on the intended purpose of using the data compression. In general, data compression allows us to dramatically reduce storage space. Just to give you an idea: 4 years' worth of historical market data compressed into 1-minute bars takes about 152 MB if saved as an American Standard Code for Information Interchange (ASCII) CSV file. The same time span of tick data will take about 1.4 to 3 GB depending on the type of tick data (whether only the last trade is transmitted as a tick or every change in bid or ask price is included).

Besides that, using data in compressed format radically speeds up the backtesting process (remember that backtesting means simulating trades generated by the algorithm using pre-stored historical price data). No surprise that processing 100,000 records is much faster than processing 1 million.

Therefore, when you use historical data from a data vendor or download it from your broker's website, most likely it will be compressed down to 1 minute, 10 seconds, or 1 second, but anyway it's unlikely to be raw tick data.

When developing trading strategies, we often use much less granular resolutions, such as 1 hour, 4 hours, 1 day, and sometimes even 1 week or 1 month.

However, using compressed data has a serious disadvantage for developers. Since individual ticks are gone, we cannot say which price came first, second, and so on inside an individual bar. In *Chapter 10, Types of Orders and Their Simulation in Python*, we will consider serious issues related to using compressed data in trade simulation and see how we can minimize the risk of making a mistake.

As we are now familiar with the concept of data compression, let's see how we can practically use it. We will start with retrieving already compressed data and then see how we can compress data in our own code.

Retrieving compressed data

Some data vendors, brokers, and trading venues use compressed data for live streaming, but most use it for historical data. In this case, you can download it as XML or—more frequently—as traditional CSV files. Contents again (as always!) depend on the data provider's free will, but at the very least it should contain the timestamp and the OHLC price data. Some data providers also include the trading volume data and even the number of upticks and downticks (moments when the price changed up or down respectively), as follows:

```
Date,Time,Open,High,Low,Close,UpVolume,DownVolume,TotalVolume,
UpTicks,DownTicks,TotalTicks
1/27/2015,13:29:00,1.12942,1.12950,1.12942,1.12949,200,150,639
,3,2,8
1/27/2015,13:30:00,1.12947,1.12959,1.12941,1.12941,230,438,888
,4,7,12
1/27/2015,13:31:00,1.12953,1.12970,1.12951,1.12965,400,240,650
,9,4,14
1/27/2015,13:32:00,1.12944,1.12944,1.12883,1.12883,90,609,749,
2,10,13
```

Now, let's see how we can efficiently read, store, and retrieve historical compressed price data:

1. First, we need some preparations. We will obviously need the `datetime` module, storage for all data (dictionary), and storage for an individual data sample (another dictionary):

    ```
    from datetime import datetime
    historical_data = {}
    sample = {}
    ```

2. Then, we need to read the data. If we're working with a CSV file, it can be done very easily, as shown here:

    ```
    file_name = '/path/to/the/data/file'
    f = open(file_name)
    ```

3. Let's read the first line (the header) to avoid possible errors when parsing price data:

    ```
    f.readline()
    ```

4. Next, we're going to read lines from the file, one by one:

    ```
    for line in f:
    ```

5. In the body of this loop, we remove any ending newline characters and parse the received line into a `values` list:

    ```
    values = line.rstrip("\n").split(",")
    ```

6. Now, we're going to merge the date and the time into a single string and convert it to a `datetime` object:

    ```
    timestamp_string = values[0] + " " + values[1]
    ts = datetime.strptime(timestamp_string, "%m/%d/%Y %H:%M:%S")
    ```

7. After that, we will gather the rest of the info into a dictionary:

    ```
    sample["open"]  = float(values[2])
    sample["high"]  = float(values[3])
    sample["low"]   = float(values[4])
    sample["close"] = float(values[5])
    sample["UpVolume"]   = int(values[6])
    sample["DownVolume"] = int(values[7])
    ```

8. Now, add the new sample to the global dataset dictionary using `timestamp` as a keyword:

    ```
    historical_data[ts] = sample
    ```

9. Now, if we check the data for the first record in the dataset, we will get the following:

    ```
    {'open': 1.12942, 'high': 1.1295, 'low': 1.12942,
    'close': 1.12949, 'UpVolume': 200, 'DownVolume': 150}
    ```

10. Now, if I want to retrieve a particular value for the closing price on a certain date and at a certain time, I may want to use something like the following:

    ```
    historical_data[timestamp]['close']
    ```

    Where `timestamp` stands for the timestamp at which you'd like to retrieve the closing price.

When running backtests, we do not retrieve data samples by their timestamp, though; instead, we'd like to have a method to continuously get samples one by one in strict chronological order. Native Python dictionaries normally contain unsorted data; however, there's a workaround that allows us to sort data by keywords—making dictionary keys sorted and automatically getting data samples sorted always in correct chronological order. Alternatively, you can use the `OrderedDict` subclass of the Python native `dict` object, which implements a dictionary with keys pre-sorted (you can find a simple tutorial on `OrderedDict` at `https://www.tutorialspoint.com/ordereddict-in-python`).

To do that, we use the built-in `sorted` method, which returns a list of the sorted values for any iterable in ascending order by default—exactly what we want:

```
for ts in sorted(historical_data):
    print(historical_data[ts])
```

The preceding code will print all data samples from the very first to the very last in strict chronological order (don't run this code with massive datasets as it will take a lot of time to display!).

Now, we can read historical data, sort it in correct chronological order, and retrieve it one by one—that's all we need to be ready for backtesting of our algorithms.

Compressing market data in Python

It is quite possible that even though a full tick data stream is available from the data provider, we still want to compress it, and not only to save disk storage space. The reason for this compression could be much more important, such as our trading algorithm can possibly generate some signals or calculate some auxiliary metrics using historical data that is compressed. Therefore, we also need to feed the algorithm with data compressed in a similar manner. And although tick data provides much more information as such, we may still want to compress it to make it compatible with the trading logic.

The most correct way to compress the data from tick to OHLC bars would be to have a method that receives ticks, recalculates OHL (open-high-low) values with each tick, and then adds the C (close) value when the time comes. For example, if we want to compress ticks into 1-minute bars, this method would create a new bar at the beginning of each minute and complete it when the minute's interval has passed. Let's look at an example to understand this better:

1. Let's assume we have historical tick data in a local file (we will see how properly written code allows us to quickly switch from files to any other source of data):

    ```
    file_name = '<your_path_name>/EURUSD 1 Tick.csv'
    f = open(file_name)
    f.readline()
    ```

    We immediately read the first line of the file and never use it as the first line as just the header.

2. Next, we don't forget to import `datetime` and create two dictionaries—one for the entire data series and another for an individual bar:

    ```
    from datetime import datetime
    bars = {}
    bar = {}
    ```

3. Next, we set the resolution for our newly formed time-based bars. I recommend using a universal measurement unit here. For example, if you work with relatively slow trading strategies, then you may want to count time in minutes. For greater precision and granularity, you may want to go down to seconds. So, let's use seconds as units and form 1-minute bars (1-minute bar equals to 60 seconds):

    ```
    resolution = 60
    ```

4. Next, we should read another line from the file, still outside the main loop, to get the first timestamp. We are going to compare all further timestamps with this one, and as soon as the distance (in time) between the two becomes greater than the resolution (60 seconds in our case), we will start a new bar:

    ```
    values = f.readline().rstrip("\n").split(",")
    timestamp_string = values[0] + " " + values[1]
    last_sample_ts = datetime.strptime(timestamp_string,
    "%m/%d/%Y %H:%M:%S.%f")
    ```

At last, the main loop starts:

```
for line in f:
    values = line.rstrip("\n").split(",")
    timestamp_string = values[0] + " " + values[1]
    ts = datetime.strptime(timestamp_string, "%m/%d/%Y
%H:%M:%S.%f")
```

Until this point, the code of the loop body is identical to what we already did—we read a new line and parse it. But then, we compare the received timestamp with the timestamp of the last formed bar or sample:

```
delta = ts - last_sample_ts
```

Here, you can feel all the beauty of using timestamps in datetime format. You can add or subtract them as if they were just regular numbers.

Note for nerds

Python supports multiple types that handle dates and times. Besides datetime, there is another useful type—timedelta, which allows easily defining time spans. If you want to learn more about timedelta and how to efficiently use it, try this tutorial: https://tutorial.eyehunts.com/python/python-timedelta-difference-two-date-time-datetime/.

---

5. Now, when the time delta between the new tick timestamp and the previous fully formed bar timestamp is greater than the resolution, we add the current bar to our bars global dictionary and start a new bar by replacing its values with the same price—the price of the last tick. Don't forget to convert strings to numbers down the road:

```
if delta.seconds >= resolution:
    bars[ts] = bar
    bar["open"]  = float(values[2])
    bar["high"]  = float(values[2])
    bar["low"]   = float(values[2])
    last_sample_ts = ts
```

Alternatively, if the time delta is still less than the resolution (in our example, it's under 1 minute), then we just update the values of the current bar:

```
else:
    bar["high"]  = max([bar["high"], float(values[2])])
    bar["low"]   = min([bar["low"], float(values[2])])
    bar["close"] = float(values[2])
```

Seems like we're done with coding. Alright—let's run our code, and we will immediately get an error:

```
File "/.../example5.py", line 36, in <module>
    bar["high"] = max([bar["high"], float(values[2])])
KeyError: 'high'
```

This means that the dictionary in which we form the current bar does not have the `high` keyword. How can this happen? Of course, it happens during the forming of the very first bar: until we save at least one bar, none of its properties (open, high, low, or close) is available. So, we fix our code by adding a `try...except` statement:

```
else:
        try:
                bar["high"] = max([bar["high"],
float(values[2])])
                bar["low"] = min([bar["low"],
float(values[2])])
                bar["close"] = float(values[2])
        except:
                print('first bar forming...')
```

Now, during the formation of the very first bar, we can see only `First bar forming...` on the screen. You can replace this message with anything or completely remove it by replacing the `print` statement with `pass`.

6. Let's run the code again, and we can see that now it's executed successfully. If we check the last 4 records in the `bars` variable, we can see that the timestamps of bars indeed have a delta of approximately 1 minute:

```
datetime.datetime(2022, 8, 8, 18, 53, 8, 64000): {'open':
1.01973,
   'high': 1.01984,
   'low': 1.01972,
   'close': 1.01972},
 datetime.datetime(2022, 8, 8, 18, 54, 8, 347000):
{'open': 1.01973,
   'high': 1.01984,
   'low': 1.01972,
   'close': 1.01972},
 datetime.datetime(2022, 8, 8, 18, 55, 10, 731000):
{'open': 1.01973,
```

```
    'high': 1.01984,
    'low': 1.01972,
    'close': 1.01972},
  datetime.datetime(2022, 8, 8, 18, 56, 12, 81000):
{'open': 1.01973,
    'high': 1.01984,
    'low': 1.01972,
    'close': 1.01972}}
```

But wait! The timestamps are OK, but why are all respective prices (comparing open to open, close to close, and so on) in all bars identical?!

Here, we have an issue that actually is one of the most prominent features of Python as a very well-developed object-oriented language. What we actually do in our code is the following sequence of actions:

1. We create object1 (bars dictionary).

2. We create object2 (bar dictionary).

3. We add object2 to object1 with a new keyword.

4. Then, we *modify* object2.

5. Again, we add object2 to object1 with a new keyword.

6. ...and then repeat this loop.

See the point? We thought we'd add a new object every time we wanted to add a new bar to bars, but in reality, we add *the same* object—the same bar dictionary—only with modified values. I know that at first, it's hard to understand, so try to think this way: the bars[ts] = bar assignment means saving a *link* to the bar object into the bars object with the ts keyword. In this case, once the bar object itself is modified, the reference to it in the bars object remains the same, so we always get modified values when we try to retrieve the bar object from bars.

But what do we actually want here? Of course, we want to save *every bar individually* so that if we update the bar object outside the bars object, its new values *will not affect* whatever is already stored in the bars object.

In fact, we want to save not the bar object itself, but *a copy of it,* which will remain unmodified when we update the bar object in the future. To do that, we just replace bars[ts] = bar with bars[ts] = dict(bar). Here, dict is a class that generates a *new* dictionary out of any iterable, mapping object, or keyword arguments. In our case, it's quite simplified as we use a ready dictionary (bar) as the mapping object.

If we run the code now, with this edit, we can see that not only timestamps are correct, but the price data in `bars` is correct as well:

```
datetime.datetime(2022, 8, 8, 18, 53, 8, 64000): {'open':
1.01982,
   'high': 1.02007,
   'low': 1.01982,
   'close': 1.02001},
  datetime.datetime(2022, 8, 8, 18, 54, 8, 347000): {'open':
1.01996,
   'high': 1.01998,
   'low': 1.01979,
   'close': 1.01981},
  datetime.datetime(2022, 8, 8, 18, 55, 10, 731000): {'open':
1.01977,
   'high': 1.01982,
   'low': 1.01965,
   'close': 1.01965},
  datetime.datetime(2022, 8, 8, 18, 56, 12, 81000): {'open':
1.01968,
   'high': 1.01971,
   'low': 1.01964,
   'close': 1.01968}}
```

So, now, we have 1-minute bars formed from tick data.

But what do their timestamps mean?

Which time do they actually reference?

And why is the seconds value of these timestamps not zero (as we would expect for a 1-minute resolution), but also differs slightly from bar to bar?

To answer the first question, our algorithm in its present form saves the timestamp *of the last tick of the time interval*. This happens because the trigger by which we start forming a new bar is `if delta. seconds >= resolution`. So, `if` starts a new bar as soon as (and no earlier than!) a new tick is received, and the timestamp of this new tick differs from its immediate predecessor by a value (which is called `timedelta`) that is greater than `resolution`. In other words, if we set `resolution` to 1 second, then we start a new bar only when we receive a tick whose timestamp differs from the start (open) of the currently forming bar by 1,000 milliseconds or more.

This also answers two remaining questions. Since the timestamp of the very first received tick (the first tick in the data file) may not be a *round* number and minutes with zero seconds, we start counting 60 seconds not from the beginning of a minute, but from an arbitrary moment.

"Is it good or bad?" you may ask.

Neither.

The correct question here would be *"Does it suit my trading algorithm?"*.

And the answer depends on the logic of your algorithm. If it only analyzes the sequence of prices (or maybe volume, if the volume is provided by the data provider) then yes—this method works well and is really easy to implement. However, if your strategy logic assumes triggering orders or doing calculations at the real edge of a minute (or any other time interval), then this method won't fit.

Luckily, we can easily modify our code so that it's generating bars with the exact 1-minute resolution. The problem is that there's no universal way of doing that, and the choice depends on whether you work with a live data stream or with saved tick data. To better understand it, let's first quickly go back to the problem of retrieving data from external data sources and keeping your trading application modular and scalable. Then, you will understand how the problem of generating correct timestamps can be elegantly solved within this paradigm. All this, coming up in the next section!

Working with saved and live data – keeping your app universal

In the previous chapter, we quickly observed various methods to get market data from LMAX, one of the most important ECNs in the FX market. Without going into too much technical detail, we can assume that most other brokers, trading venues, and data vendors use more or less the same protocols and APIs based on socket connections. So, it should not be a problem to re-adapt your code to start retrieving data from a new source.

However, from the previous chapter, I hope you also remember that despite similarities in the transport layer of the connection, almost every data source has its own features that can only be found in its documentation (and sometimes, unfortunately, only in direct talks with its technical support).

This means that even if you implemented—for example—**Financial Information eXchange** (**FIX**) protocol version 4.4 with one broker, it is quite possible that you will have to modify something in your code or FIX dictionary when you want to connect to another broker. With proprietary APIs, the situation is obviously more complex, and sometimes the entire code should be rewritten (everything on top of the transport layer, such as the socket connection).

So, a good practice when building a trading application is to make sure that it has a modular structure where modules have interfaces talking to each other using an internal, built-in, universal transport infrastructure. Such an infrastructure should transfer price information between modules regardless of their particular implementation, even if they are provided by third parties. In this case, you don't have to modify the entire application once you want to switch to another data source: you just need to write a new module, and a new plugin if you want, which would connect to the new source but deliver data in the same internal format compatible with the rest of the app's modules.

In general, we want to create an architecture as shown in *Figure 5.2*:

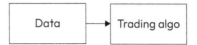

Figure 5.2 – The most simplistic data transport infrastructure for a trading app

However, this simplistic architecture has prominent flaws:

- It supports only one source of data
- It supports only one trading algorithm

So, we may want to upgrade our architecture a bit to add multiple data streams to our trading algorithm, as follows:

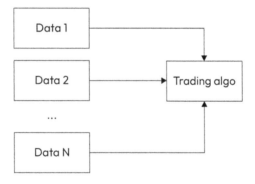

Figure 5.3 – Multiple data sources with a single trading algorithm

Well, this architecture reveals a new problem: how to sync multiple data streams? How to decide which tick to pass to the algo if we have multiple sources? How do we request these sources? If we do that from our global infinite loop (for line in file for data read from a file or while True for socket connections), then we will have a really hard time switching to another data source because it will require rewriting almost the entire code.

Moreover, if we want to run a number of trading algorithms in parallel using a number of data sources, we quickly come to a complete mess:

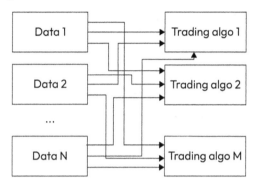

Figure 5.4 – Using multiple data sources with multiple algorithms in a bad way

Now, we clearly understand what we actually need to build a robust infrastructure. We need:

- To be able to run multiple processes of retrieving data *concurrently* without interfering with one another

- To be able to store received data in universal elastic storage that is being filled with new data and then emptied as older ticks are processed by the trading algorithms

So, we are talking about an architecture as shown in *Figure 5.5* with multiple data connectors, each of them having methods to connect, get data, and write it to a kind of a queue, and multiple trading algorithms (about whose internal architecture we don't know anything yet) exchanging information using universal *elastic storage*, as described in the preceding list:

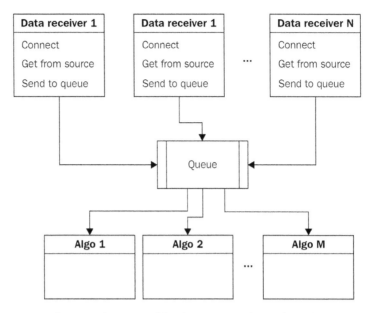

Figure 5.5 – A better architecture of the data transport layer of a trading application

Python does offer native solutions to both problems in an exceptionally streamlined and convenient way (as always, though). The ability to run data connectors concurrently is provided by *threads*, while the "elastic storage" mentioned previously is a *queue*. Let's give both some insight.

A **thread** is a separate branch of execution of the program's code that runs *concurrently* with the main code or in parallel with other threads. It can be implemented only within the paradigm of **object-oriented programming** (**OOP**) where we no longer have a single algorithm with a single start and a single end point, but instead, we have objects with their own behavior that can co-exist without interfering with one another or interacting with each other, depending on the will of their creator. So, a thread is an object that runs a function (a method) in parallel with everything else. Exactly what we need for retrieving data from multiple sources without syncing, right?

A **queue** is... well, a queue that you can see at a cash desk around Christmas time. Customers are served on a first-come, first-served basis. The data in a Python queue is treated the same way: whatever gets into the queue is moving along as older data is being processed. The moment a new element is retrieved, it is removed from the queue, freeing up space for newer data.

To better understand how queues work, let's consider a very simple example:

```
import queue
q = queue.Queue()
q.put("Sample 1")
q.put("Sample 2")
print(q.get())
```

If you run this code, it will print `Sample 1` because the very first element in the queue was the `Sample 1` string. However, if you work in an interactive console and type `print(q.get())` again (or just add another `print(q.get())` statement to the code), then this second `print` statement will print `Sample 2` because `Sample 1` was already retrieved by the `.get()` method and deleted from the queue.

Now that we know what threads and queues are, we can suggest a final draft for the architecture of the data transport layer of our trading application:

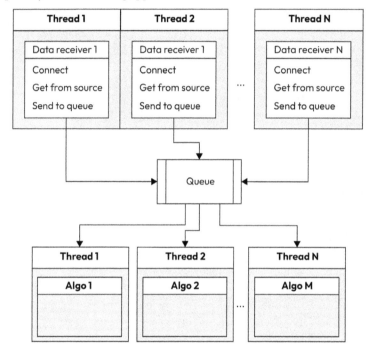

Figure 5.6 – The final draft of the architecture of the data transport layer of a trading app

Let's now try to implement it in code.

Universal data connector

Let's start with the necessary preparations:

1. We will need to specify the source data file, read the header, and do some imports:

```
file_name = '<your_file_path>/EURUSD 1 Tick.csv'
f = open(file_name)
f.readline()
```

```
from datetime import datetime
import threading
import queue
import time
```

2. Now, let's create a universal data stream, something into which all retrieved data will be written. Of course, it's an instance of Python's queue class:

```
datastream = queue.Queue()
```

3. And now, let's create our first method that retrieves data, this time from a local file:

```
def get_tick():
    tick = {}
    values = f.readline().rstrip("\n").split(",")
    timestamp_string = values[0] + " " + values[1]
    ts = datetime.strptime(timestamp_string, "%m/%d/%Y
%H:%M:%S.%f")
    tick[ts] = float(values[2])
    return tick
```

Can you see the already familiar code? Yes, of course—this is just a copy of what we did in the previous section, but this time wrapped into a function. So far, no different from what we did before. The difference comes with the following two functions:

```
def emulate_tick_stream():
    while True:
        time.sleep(1)
        temp = get_tick()
        datastream.put(temp)


def trading_algo():
    while True:
      temp = datastream.get()
        print('Received tick ', temp)
```

The first function, emulate_tick_stream(), reads a new tick from the file every second and puts it into the datastream queue.

> **Note**
>
> This 1-second delay is added here only for demonstration purposes—real data retrieval methods should not contain any delays!

The second function is simply a prototype—a dummy trading algorithm. It does nothing but report that it successfully received a new data sample.

4. Now, it's time to run both processes—retrieving and processing data—in parallel. The time has come for Python threads:

    ```
    data_source_thread = threading.Thread(target = emulate_
    tick_stream)
    data_receiver_thread = threading.Thread(target = trading_
    algo)
    ```

    This way, we create two instances of the `Thread` class, one for retrieving data (`data_source_thread`) and one for processing data (`data_receiver_thread`). As the only argument, we pass the name of the function that we would like to run within this thread.

> **Note**
>
> We pass the function name and do not call the function itself! If you type something such as `threading.Thread(target = trading_algo())`, the function will be called right *at the point it is passed* into the thread, so *the thread will never actually start!*

5. All we need to do now is to run the two threads concurrently:

    ```
    data_source_thread.start()
    data_receiver_thread.start()
    ```

    That's it! Now if we run the code in a new console window, we will see something like this:

    ```
    ('Received tick ', {datetime.datetime(2022, 8, 8, 13, 50,
    30, 446000): 1.01896})
    ('Received tick ', {datetime.datetime(2022, 8, 8, 13, 50,
    31, 505000): 1.01895})
    ('Received tick ', {datetime.datetime(2022, 8, 8, 13, 50,
    33, 619000): 1.019})
    ('Received tick ', {datetime.datetime(2022, 8, 8, 13, 50,
    36, 793000): 1.01901})
    ```

A new line will appear every second (because we have a delay of 1 second in the `get_tick()` function).

Even in this simple example, we can see the power of using an object-oriented approach to developing trading apps and especially using threads and queues. Now, you can rewrite the `get_tick()`

function to connect to a totally different data source, and the rest of your code will remain completely, absolutely untouched! You can replace reading from a file with reading from a socket, from a REST API, or from whatever you (or your broker) might imagine. It won't ever affect the rest of your code, given your new `get_tick()` function returns data in the same format.

And now, we can get back to the discussion on data compression, which we somehow abruptly dropped in the previous section.

Data compression revisited

Remember that we compressed tick data into 1-minute bars, but the actual beginning and end of a minute was not when the number of seconds was zero, but at an arbitrary point inside a minute interval? That time, we were unable to solve this problem because we only read data samples one by one from a file at a speed that was unknown to us.

But with the power of threading and queuing, we can form *correct* 1-minute (or any N-minute) bars with perfect precision when the new bar starts at exactly 00 seconds. All we need is to add a new function and run it in a thread.

> **Note**
>
> Note how easy it is now to customize data processing. We no longer rewrite the entire code—we only add new functionality or modify a single function.

So, let's create a function that will break our incoming data stream into 1-minute bars simply by using a system timer:

1. We will start with creating a dictionary for the currently forming bar (as in the previous example), and, as always with functions that are supposed to work inside threads, we start with an infinite loop:

    ```
    def compressor():
        bar = {}
        while True:
    ```

2. Then, we will read data from the data stream:

    ```
    tick = datastream.get()
    ```

    Note that this call is universal for any data recipient, be it a trading strategy, a data compressor, a database, or whatever.

3. Next, we will check the current time (system time), and if its seconds value is zero, we will save the formed bar and start a new one:

```
current_time = datetime.now()
if current_time.second == 0:
    bars[current_time] = dict(bar)
    bar["open"]  = tick.values()[0]
    bar["high"]  = tick.values()[0]
    bar["low"]   = tick.values()[0]
    print(bars)
```

The rest of the code is the same as in the aforementioned example and handles exceptions that are raised when the first bar is not complete:

```
else:
    try:
        bar["high"] = max([bar["high"], tick.values()[0]])
        bar["low"] = min([bar["low"], tick.values()[0]])
        bar["close"] = tick.values()[0]
    except:
        print(str(current_time), ' bar forming...')
```

You can see that this function almost completely copies the code we used in the *Compressing market data in Python* section, with the only important modification being that now, instead of comparing timestamps of individual ticks, we finalize the bar *by a system timer*. As soon as the *system time* passes a minute, which means that its seconds value is zero, we start a new bar.

In fact, synching time is one of the greatest problems in algo trading. The system time on the trading server may differ from the clock at the data vendor's, and the clock at the broker or ECN may again differ from both. Luckily, in the further examples, we are going to use only 1-second snapshots of live data and 1-minute bars of historical data, so the problem of clock synchronization can be set aside for now.

If you run this code using pre-saved historical tick data, you will see something like this:

```
{datetime.datetime(2022, 8, 10, 20, 4, 0, 287224): {},
datetime.datetime(2022, 8, 10, 20, 5, 0, 456837): {'high':
1.01947, 'close': 1.01947, 'open': 1.01918, 'low': 1.01918},
datetime.datetime(2022, 8, 10, 20, 6, 0, 639863): {'high':
1.0195, 'close': 1.01925, 'open': 1.01945, 'low': 1.01925}}
```

You can see that the first bar does not have price data as it was started before the first minute ended. All the following bars have OHLC values that correspond to the *last ticks of the minute* by the time the system timer triggered a new bar.

Now, I hope you understand why historical compressed data from a broker always has nice *round* timestamps: they do not correspond to actual ticks; they are simply split into bars by the system timer.

You can see that this method works perfectly with live data that is received from a broker, a trading venue, or a similar source. It doesn't really suit for processing pre-saved historical data because it can be read back from disk at speeds that seriously exceed the real speed at which ticks are being received from the market. So, with historical data, it's better to use the *tick-to-tick timestamp compare* approach that we considered in the *Compressing market data in Python* section earlier in this chapter.

If you are not familiar with threads and queues and want to learn more about the ways you can use them in your trading apps, I'd recommend starting with a simple tutorial here (`https://realpython.com/intro-to-python-threading/`) and then referring to the official Python documentation here (`https://docs.python.org/3/library/threading.html`) for tips and tricks and deeper understanding.

Summary

In this chapter, we learned how to process both live and historical market data and, most importantly, how to do it in an efficient way. We are now familiar with time-based bars, which are most heavily used in trading strategies. We also learned about the solution that helps keep our trading applications flexible and quickly switch from one data source to another, which will help when switching from testing to production in the future.

Now, we are ready to move on to using the processed market data in our trading strategies. Let's see how we can do this in the next chapter.

6

Basics of Fundamental Analysis and Its Possible Use in FX Trading

I am sure that almost anyone who has ever been curious about trading has heard about fundamental and technical analyses. As with many popular terms, there's a good deal of misunderstanding with both.

Most likely, you know that there is an analyst profession and that this profession is in demand in the financial industry. You might have even considered this profession for yourself because you heard that modern analysts use advanced computer technologies and come from the world of data science. However, there is a crucial difference between the two concepts; thus, the mathematical and computer inventory used with each of them is radically different. Moreover, their use in actual trading algorithms is also quite different. Let's have a deeper look into both and see how (and if) we can use them in our applications.

We will review the key principles of fundamental and technical analyses, learn how markets react to important economic, political, and other events, and get familiar with two approaches to analyzing price behavior: one based on non-price information and the other using price time series only.

In this chapter, we will cover the following topics:

- Fundamental analysis
- Economic news from a fundamental analysis perspective
- Political events
- Industry-specific information

Fundamental analysis – intuitive but of little practical use

The idea of fundamental analysis is easily understandable: markets are known to react to various external information, so let's study this reaction to help us to predict the market's behavior. The *external information* in question depends on the market and can differ significantly.

Let's start with probably the most evident factor that clearly affects the market prices: economic news.

Economic news

This is the most well-known type of fundamental data. In layperson's terms, the better the economic situation, the greater the price of the asset. For example, if the nationwide economy shows growth, the most liquid stocks also grow. Yes, of course, there are exceptions, nuances, and so on, but overall, there is a positive correlation between the major macroeconomic indicators and the stock market's growth.

But wait, why are we talking about stock markets while our main point of interest is **forex (FX)**?

With the FX market, economic indicators such as **gross domestic product (GDP)**, **jobless rate**, **core price index** (**CPI** – the main inflation indicator), and others do not have any real long-term effect. Why? Because currencies have one feature that makes them completely different from any other asset class: they have *interest rates*.

To understand the concept of the interest rate, we should recall the mechanism that brings money into the economy. The central bank or a similar institution (such as the Federal Reserve of the United States) *emits* money. In earlier days, it meant minting coins, then printing the bills, and today, it also (and mostly) means making changes in databases electronically.

But in any case, the path of money into the economy goes through banks. The central bank doesn't just give money away to banks for free – banks pay *interest* to the central bank at a rate that is consequently called the *interest rate*. Banks also lend money to their clients – retail, businesses, and other banks – at different interest rates, which are, of course, greater than the rate at which they borrow from the central bank. And when your broker provides you with a credit line to facilitate margin trading (see *Chapter 3, FX Market Overview from a Developer's Standpoint*, in the *Trade mechanics – some terminology* section), they do not provide it for free, but rather at a rate that is, again, slightly higher than the rate at which they can borrow it.

This structure may look a bit confusing at first glance, but the key things you should remember are the following:

- Whatever you do within a single working day between the bank settlements does not count toward any interest

- As soon as you hold your FX position overnight, you either pay interest or receive it – depending on the difference in interest rates between currencies in the traded currency pair

Let's consider an example. In 2007, the Japanese yen could be borrowed at a rate close to zero, and the British pound at a rate of over 5%, peaking at 5.75% in July 2007. If you bought GBPJPY in 2007 – remember that this means that you buy the British pound by selling the Japanese yen – you benefit from an interest rate differential of about 5% per annum, which you *receive* every night. On the contrary, if you sold GBPJPY in 2007, then you would *pay* the interest every night. Now, multiply these numbers by the leverage provided by the broker (and back in 2007, in certain cases, it could reach 700:1 for select clients!) and you can imagine a sort of a Holy Grail of FX trading, which is called **carry trading**.

Carry trading

Carry trading refers to buying an asset and holding it for a considerable time, not only aiming at making a profit by selling the asset later at a higher price, but also collecting interest. If you are interested in learning more about carry trading, I'd recommend starting with an introductory article at Investopedia: `https://www.investopedia.com/articles/forex/07/carry_trade.asp`.

Of course, carry trading doesn't last long because interest rates change, and since the introduction of the **zero interest rate policy** (**ZIRP**) after the financial crisis of 2008, carry trading degraded substantially. However, understanding the fact that no money is free on the market helps understand why macroeconomic indicators don't have such a long-term impact on the currency market as they do on stocks and equities.

Nevertheless, macroeconomic news does have some impact on the currency market. The point here is that although stocks and equities are more affected by the economic news background, they are all purchased *for money*. So, although not immediately, interest rates also affect the cost of investment into stocks and equities. Therefore, releases of important macroeconomic news (especially GDP, jobless rate, and CPI) are closely observed by currency traders, and that's why we normally expect fast price movements in currencies before and after the publication of these economic indicators.

To illustrate this, let's look at a couple of examples from history.

US non-farm payrolls

The US **non-farm payroll** (**NFP**) is one of the most observed key macroeconomic indicators. It represents the number of new jobs countrywide in all industries except for agriculture. Normally, the greater the reading of this indicator, the better the state of the country's economy is considered to be. Consequently, the stock markets normally grow with the growth in new jobs and the domestic currency appreciates versus others.

In the FX markets, quite often, we observe sharp price movements at the moment when the US NFP is released. It usually happens when the published reading deviates significantly from the previously forecasted values. It is not so much important whether the reading itself is even positive or negative. For example, if a forecast predicted growth in new jobs by 5% and the actual published value is only 2%, then despite this value being positive, the market reaction will most likely be negative – because this value falls short of expectations. *Figure 6.1* shows a nice example of such a price movement in EURUSD a few seconds after the release of the US NFP on August 5, 2022:

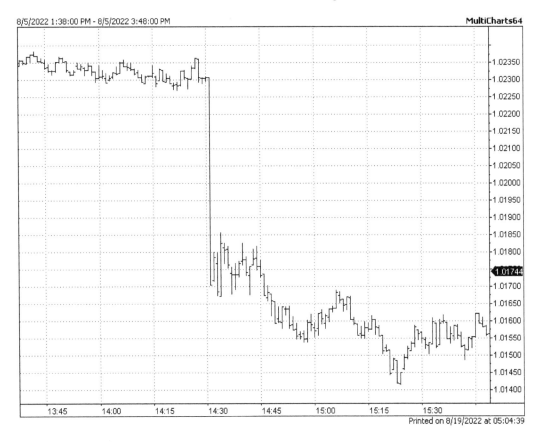

Figure 6.1 – Sharp price movement in EURUSD following the release of US NFP

Such a move can be explained in terms of liquidity (see *Chapter 3, FX Market Overview from a Developer's Standpoint*). Let's try to reconstruct the situation step by step:

1. Several minutes before the release of the news, liquidity providers prefer to withdraw liquidity from order books before the publication to avoid possible losses. And we already know that the less the liquidity, the faster and greater the price movements.

2. At the moment of the new release, liquidity in the order book is minimal, if any. Spreads may reach 10 times the normal, or even more.

3. The first order sent by a price taker after the news release may move the price dramatically. This is normally seen as a very quick jump if observed live on charts.

4. Consequent orders may move the price even further in the original direction or reverse it partially or completely.

5. Some time after the news release, liquidity goes back to the market and the amplitude of price movements returns to median values.

Let's zoom into what happened on August 5 and look at the individual ticks. *Figure 6.2* shows historical data tick by tick around the moment when the US NFP was released:

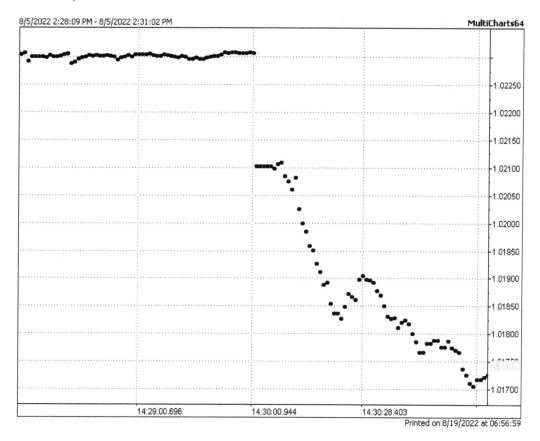

Figure 6.2 – Tick by tick chart of EURUSD around the release of the US NFP on August 5, 2022

So, we can see now that the liquidity was so thin at the time of the event that the price fell 20 pips in one tick.

> **Note**
>
> This means that there actually was no opportunity to trade at any price between 1.0210 and 1.0230. If you tried to send a market order at that moment, it would most likely be executed at an even lower price because chances are, you would not be the fastest trader in the liquidity pool.

Gross domestic product (GDP)

Let's consider another example of a similar event – this time, the publication of UK GDP data on August 12, 2022. *Figure 6.3* shows a 1-minute chart of GBPUSD (the British pound to the US dollar), which exhibits the price movements around the event. We can see that this time, the picture is different; we can see a sharp price movement right after the event (at 8:00 a.m. on the chart, the time is GMT+2), but then it almost immediately dwindled and the price quickly returned to the levels where it used to be before the event:

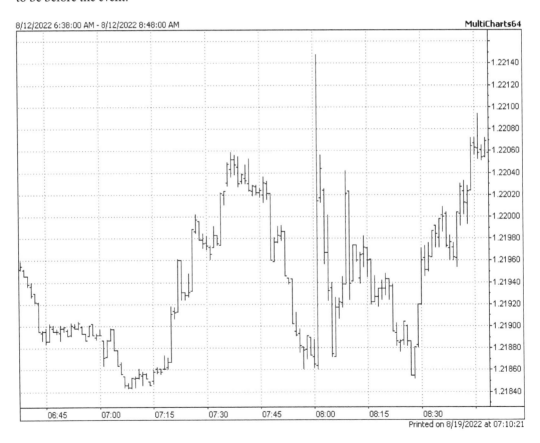

Figure 6.3 – Publication of UK GDP on August 12, 2022, 1-minute chart

Let's see what was going on in the market by looking at actual trade data. *Figure 6.4* shows a tick-by-tick chart of the same price movements around the same event:

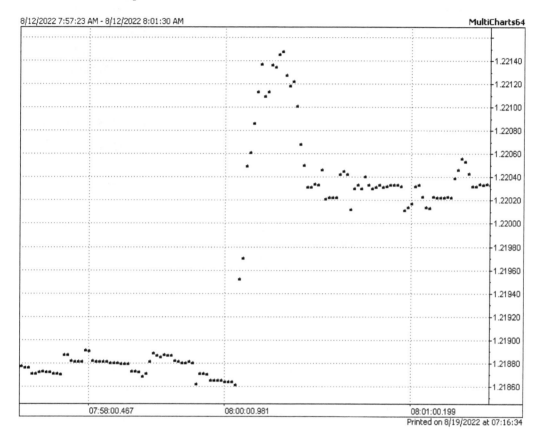

Figure 6.4 – Trade by trade chart of GBPUSD during publication of UK GDP data on August 12, 2022

Again, as in the case with the US NFP, there was almost no liquidity right after the release of this economic news, and therefore, any attempt to trade immediately after or immediately before it was really problematic. We can see that the price stabilized only 1-2 seconds after the event at a price level that is about 16-20 pips higher than immediately before it. This means that liquidity providers were back in the market by that time, but now, their bids and offers were significantly higher than just a couple of seconds before.

Economic news from a fundamental analysis perspective

So, what would a fundamental analyst say in both cases? Let's read one of the typical market reports:

"Today's weekly Initial Jobless Claims came in at 234k above the expectations of 220K the 8:30 am release had little effect on the USD against its peers. We have Existing Home Sale figures for the month of April released at 10 am. Market participants will be interested in comments on yesterday's FOMC minutes from Philadelphia Fed President Harker and Atlanta Fed President Bostic at a conference in Dallas today." (By OFX, `https://sitecore.prd.ofx.com/en-us/forex-news/daily-and-weekly-market-news/20180524/fomc-minutes-followed-up-by-fed-speakers-todays/`.)

We can see here only a statement of a few known facts with a vague reference to *market participants* who *will be interested in comments*. So this analysis is useless for practical immediate trading: it does not give us any idea about possible scenarios of further price movements that could potentially be exploited.

Institutional fundamental research is way more complex and includes a great number of factors, but in the long run, they can produce only long-term forecasts or investment advice. This happens because modern markets are so tightly connected to one another and these connections are so complex (and at the same time, factors that affect the market price are so numerous) that it becomes really problematic to use fundamental analysis of macroeconomic events for practical trading.

Does it mean, then, that we can safely disregard fundamental analysis and macroeconomic events?

Of course not!

The preceding examples clearly demonstrate what normally happens in the FX market on its micro-level around the release of important economic indicators. While it's hard to predict the exact direction of price movements after the news release, we can say that with a probability of almost 100%, there will be thin liquidity and sharp price movements, and overall, it will be too risky to place trades. I never suggest taking my words for granted – I encourage you to download historical FX price data along with a list of past economic events and see other examples of such a price behavior around the time important indicators were released. You will see it yourself: around 9 out of 10 cases only confirm the following important conclusion.

> **Note**
> Do avoid trading around the time of an important macroeconomic news release. You can stay with an already open position if it is suggested by your trade logic, but do refrain from opening or closing positions immediately before or after the event until liquidity returns to the order book.

Political events

Political events (such as presidential elections, wars, global treaties and declarations, and so on) also affect the markets, and the price behavior before and soon after such an event is somewhat similar to that of a reaction to regular economic news. This isn't surprising because the mechanics behind the scenes is the same – everyone knows that this is a major event, no one wants to take excessive risk, liquidity providers withdraw liquidity from the books, and any new order, even small in size, can momentarily drive the price anywhere.

The difference between political and regular economic events is probably in the duration of the price movement after the event. Let's consider a couple of examples.

US presidential elections, November 8, 2016

On this day, Donald Trump was elected the President of the US. His victory was not smooth: he was only the fifth president who lost the popular vote but was nevertheless elected. Therefore, if we look at the chart of EURUSD on that date, we can clearly see how the market sentiment changed from optimistic (that Trump wouldn't win) to pessimistic (when it began to be clear that his chances were higher than expected). *Figure 6.5* tells that epic story in a 1-minute chart:

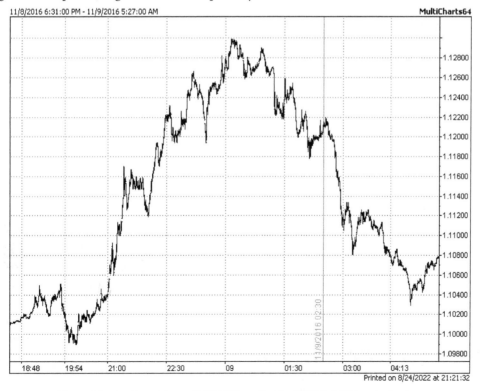

Figure 6.5 – 1 minute chart of EURUSD on the day of Donald Trump's election

We can see a much steadier price movement than what we observed during regular economic news releases. First, the price moved up to almost 300 pips in just 3-4 hours, which is really huge for this market, and this movement was fueled by expectations that Hillary Clinton would win the race. But then, around midnight, the picture became not so clear, and after The Associated Press officially called the election for Trump at 2:30 a.m. (marked with a vertical red line on the chart), the price of the US dollar sharply increased (don't forget that we're looking at the euro versus the US dollar pair: the higher the dollar, the lower the rate – hence, when we say *the US dollar goes up*, visually, the chart of EURUSD goes down).

UK Brexit, June 23, 2016

The year 2016 was full of unprecedented political events, and Brexit was by far not the least one among them. There was no clear consensus on the possible outcome of this poll, but all analysts agreed that if the UK left the EU, the value of its domestic currency (the British Pound, GBP) would fall sharply. This is exactly what happened, and we can revisit the scene by looking at a 1-minute chart of GBPUSD on that date:

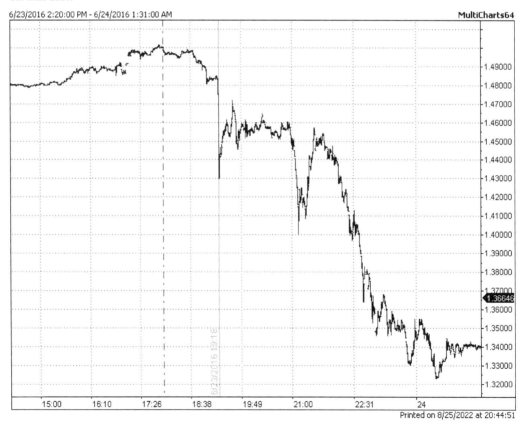

Figure 6.6 – 1 minute chart on GBPUSD on the date of Brexit

You can see that the publication of the official poll results caused the rate of GBPUSD to fall 600 pips in 2 minutes. This is one of the fastest movements in major currency pairs throughout the entire history of the forex market. This sharp fall was almost completely played back in the following 20-30 minutes, and again, there was no surprise in it because the liquidity was returning to the market. However, the following downward price movement continued and lasted not just for minutes and even not for hours, but for days. So, at least theoretically, Brexit again provided an opportunity for a speculative trade – to sell GBPUSD on Brexit day and exit the position a few hours or even days later.

We can see that the main difference between a major political event and a release of a regular economic indicator is that the price movement in the former case is much longer in duration. Therefore, these events are probably the best occasions when fundamental analysis really works and helps us make some profits.

Having now considered the *all-markets* news, so to say, let's have a quick look into fundamental factors that affect only a certain market, or sometimes, even a certain asset.

Industry-specific information

Normally, fundamental information of this sort almost doesn't affect the currency rates because the scope of its effect is too narrow. You can think about a currency as the largest market index, which includes all industries and all aspects of the economy of a particular country and compares them to those of another country in a currency pair. Most developed countries make every effort to keep their economies balanced and diversified. So, in case something happens, say, only in microelectronics, car manufacturing, agriculture, or healthcare – well, yes, it may affect the currency rates for a very limited time, but the effect will be so small, almost negligible, that normally, currency traders disregard fundamental information of this sort.

There are some notable exceptions though. There are countries whose economies are very tightly connected to only one or two industries. For these countries, fundamental factors that are specific to the key industry *do* affect the entire economy. Let's consider the most prominent example of how industry-specific news and prices of just a single commodity may be highly correlated with the rate of the domestic currency.

Crude oil and the Canadian dollar

The Canadian economy is known to be tightly connected with oil. No surprise that the Canadian dollar versus the US dollar rate shows a strong correlation with the price of crude oil. *Figure 6.7* shows this correlation very clearly.

> **Note**
>
> To compare apples to apples, we need both instruments in the same chart to be quoted in the same currency. However, this is not the case in the following chart. The rate of the Canadian dollar is shown as USDCAD, which means *how many US dollars there are in one Canadian dollar*. Thus, the top chart shows not Canadian dollars in US dollars, but US dollars in Canadian dollars. And the bottom chart shows prices of US crude oil in US dollars. Therefore, we should (mentally) invert the top chart to have both instruments (CAD and US crude) quoted in the same currency (USD).

Figure 6.7 – The Canadian dollar and oil prices show a strong correlation

In this figure, we can see daily charts of both the Canadian dollar and US crude oil from mid-2018 till about the end of 2021. We can see that the bottom chart is very close to a mirrored version of the top one, which shows a very high positive correlation if we remember that the rate of USDCAD is *mirrored* to CADUSD.

Moreover, even if we zoom in and look at intraday data, we will still see a strong correlation between CAD and US crude oil. *Figure 6.8* shows an example of this correlation in 1-hour charts (don't forget, we should invert the chart of USDCAD to compare both prices in USD).

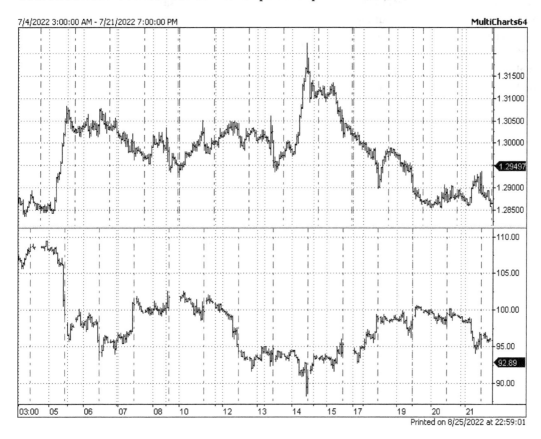

Figure 6.8 – Intraday (hourly) charts of USDCAD and US crude oil

Therefore, we can assume that fundamental factors that come from the oil industry may affect USDCAD and can potentially be used for trading this currency pair.

Summary

We can see that fundamental factors do affect the prices of currencies, but we also can see key problems with using these factors in automated trading, such as the (a) releases of macroeconomic news mostly cause the unpredicted direction of price movements, and these movements frequently do not last long enough to trade, (b) political events cause longer price movements and are potentially tradable, but they are rare, and it's easier to trade them manually than programmatically, (c) using industry-specific fundamental factors is potentially the most promising, but requires a thorough analysis of the respective industry and works only for specific currencies.

In any case, systematic traders (those who prefer entering and exiting positions basing their decisions on a set of rules rather than intuition or sentiment) have long searched for an alternative, *quantitative* way of analyzing market data as opposed to *qualitative* fundamental analysis. This quantitative analysis could open lots of new opportunities because it removes human discretion, emotions, and any bias, as all trading decisions are based only on numbers. Such quantitative analysis is called **technical analysis**. We will learn more about this analysis type in the next chapter.

7

Technical Analysis and Its Implementation in Python

In the previous chapter, we considered fundamental factors and saw how they may impact market prices. We noted that, although such an impact may be significant and potentially quite lucrative for trading, most of the time, it's difficult to suggest a quantitative model that could generate unambiguous trading rules (when to enter the market, to which direction, and when to exit it) that wouldn't require human discretion. For clarity's sake, let's note that there exist various fully quantitative approaches to evaluating fundamental factors, even political ones, but they are based on complex cross-discipline subjects, such as semantic analysis, and thus require solid knowledge of respective sciences. Is it possible to avoid this complexity and find a method to analyze market behavior using only price data? Or, maybe, some additional data, but only in numeric form?

The answer is yes, and this kind of market analysis is called **technical analysis**. In this chapter, we will consider its premises, learn about the most common technical indicators, and discover how they may be used to quantitatively describe various processes that go on in the market. We will also consider the implementations of key technical indicators in Python and introduce the concept of the sliding window, which will be used throughout all future codes.

In this chapter, you will learn about the following topics:

- Technical analysis – ideal for computing, but missing real market processes
- Momentum and RSI as indicators to measure the velocity of the market
- Digital filters and moving averages
- Range indicators
- Volatility indicators
- Implementation of technical indicators in Python

Technical analysis – ideal for computing, but missing real market processes

The main idea that lies in the foundation of **technical analysis**, or **TA** for short, is that *price includes everything in itself*. From this standpoint, if we see a price movement up or down, large or small, we don't really want to know the reason behind this movement; instead, we just acknowledge that it was caused by some fundamental factors and try to focus on the future price development in regard to the observed price movement only.

Of course, TA can analyze a *series* of data and not just a single data point. In this regard, TA studies help in identifying *patterns* or repeating sequences in price time series that bear resemblance to each other. TA suggests that if we observe a pattern that we already saw in the past, then the following price development will also be similar to what happened in the past; therefore, we can be prepared and exploit it.

With TA, we don't want and don't need to know the actual fundamental factors that affected the price, we are only looking for *footprints* of something that happened behind the scenes and will then take action depending on the form of these footprints.

Now that we understand the difference in the foundations of fundamental and technical analyses, let's see how this difference impacts the two main practical points of any market analysis: its time horizon and precision.

Fundamental analysis focuses on macroeconomic factors, which are always longer term by nature, so the time horizon for fundamental forecasts is normally days and above, up to years. On the contrary, technical studies may analyze extremely short-living processes (for example, momentary imbalances in the order book), and therefore, it's normal that technical studies may have a forecast horizon of 1 second, 1 millisecond, and sometimes even a few microseconds.

The main differences between fundamental and technical analyses are summarized in the following table:

	Fundamental analysis	**Technical analysis**
Key focus	Macroeconomics, politics, industry news, and the sentiment of investors	Price, volume, open interest, spreads, liquidity, and other quantitative parameters
Forecast horizon	Days to years	Microseconds to days, and rarely, weeks and months
Forecast precision	Very volatile	Depends on the timeframe

Table 7.1 – Key differences between fundamental and technical analyses

The building block of any TA study is an **indicator**. It is a combination of price, time, volume, and/ or any other market data that can be quantitatively measured.

Indicators are usually plotted as lines, dots, histograms, and other graphical objects *on* a price chart, *below* a price chart, or both. Normally, technical analysts use two to five indicators, each of them showing a particular feature of the examined price time series. *Figure 7.1* shows a typical example of such a combination of TA indicators in a single chart:

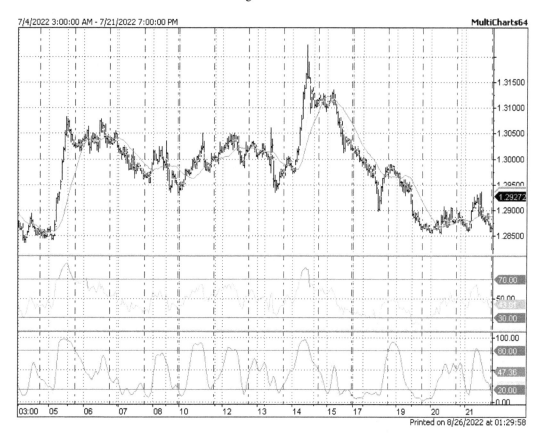

Figure 7.1 – Typical layout of TA indicators with a price chart

Excessive use of TA indicators may lead to a mess when it's really hard to understand what each of them shows and what the author of this mess really wanted to achieve. You probably can't believe it, but the example in the following figure is not my fantasy, but something similar to what I saw with my own eyes so many times on various trading forums!

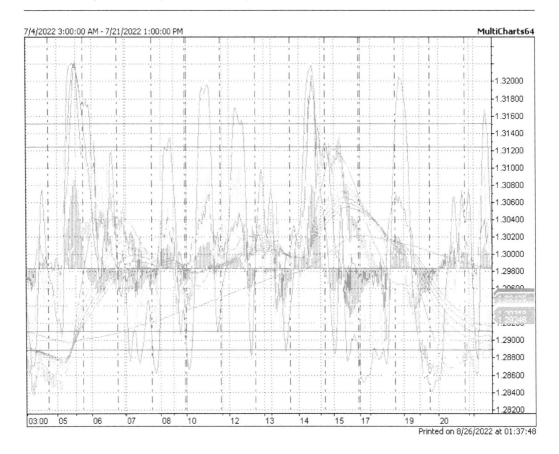

Figure 7.2 – How the excessive use of TA indicators may lead to abuse

There is one thing common for all TA indicators – their values are always synchronized with the original price time series on which they are based.

This means that if we build an indicator based on a 1-minute chart, then the values of this indicator will be updated every minute; for an hourly chart, the values will be updated every hour, and so on.

As you can see, if we use a tick chart as the source data to calculate the values of a TA indicator, then these values will be updated on every tick. When we work with live data feeds, TA indicators show fixed, unchanged values for all historical bars (well, we can't change history, can we?), but update the latest reading with every new tick that comes in for a bar that is not completed yet.

Regardless of their complexity, almost all TA indicators can be classified into four major groups: velocity of the market, digital filters, range indicators, and volatility indicators. Let's consider each of them.

An important note before we proceed

In all the following discussions about technical indicators, we will use the term **current bar**. This doesn't mean that we are talking only about the last (rightmost) bar on the chart. This means that when we plot charts, indicators, backtest strategies, and so on, we always move (imaginarily) from left to right, from historically older data to historically present, and we calculate anything *on every bar that we encounter*. This bar, for which we are calculating any values *at the moment*, is referred to as the **current bar**. We use this term because when we go live with our developments, the current bar will actually mean the price data that we receive *at this very moment*, so we don't have to modify anything in our study or strategy code.

With this important note in mind, let's go ahead.

Velocity of the market

These indicators try to answer the question, *How fast is the price moving?*. Indeed, if we compare a normal average day in the FX market with a release of important economic news or a political event, then we clearly see the difference. And of course, it would be nice to assess this difference quantitatively. We will consider only the two most well-known indicators of this kind – momentum and RSI – but any more sophisticated market speed indicator will be inevitably built on the same principles.

Momentum

This is probably the oldest technical indicator and definitely the simplest. It is really hard to imagine a simpler formula:

$$M = C_0 - C_{-1}$$

Here, C_0 means the current closing price and C_{-1} means the closing price of the previous bar.

If we calculate these differences for every bar, store them in an array, and plot the indicator below the chart, we will see that its values no longer follow the price movements and, overall, it looks more like noise rather than a clear trending price pattern. However, this noise is quite informative. Even from a quick glance at the chart in *Figure 7.3*, we can conclude a number of important points:

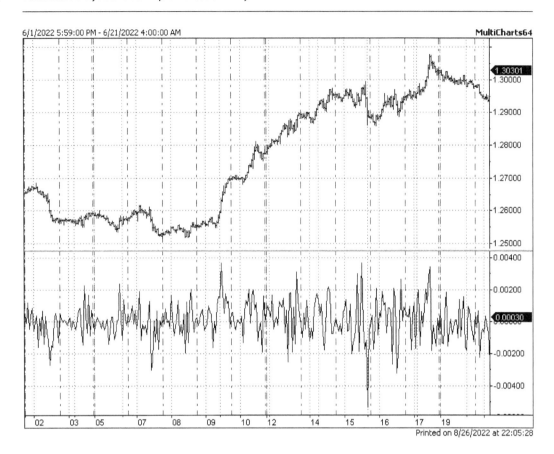

Figure 7.3 – Basic momentum plotted below a price chart

First, we can see that the readings of momentum seldom remain in the positive or negative zone for more than two or three data points in a row. Since the momentum's value is the difference between the current and the previous closing prices of just two adjacent bars, we can say that it's not usual for this market that the price grew or declined steadily for more than three bars in a row. In other words, if we see more than two bars closing up, we may expect a bar to close down rather than another bar closing up. Technical analysts call these bars **corrections**; they may even appear inside quite long and steady trends, as in *Figure 7.3*, but they do not break the trend. So, overall, we can say that this market is really prone to corrections.

Second, if we estimate the amplitude of the momentum indicator, we can see that it is different during different market regimes. While the market remained more or less *flat* (at the beginning of the chart), the amplitude of the momentum hardly exceeded 0.002 points, but as the uptrend was developing, its values increased to 0.004 by absolute value – that is, two times the *idle* market. So, we can assume that the *market speed* has some correlation with the market regime and could potentially use it in our own studies.

Normally, the momentum indicator has one parameter – the number of bars between which we calculate the difference. In the classical formula at the beginning of this section, we compared the closing prices of two adjacent bars; of course, we can compare the price of the current bar with that of any bar in the past. If we continue doing that for every bar, we will get to a modified formula:

$$M = C_0 - C_{-n},$$

Here, n means the number of bars *back* from the current bar.

For example, if we set n to 24, then we calculate the difference in closing prices between the current bar and 24 bars ago (which, for an hourly chart, means the price strictly 24 hours or 1 day ago), we will see a somewhat different picture, as shown in *Figure 7.4*:

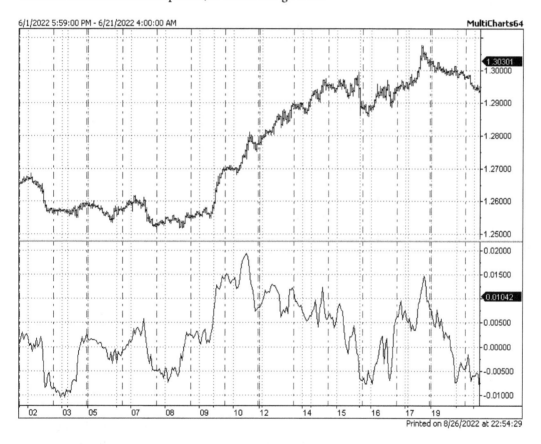

Figure 7.4 – A 24-bar momentum based on a 1-hour chart means the price rate of change for 24 hours

We can see that the *market speed*, or the price rate of change for 24 hours, looks totally different from the preceding chart, where we considered the difference in closing prices of just two neighbor bars. There's no *noise* here anymore; instead, we observe longer-term changes in the momentum values. But the observations we made previously (regarding the corrections and correlations between *market speed* and range/trend markets) remain valid, as only the scale and proportions of these phenomena increased.

So, to summarize, the momentum indicator is useful to determine the idle market phases (when its readings are close to zero) and the highly active market (when its readings exceed a certain threshold). However, I hope you can see the evident shortcoming of this indicator in its present form – to decide whether the present market is active or not, we must specify this very *certain threshold* we just mentioned.

What is this threshold? In the first example (*Figure 7.3*), the momentum values never exceeded 0.006, while in the second one (*Figure 7.4*), it reaches almost 0.02, which is *a order of magnitude* greater. So, if we say that market speed above 0.004 is *abnormally big*, then we have to agree that in the second example, the market is in *abnormally big* mode half of the time.

It becomes clear that for the classical momentum indicator, there is no such threshold as a single unique numeric value. It depends on the market, the data resolution, and the momentum period. And it would be great if we could adjust the threshold value automatically, without the need for doing that manually every time, and consequently, eliminating possible human discretion bias.

So, how can we get rid of subjectivity when setting such a threshold?

RSI

The problem of answering the key question, *Is it big enough or still small* discussed in the previous section was solved for the momentum indicator by *J. Welles Wilder Jr.* in 1978. In his book, *New Concepts in Technical Trading Systems*, he introduced the **relative strength index** (**RSI**), a new TA indicator that he suggested using in order to determine the *overbought* and *oversold* states of the market. In his terminology, *overbought* corresponds to the situation when prices grow *too quickly*, basically meaning that the market speed we discussed previously is too high. *Oversold* zones correspond to situations when prices fall *too quickly*, meaning the momentum is still greater than average by its absolute value but has a negative sign.

RSI solves the problem of specifying a universal threshold for the momentum indicator by *normalizing* its values. Normalization is a process of scaling data so that all values fit into a certain range. For example, we have two datasets:

```
{0, 1, 2, 3, 4, 5, 6, 7, 8, 9, 10}
{0, 0.1, 0.4, 0.05, 0.1, 0.3, 0.2}
```

We want to be able to compare *apples to apples*, and thus we want to scale both of them so the minimum and the maximum values of each dataset are the same. Typically, a range of 0 to 100 is used (it's convenient: if we normalize data to this range we can then consider the values as a percentage). So, if we scale the first dataset to the range *0:100*, we will get an obvious sequence:

```
{0, 10, 20, 30, 40, 50, 60, 70, 80, 90, 100}
```

But when we scale the second one, then 0 remains 0, and the maximum value, which is 0.4, becomes 100, so the scaling coefficient is *100/0.4 = 250*. Then, the normalized dataset will look as follows:

```
{0, 25, 100, 12.5, 25, 75, 50}
```

Now we can compare, for example, the rate of change of data points in both datasets using the same metrics, despite the fact that, originally, the second dataset contains values of *a order of magnitude smaller* than values in the first one.

So, the idea of the normalization of TA indicators is to scale them *automatically* so that their values always remain in the *0:100* range, or sometimes, *-100:100*. Let's do it for the momentum.

Welles Wilder suggests calculating RSI in two steps: first, we calculate the **relative strength (RS)**, and second, the RSI.

> **Note**
>
> Don't forget that as with any other TA indicator, RSI uses *period*, a parameter that determines the number of data points we take into consideration. In the first example of the momentum indicator from the previous section, the period was just 1, and in the second example, it was 24.

To calculate the RS, we should first calculate the *gains* and *losses* for the period. A gain, in Wilder's terminology, happened when a bar closed up, and a loss when a bar closed down. Then, we calculate the average of gains and the average of losses separately. And finally, we calculate the relative strength for the period:

$$RS = \frac{Average gain}{Average loss}$$

This formula is similar to the original momentum, only the momentum measures the *difference* between prices, and the RS measures the *ratio*. Using ratios is always preferred when we want to become independent of the original value range, where subtracting 0.01 from 0.1 will result in 0.09, while subtracting 10 from 100 results in 90, and it's evident that 90 and 0.09 differ by *4 orders of magnitude*, so it's impossible to compare them directly. However, dividing 0.01 by 0.1 and dividing 10 by 100 produces exactly the same value, that is, 0.1, so in terms of market speed, this value is indeed the same.

Now, we normalize the RS by keeping it always within the range of 0 to 100:

$$RSI = 100 - \frac{100}{1 + RS}$$

If we now plot the RSI along with the momentum on the same chart, we can see that the two indicators are very similar:

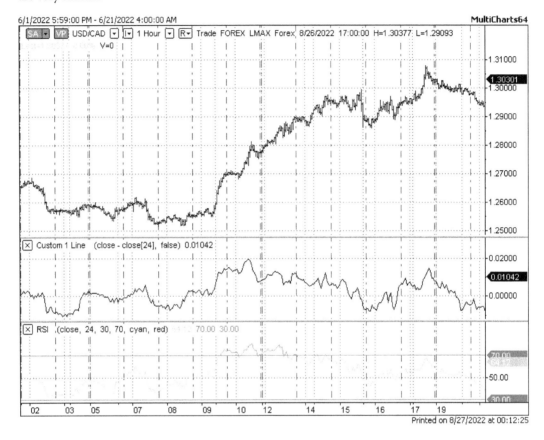

Figure 7.5 – Momentum (top) and RSI (bottom) plotted on the same price chart

Since RSI is normalized to a range of 0 to 100, typically, the values above 70 are considered an *overbought* market, while values below 30 are spoken of as *oversold*. In the preceding chart, the *overbought* market corresponds to an uptrend, and absence of *oversold* state can be interpreted as a strong upside bias in the market sentiment.

There are more market speed indicators than momentum and RSI, but all of them are used to determine the following market regimes:

- Idle versus active market (prices move slowly or quickly)
- Overbought/oversold zones (prices went *too high* or *too low*)
- Sharp bursts of prices mostly caused by liquidity issues (*spikes* on momentum charts)

So, momentum is good for detecting relatively short-living market situations. But what about something longer-term? Are there indicators that could show us a more global sentiment, a long-term tendency? Let's move on to another class of TA indicators that is normally used for this very purpose.

Digital filters

If you listen to music of any genre, and I hope you do, there's a good chance that you are familiar with high-pass filters, low-pass filters, and equalizers. Any car audio, desktop, or mobile audio player offers this functionality. And I do hope that if you played with audio settings at least once in your life, you will remember what happens if you turn off treble and boost the bass to the maximum – that is, instead of music, you now hear only *boom-boom-boom*.

However, cutting off higher frequencies can also be quite useful if you want to focus on the rhythm, on the bass line, and probably on the chords and base (as opposed to harmonics) tones. And this is what lots of technical analysts dream of – to strip away all the *noise* from the market prices, leaving only the *bass line* or *rhythm*, – that is, the key trends and major price movements that last relatively long and, potentially, bring profits.

Surprisingly, or not, all TA indicators that do this job work *exactly* the same as low or high-pass filters in audio because they are based on *exactly the same* mathematical principles. That's why we put them all in one section: digital filters.

Moving averages

A moving average is also one of the oldest technical indicators. It is calculated as the average of prices for the period and recalculated on every bar.

> **Note**
>
> When we discuss TA indicators, we always use two terms: *period* and *current bar*. So let me just quickly remind you that a *period* means a number of data points (ticks, bars, any other samples from a time series) that the TA indicator analyzes, and the *current bar* changes one by one, left to right, as we reconstruct the historical values of the indicator, along with the historical values of the market price itself.

To give you a simple example, let's consider the following dataset:

```
A = {0, 1, 2, 3, 2, 1, 0, 1, 2, 3}
```

Let's calculate an average of three data points starting from the leftmost one. For the first element in the original dataset, it's impossible to do because we have only one data point and we require three. The same for the second data point. So, we can start calculating the moving average from the third data point, and its value will be as follows:

$$MA_3 = \frac{a_0 + a_1 + a_2}{3} = \frac{0 + 1 + 2}{3} = 1$$

Then, we move on to the fourth data point and again calculate the value of the moving average, but this time, we start calculating from the second element in our dataset:

$$MA_3 = \frac{a_1 + a_2 + a_3}{3} = \frac{1 + 2 + 3}{3} = 2$$

Proceeding in this way, we will get a new dataset that represents the average values of three data points in a row, recalculated for each data point from left to right. Therefore, for the first two data points, we don't have any value (as the number of original data points was insufficient to calculate a three-point average):

$$\bar{A} = \{\text{NaN, NaN, 1, 2, 2.33, 2, 1, 0.66, 1, 2}\}$$

> **Note**
>
> I hope you got the point: we always take three samples from the dataset, calculate the average, store this value in a new dataset, and move on to the next sample. This technique is called the **moving window** and is the basis for the calculation of all TA indicators.

Normally, **moving averages** (**MAs**) are calculated based on the closing prices of bars, but nothing prevents us from using them with any other price (such as high, low, or trade) or non-price data (such as volume, liquidity, and so on).

It's evident that an MA with a period of one equals the original time series. How will values of MAs with greater periods correspond to the original data?

Let's plot the original price time series in form of just dots, not bars, where each dot will denote a closing price of the bar. And let's plot 3 different MAs along with the original series with periods of 2, 3, 5, and 10, respectively:

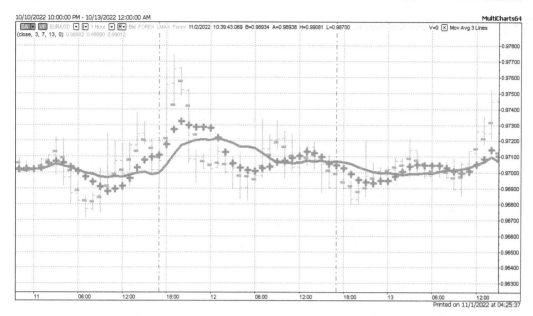

Figure 7.6 – 3, 7, and 13-period MAs on top of a 1-hour chart of EURUSD

Figure 7.6 plots the original time series as bars, and 3, 7, and 13-period MAs as dashes, crosses, and solid lines, respectively. We can see that the smaller the period of an MA, the closer its values are to the original series, and the greater the period, the *smoother* the change in the MA's values.

This *smoothing* is the very effect of a low-pass filter. Surprisingly, an MA, calculated using simple mathematics, *is* a digital filter, pretty close to those used in audio processing. The greater the period of the MA, the lower the maximum frequency passed by such a filter. So, if applied to an audio signal, such a filter will leave us with *boom-boom*, and now we can see this *boom-boom* in the market prices. Ultimately, using MAs with a period of 20, 50, or 200 will show only longer-term changes in the market prices, considering minor price movements as high-frequency noise.

Figure 7.7 shows the same hourly chart of EURUSD with closing prices only, plotted as big black dots, and 20-, 50-, and 200-period MAs on top of it:

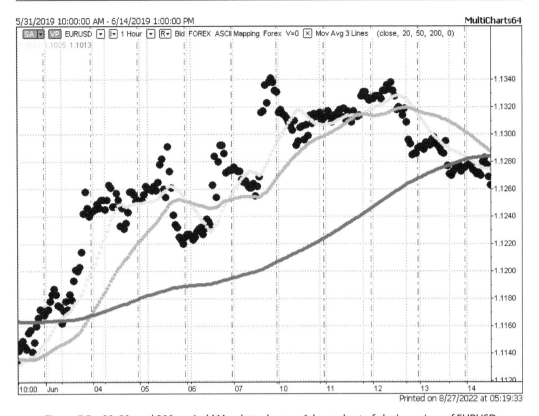

Figure 7.7 – 20, 50, and 200-period MAs plotted over a 1-hour chart of closing prices of EURUSD

In this example, we can see that the MA with the greatest period (200) only grows with slight changes in the growth rate, while MAs with shorter periods grow and decline, and the smaller the period of the MA, the closer its values are to the original series.

So, MAs are the simplest digital filters and are designed to detect *tendencies* rather than immediate activity. They are used in TA to solve the following problems:

- To determine long- and medium-term trends
- To distinguish bullish and bearish markets (normally, when daily prices close above the 200-period MA, the market is considered bullish, and vice versa)
- To smoothen *occasional* or *abnormal* sharp price movements

Very frequently, MAs are used in combination with momentum indicators – for example, an MA can be used to determine whether the market is bullish (closing prices above 200-period MA), and momentum can determine the moment when the market speed is high, so potentially, it could be a good time to buy.

However, you probably already heard about traders who lost their fortune buying when prices were already too high or selling when prices were already too low. I hope now that we have so thoroughly examined the design of market speed indicators and digital filters, you have already spotted the bottleneck here – *too high* or *too low*. But how do we decide that it's already *too high* or still *not so high*? The answer is in the following section.

Range indicators

One of the most common methods to solve the problem of identifying whether the current price is in any extreme zone (too high or too low) is using range indicators. Normally, a **price range** is a difference between the maximum price and the minimum price for, well (I'm sure I heard you say that), a *period*. As always, with technical indicators, we're bound to a certain timespan, a moving window that we slide along the chart from left to right. So, when we talk about range, we have to define the period for which this range is calculated.

Let's look at the chart shown in *Figure 7.8*. The rectangle shows the maximum and minimum price of a 24-bar span (since it's an hourly chart, this means the rectangle corresponds to 1 day):

Figure 7.8 – A 24-hour price range with 2 closing prices shown as percentage of range, EURUSD, 1-hour

Two closing prices are marked with small arrows. Horizontal lines are drawn through these closing prices to visualize the price levels relative to the range rather than absolute values. So, for the first (left to right) closing price, the absolute value is 1.1260, but relative to the range, it's right at 50% of it. The second closing price is 1.1292, but relative to the range, it's about 85% of it.

Got the point? We can replace absolute price values that don't say much with relative price levels, which could be interpreted pretty much as we interpreted RSI values (see the *RSI* section). For example, we can say that when the price is above 80% of the range level, then the price is *too high*, and when the price is below 20% of the range level, then the price is *too low*.

The first and the most well-known range indicator is the **stochastic oscillator**.

Stochastic oscillator

Stochastic is quite a popular word among traders, but unfortunately, it is often used improperly. In mathematics, the term *stochastic* means a variety of random processes. To understand what it means, let's consider an example.

If you go out to buy some bread, then you will most likely go down the same streets, end your route at the same local grocery store, and spend more or less the same amount of time as usual. This is an example of a *deterministic process* – although there can be some *fluctuations* or deviations down the road (for example, you decide to walk on this or that side of the street), the overall route and destination remain the same.

Now, imagine that you go out with no particular goal in mind and stop at any shop, bar, or movie theater you like, spend any amount of time in each, and decide where to go next by tossing a coin. Every time you take such a trip, its trajectory, destinations, and time spent, both on each leg and the entire journey, will differ. Although the area where you're traveling is confined and you visit the same places, the map of your actual movements will be different because of the *randomness* of your decisions. Such a process is called *stochastic* or *random* or *probabilistic*.

Market price movements are also considered random or stochastic processes by many researchers, who have suggested various probabilistic models that describe price behavior. Although this standpoint can also be criticized, such an academic debate is definitely outside the scope of this book, so the main points we should take away from this brief *lyrical digression* are as follows:

- Processes with a definite trajectory, target, and time are called **deterministic**
- Processes where every next step has just some probability and you never know for sure where and when it reaches any target are called **stochastic**
- Changes in market prices can be considered a **stochastic process**
- The stochastic oscillator has nothing in common with **stochastic processes**

The stochastic oscillator in its original form shows exactly what we considered at the very end of the previous section – it shows where the current price is as a percentage of a certain price range. So, in order to calculate the stochastic oscillator, we should choose a period (number of data points), then find the maximum and the minimum price for this period, and then calculate the value of the stochastic oscillator:

$$SO = \frac{P_0 - L}{H - L} \cdot 100$$

Here, P_0 means the current price, L means the lowest price for the period, and H means the highest price for the period.

Let's again open an hourly chart of a currency pair, but this time, the Japanese yen for a change, and let's plot this indicator with a period of 24 below it (thus tracking changes in price as a percentage of a day's range):

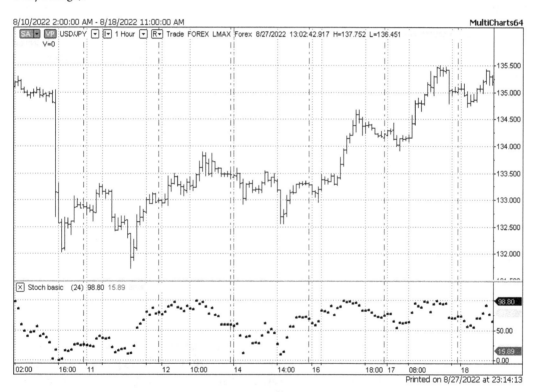

Figure 7.9 – Basic 24-period stochastic oscillator below the 1-hour chart of USDJPY

In *Figure 7.9*, we can see that the stochastic oscillator indeed *oscillates* in a range from 0 to 100 (what a surprise). During trends (right half of the picture), it tends to stay above 50, and in sideways markets (middle part of the picture) it can oscillate full scale.

So, what's the possible application of the stochastic oscillator?

First and foremost, it's used to answer the question of whether the price is *too high* or *too low* (I hope you remember this Shakespearean question from the end of the previous section). We can say, for example, that when the price is above the level of 80 – which means that the price is greater than 80% of the price range – then it is indeed *too high*. Likewise, being under 20% of the range could mean that the price is *too low*.

Second, some technical traders like to use stochastic and similar oscillators to determine trends. We already saw that, during trends, the stochastic oscillator tends to remain above (for uptrends) or below (for downtrends) 50% of the range for quite a long time. It's no wonder that trends are special market regimes where corrections in prices are much smaller and last for a much shorter time than the movements in the direction of the trend. So, prices will indeed remain in the upper or lower half of the range for many hours, days, or sometimes even weeks.

There are numerous modifications of the stochastic oscillator. For example, adding an MA to its values (and we remember that we can add an MA to any time series, not necessarily price) gives us a so-called *slow stochastic*. Some authors suggest using the original indicator and the averaged one on the same chart, but the essence remains the same – this is a range oscillator and can, therefore, be used to solve the following problems:

- Identifying whether the price is *too high* or *too low*
- Identifying trends as long-term periods when prices are above or below 50% of the range
- Suggesting buy signals when the oscillator starts going up from *too low* levels
- Suggesting sell signals when the oscillator starts going down from *too high* levels

Now that we have a speed indicator (momentum or RSI) that tells us that the market is moving fast, a digital filter (MAs) that confirms that the main tendency in the market is still positive, and a range indicator (stochastic) that shows that the asset is currently oversold, it may look like it's a good time to buy.

But!

Even if we calculated the timing of our entry with the highest degree of perfection, markets still remain stochastic processes (remember what we started with at the beginning of this section?) and it is normal that price may go against you for some time. The key question here is whether this adverse price movement is only a small correction and it's wise to just wait till red turns green, or you were wrong with your trading decision (which, by the way, is also absolutely normal) and should liquidate your losing position before it drains your account completely.

Normally, this problem is solved by adding volatility studies to the trading strategy logic.

Volatility indicators

If we look up the definition of volatility in Merriam-Webster, the first suggested meaning would be *a tendency to change quickly and unpredictably.* Sounds good, but how can we measure this tendency, this ability to change?

Wikipedia (`https://en.wikipedia.org/wiki/Volatility_(finance)`) suggests a different definition: *"volatility (usually denoted by σ) is the degree of variation of a trading price series over time, usually measured by the standard deviation of logarithmic returns."* If you are not familiar with mathematical statistics, this may sound like a foreign language to you, but don't worry, let's take a quick tour of the theory of probability.

Let's use the same example with a random walk around bars and movie theaters. Let's measure the distance between the starting point (your home, presumably) and the ending point (where you decide to finish your walk for the day). Every day, we will get different values because you make your travel decisions randomly. However, we can calculate the average value and say that, on average, you walk, say, three kilometers per walk.

The devil is always in the details, and the devil of averaging is called **dispersion**. This is a measure of how much the actual values of a certain random variable differ from the average, or *mean* value. Let's consider two examples.

First, let's go back to a deterministic process when you go out to a local grocery. We record travel distances for each trip and put them into a dataset:

```
S = {1.8, 1.9, 1.85, 1.79, 1.78, 1.81, 1.85, 1.82, 1.89, 1.2}
```

Now, let's calculate the mean value of this dataset:

$$\bar{S} = \frac{S_0 + S_1 + \ldots + S_n}{n} = 1.769$$

Now, subtract this mean value from each element of the original dataset:

```
D = {0.03, 0.13, 0.08, 0.02, 0.01, 0.04, 0.08, 0.05, 0.12,
-0.57}
```

We can see that the difference between almost all recorded values and their mean is *a order of magnitude smaller* than the mean itself. The only exception is the last values in the D dataset: the difference between it and the mean is comparable to the value itself. Such a value is called an **outlier** and is most likely explained by incorrect measurements or something exceptional that happened to you down the road.

Now, let's record the distances traveled each time you took a random walk around the local bars and movie theaters. In some cases, you found a nice place to stay almost as soon as you left your house;

in other cases, you walked quite a lot and still returned home unsatisfied, hence the difference in the distance you traveled each time. We will get a dataset like this:

```
S1 = {0.7, 2, 1.5, 0.3, 2.6, 1.1, 1.8, 0.45, 3.1, 2.9}
```

Its mean value is 1.645. If we now do the same as previously (that is, subtract this mean from each element of the dataset), we will see that the differences now are quite comparable to the mean value, and in some cases, nearly exceed it:

```
D = {-0.94, 0.35, -0.14, -1.34, 0.95, -0.54, 0.15, -1.19, 1.45,
1.25}
```

The process in which the differences between values and their mean are way smaller than the values themselves is a *deterministic process*, and now we have a more math-looking definition of it (although it's still not formally correct). Conversely, the process where the differences between values and their mean are comparable to the mean itself is a *stochastic* or *random* process.

So, back to the market stuff. If we do the same math with prices (for example, recording the changes in price for each bar and then calculating their mean value and the difference), then we can use this difference as the measure of *volatility*. It will indeed match the Merriam-Webster definition – the greater the differences in question, the less predictable the values and the quicker the possible changes in prices.

In practice, a bit more complex calculation is used to determine market volatility. One of the commonly used metrics that estimate *how far the values of a dataset are from their mean* is called **standard deviation**. If you are interested in learning more about it and the mathematics behind the concept of volatility, I encourage you to first read the basics about mathematical statistics to get familiar with the terminology and the key concepts. The article in Wikipedia (`https://en.wikipedia.org/wiki/Mathematical_statistics`) could be a good starting point. In the meantime, we continue in a somewhat informal manner and remember that standard deviation is used to estimate the volatility in any stochastic process and market prices in particular.

I am sure you now perfectly understand that **standard deviation** (or **stddev** for short) also requires a period quite like any other TA indicator. This period is the length of the dataset for which we measure the volatility. So, what we're plotting is as follows:

```
S = stddev(close, 24)
```

This can be shown in the form of an equation like so:

$$\sigma = \sqrt{\frac{\sum_{i=1}^{24} (c_i - \mu)^2}{24}}$$

Here, c_i means the closing price of the i-th bar, μ denotes the mean value, and *24* means the number of data points (closing prices of bars) for which we calculate `stddev`.

Figure 7.10 shows the same 1-hour chart of GBPUSD as in the previous example, but now with the 24-period standard deviation indicator below it:

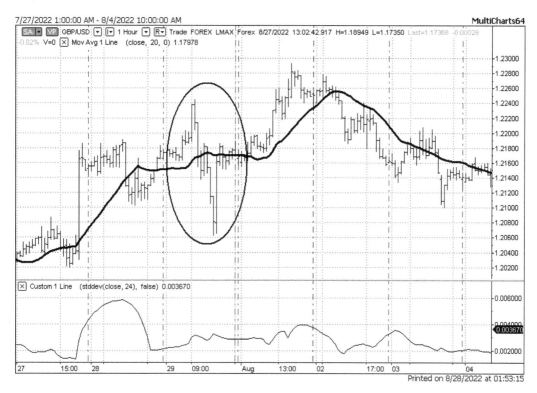

Figure 7.10 – Hourly chart of GBPUSD with a standard deviation of closing prices

We can see that volatility is something that doesn't have any evident relationships with the direction of the market prices or with trend/sideways market regimes. What we *can* see though is a number of important observations:

- Standard deviation is always positive; it disregards the direction of the price movement
- A sudden increase in the market activity does increase values of the standard deviation of closing prices
- The longer the price remains at new levels (see the jump in price on July 27 and a congestion zone following it the next day), the greater the increase in values of the standard deviation
- Maximums and minimums in the `stddev` indicator do not correspond to maximums and minimums in the price chart

Interesting picture, but there's one questionable assumption here, and I hope you already exclaimed, *"Wait! But we measure the standard deviation of an incorrect dataset! Why do we measure it for the price itself when we should have done that for price increments?"*.

Indeed, the market process can be considered a stochastic process from a number of standpoints. We can consider every closing price as an independent value of a random process, or we can look at price movements as a random walk process, where we're interested only in how much the price changed since the last observation (bar). So instead of calculating the standard deviation of *closing prices*, we should rather calculate the standard deviation of *changes in price* for each bar:

$$=\Delta = C_i - C_{i-1}$$

$$S' = stddev(\Delta, 24)$$

Here, C_i means the current bar, C_{i-1} means the previous bar, and the delta symbol means the price increment per bar (positive or negative – and this is the key difference from calculating standard deviations for prices, as they can only be positive).

Let's see whether there's any difference between the standard deviation of closing prices and the standard deviation of *differences* of closing prices. *Figure 7.11* still shows the same chart of GBPUSD with both standard deviations plotted below it:

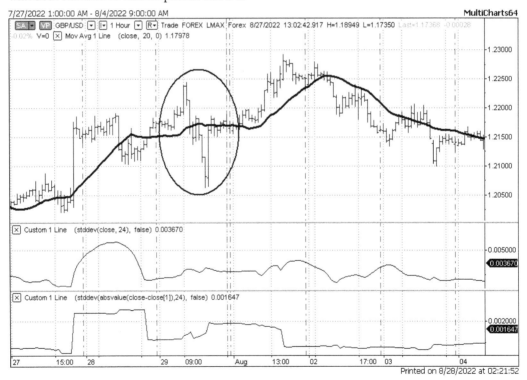

Figure 7.11 – Two versions of the standard deviation-based volatility indicator

The difference is pathetic! There are no longer *smooth* changes in volatility. Instead, we observe periods of high and low volatility abruptly switching from one to another. Now the picture is more adequate to what we observe in the market itself:

- Sharp price movements always and immediately cause our volatility indicator to jump

- High volatility often means a reversal in price

- Longer-term trends (the right part of the chart) are accompanied by low volatility (surprise!)

The fact that sharp price movements cause volatility to also increase sharply is used in *volatility breakout* strategies; the idea is buying or selling the asset in the direction of the already started sharp price movement. And the fact that the volatility is relatively low during trends is used in various *trend-following* or *mean-reversion* strategies.

Our study on volatility would definitely be incomplete without one of the most well-known and popular TA indicators, Bollinger bands.

Bollinger bands

This indicator was introduced by John Bollinger in the 1980s. The idea is to determine whether the price of an asset lies outside of the *normal* range. In this indicator, the *normal* range is defined as the mean value plus or minus two standard deviations (or two *sigma*). Therefore, Bollinger bands consist of *two* lines, one always going above the price (*B+*) and the other, always below (*B-*):

$$B+ = mean + 2 * stddev(close, period)$$

$$B- = mean - 2 * stddev(close, period)$$

Why two *stddev*, not one? If you want to learn the correct, formal answer, I would recommend that you refer to any book on mathematical statistics or the same Wikipedia article as earlier. Without going into details, let us just take it for granted that for a stochastic process, 90% of data points fall into the mean ± *2* sigma range. So, the idea of Bollinger bands is that drawing lines in a *2* sigma distance from the mean could help isolate outliers – that is, the prices that lie outside the ±*2* stddev range.

Let's see what it looks like in reality. *Figure 7.12* shows a 1-minute chart of AUDUSD with 20-period Bollinger bands on it:

Figure 7.12 – 1-minute chart of AUDUSD with Bollinger bands

This chart represents the mean or moving average (solid line in the middle) and two Bollinger bands (gray lines above and below). Bold black dots mark the closing prices that lie above the upper band or below the lower band. Both are *outliers*.

Technical traders use Bollinger bands for various purposes as other TA indicators as well, though:

- Outliers can be interpreted as breakouts – moments when the price starts its movement to a certain direction – so can be used in strategies that attempt to buy or sell *along with* the movement

- Outliers can be interpreted as liquidity issues and thus considered as good points for mean reversion – so can be used as entry points to buy or sell *against* the current price movement

Key takeaways – what TA indicators are all about and how to use them

The world of technical indicators is really vast. However, most of them are just variations of the same old classical indicators of the four main types:

- Momentum, or *market speed*
- Digital filters

- Range
- Volatility

Don't forget this when you stumble upon a new *unique* indicator that promises *fantastic* results. Give it a thorough examination first and you will see what it actually shows.

Don't forget that no indicator can build you a robust trading strategy. They serve only to quantitatively identify various situations in the market, and it is still up to you as the trading strategy developer how you actually exploit these situations in the logic of your code.

Now, it's time to see how we can implement technical indicators in native Python code.

Implementation of TA indicators in Python

I am sure you remember that any TA indicator uses a certain period as a parameter. This period means a number of data points that we take into consideration. To calculate an indicator on every bar, we start from the oldest one (the leftmost on the chart) and then move one by one, updating our dataset with each new bar.

Since we are talking about an absolutely essential thing that lies in the foundation of all TA, let me be very detailed here – probably too detailed – but I want to leave no place for ambiguity or misunderstanding in the following concepts and code samples.

Let's start with the core concept of time series processing: the sliding window.

Sliding windows

Let's go back to the example of a random walk (around bars and movies) that we considered in the previous section. The entire dataset, or historical data, consists of 10 data points:

```
S1 = {0.7, 2, 1.5, 0.3, 2.6, 1.1, 1.8, 0.45, 3.1, 2.9}
```

Now, if we are interested in analyzing the activity only for the last 3 days, then we get the following subsets:

```
S1_1 = {0.7, 2, 1.5}
S1_2 = {2, 1.5, 0.3}
...
S1_8 = {0.45, 3.1, 2.9}
```

Then, we apply a TA indicator to each subset, one by one, left to right, older to newer.

This technique is known as the **sliding window**, and is the cornerstone of all technical trading, from plotting simple indicators to backtesting and optimization.

Peeking ahead

The main problem of working with historical data while using sliding windows is the potential ability to *peek ahead*, or look into the future (see *Chapter 4, Trading Application – What's Inside?*, in the *Trading logic – this is where a small mistake may cost a fortune* section, for the discussion on the peeking ahead issue). If we reconstruct your random walk movements from the S1 dataset (see the *Stochastic oscillator* section in this chapter), we should take particular care about *not* using data from *tomorrow* when we analyze what happened *today*. Let's add dates to our data samples to give them more clarity:

```
S1 =   {{01/01/2001,0.7}
        {01/02/2001,  2}
        {01/03/2001,  1.5}
        {01/04/2001,  0.3}
        {01/05/2001,  2.6}
        {01/06/2001,  1.1}
        {01/07/2001,  1.8}
        {01/08/2001,  0.45}
        {01/09/2001,  3.1}
        {01/10/2001,  2.9}}
```

If we reconstruct what happened on or before January 6, 2001, we are allowed to take into consideration only data from the prior period. We *cannot, should not, and have no right* to use data from January 7 or later. If we do, we face this peek-ahead issue.

Now, imagine that you're developing a trading strategy and want to test it using past data. The goal of such a test is to reconstruct what *would have happened* on that particular day at that particular time *if* your strategy actually worked then. If you reconstruct what your strategy would have done on January 6, you have no right to peek ahead and use data from January 7, even 1 second past the test date, because you have no time machine (or so I assume) and when you run your strategy *live*, you will be also unable to retrieve data from the future.

However, peeking ahead is, surprisingly, quite a common mistake, and this is why I go into so much detail on this issue here. Remember that *if your strategy delivers unrealistically good returns, then most likely, they are indeed not realistic and are caused by peeking ahead.*

How is it possible to peek ahead non-intentionally, occasionally? Well, it's very easy if you store price time series in a list or any similar iterable structure, and retrieve data to do calculations by an index. In the previous example, I can get data from January 7 while testing a strategy for January 6 simply by calling S1 [4 : 7]. Even if you use dictionaries, you can get erroneous data by retrieving it with an incorrectly specified datetime index.

But having said all that, is there a method to guarantee that your code will never try to retrieve data from the future? Let's find out!

The ultimate solution to the peek-ahead issue

To suggest such a solution, we should recall that when we use *live* data, we are physically unable to get data from the future because ticks or any other data packets arrive at your trading application one by one. So, if we want to fully guarantee no peeking ahead during the testing phase of the development, we may want to emulate the very incoming data stream and write the rest of the code as if we plan to work with live data, not historical data stored on disk.

The first step toward this universal architecture was made in *Chapter 5, Retrieving and Handling Market Data with Python*, where we suggested using queues and threads to accommodate for receiving large amounts of incoming ticks. Now, let's look at the problem of calculating TA indicators from the same standpoint.

I'm sure you remember that *any* TA indicator analyzes a subset of price time series, and the length of this subset is called a **period**. When we looked at charts, we always noted that for the reconstruction of the indicator's values on historical price data, we need to move this period from left to right, from the oldest to the newest data points. We called this approach a **sliding window**.

But now let's think about what we should do in case we try to build the indicator's values *on the fly*, live, as market data is coming in. There's no history, no stored values, only live ticks. So how can we create such a sliding window?

The answer is obvious: we do create a *window*, but we don't create a *sliding* window because there's nothing to slide on.

Let's recall how a queue works (see also *Chapter 5, Retrieving and Handling Market Data with Python*). Generally speaking, a queue is a list with the following properties:

- When a new element comes in, it is added to the end of the queue
- When we retrieve an element from the queue, it is taken from the beginning and removed

Now, let's create a special queue where the oldest elements (those at the beginning) are not retrieved, but automatically removed as soon as a new element is added. Let's look at the diagram in *Figure 7.13* to see how it works:

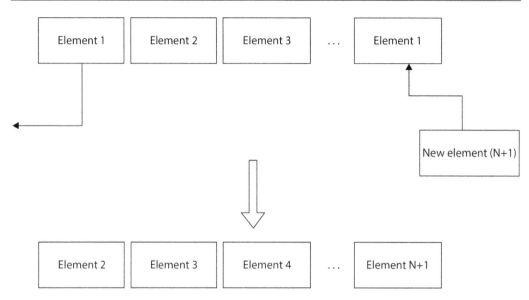

Figure 7.13 – Queue with a fixed length and automatic removal of
the oldest element upon arrival of a new element

Now, let's start filling this queue with price time series, starting from the oldest data points. What do we get then?

Let's do it with our S1 sample data from the preceding example. Imagine that we created such a queue with a length of three. Then, we start pushing data points to this queue, removing the oldest points as new points come in. We will get the following subsets:

```
S1_1 = {{01/01/2001,0.7}
        {01/02/2001, 2}
        {01/03/2001, 1.5}}
S1_2 = {{01/02/2001, 2}
        {01/03/2001, 1.5}
        {01/04/2001, 0.3}}
S1_3 = {{01/03/2001, 1.5}
        {01/04/2001, 0.3}
        {01/05/2001, 2.6}}
    . . .
```

And so on.

What are these subsets now?

Wow, these are exactly what we got using a sliding window!

Now, instead of storing data in a database or any other storage and then retrieving it for the purpose of building a TA indicator, we do that *on the fly* as new data is coming in. In this case, we will never be able to peek ahead because we will never be able to receive data from the future. All we need to do is emulate the data feed using historical data.

This solution has another evident and huge benefit: if we develop our application using an emulated data feed, then we can switch to a live data feed *without changing a single line of code*. So, this approach not only guarantees that the results of our tests are always honest but also that we save a massive amount of time by developing a *universal* application from the very beginning.

Enough talk, let's get to coding.

Sliding window as a queue

Now, we're ready to implement the sliding window using a Python queue:

1. Let's create a class for our sliding windows first:

    ```
    class sliding_window:
        def __init__(self, length):
            self.data = ([0]*length)
    ```

    Here, we create a container for our sliding window and fill it with zeros.

2. Now, let's add the only method that appends a new element to this window and immediately deletes the oldest one:

    ```
    def add(self, element):
        self.data.append(element)
        self.data.pop(0)
    ```

3. Now, create an instance of this class with a length of just 5 (for demo purposes):

    ```
    sw = sliding_window(5)
    ```

    That's it!

4. Now, let's use the code that we created in *Chapter 5, Retrieving and Handling Market Data with Python*. It already contains the global queue (data stream) that can be used to transfer any data from any object or module to any other. All we want now is to add two functions: one that reads data from a compressed file (bars) and sends it to the global data stream, and the other that reads bars from this data stream and pushes them to the sliding window:

    ```
    def get_sample(f):
        sample = {}
        values = f.readline().rstrip("\n").split(",")
    ```

```
        timestamp_string = "0" + values[0] + " " + values[1]
        ts = datetime.strptime(timestamp_string, "%m/%d/%Y
%H:%M:%S")
        sample["open"] = float(values[2])
        sample["high"] = float(values[3])
        sample["low"]  = float(values[4])
        sample["close"]= float(values[5])
        sample["UpVolume"] = int(values[6])
        sample["DownVolume"] = int(values[7])
        sample["Datetime"] = ts
        return sample
```

You can see that we have completely reused the function that we created in *Chapter 5, Retrieving and Handling Market Data with Python*, when we learned how to handle data stored in files. Here, we read a bar from a CSV ASCII file, parse it, and convert it into a dictionary.

5. Now, let's send this sample to the global queue:

```
def emulate_bar_stream():
    while True:
        time.sleep(1)
        datastream.put(get_sample(f))
```

Again, this is similar to what we did in the previous chapter, the only difference is that we now use a different function that gets data from a file. Anyway, the result is the same: we put the new sample into the global data stream.

Note

Don't forget that the delay here is added only for the sake of debugging and demonstration to emulate samples arriving at the application one by one.

Now, we have finished the code that emulates the incoming data. Let's look at it: any code written from this point and retrieving data from the global queue will be *independent* of any particular data source. If you want to replace the source or switch from testing to live trading, then all you need to do is to re-write the `emulate_bar_stream()` function. The rest of the code will remain unchanged.

Finally, we need a function that reads from the global data queue and does something meaningful.

6. In our present case, we will take only the closing price of the bar, push it to the sliding window, and then call any function that calculates a TA indicator:

```
def retrieve_bars():
    while True:
        sw.add(datastream.get()["close"])
        # calling a TA indicator function here
        print(sw.data)
```

Making output to the console from a function is definitely a bad practice, but it's added here only temporarily, to quickly check the correctness of the code during debugging.

7. Now, let's start two threads: one that reads data from a file (or, in the future, from any other source) and the other that processes the received data. Don't forget to import the `threading` module:

```
import threading
data_source_thread = threading.Thread(target = emulate_
bar_stream)
data_receiver_thread = threading.Thread(target =
retrieve_bars)
data_source_thread.start()
data_receiver_thread.start()
```

If you did everything correctly, you should see something like this in the console:

```
[0, 0, 0, 0, 1.12949]
[0, 0, 0, 1.12949, 1.12941]
[0, 0, 1.12949, 1.12941, 1.12965]
[0, 1.12949, 1.12941, 1.12965, 1.12883]
[1.12949, 1.12941, 1.12965, 1.12883, 1.12894]
[1.12941, 1.12965, 1.12883, 1.12894, 1.12925]
```

You can see now how our sliding window is being filled with values from right to left, pushing older values out – *exactly* like a bar or tick chart on screen. So at any given moment, we have a *ready* sliding window of the specified length filled with any data we need to calculate an indicator – or to do any other thing we only could imagine.

Let's now see how easily we can build indicators using this approach.

Moving average – implementation

To calculate an MA with our setup, we only need to calculate an average of all values in the window:

```
def moving_average(data):
    return sum(data) / len(data)
```

It is indeed that simple! We don't have to worry about any parameters because we already specified the length of the sliding window when we instantiated from the `sliding_window` class and specified the type of data (in our example, closing prices) when we fill the window with data.

If we run our program now, we will get something like the following:

```
0.225898
0.45178
0.67771
0.903476
1.129264
1.129216
1.129208
```

This explains why we always disregard the first *N-1* values from a sliding window with a length of *N*; until *all* elements of the window are filled with meaningful data, the indicator's value is meaningless and should be ignored. So, since in our example $N == 5$, we disregard the first 4 values.

Stochastic oscillator – implementation

Let's now see how we calculate a range indicator like a stochastic oscillator. Since this indicator requires three values per bar (`high`, `low`, and `close`), we may want to modify our code slightly:

1. First, let's replace the generic name of our sliding window from `sw` to `close` and add two more sliding windows for highs and lows:

    ```
    close = sliding_window(5)
    high = sliding_window(5)
    low = sliding_window(5)
    ```

2. Now, let's write the function that calculates the stochastic indicator:

    ```
    def stochastic(high, low, close):
        max_price = max(high)
        min_price = min(low)
    ```

```
        return (close[-1] - min_price) / (max_price - min_
    price)
```

Here, `close[-1]` stands for the last available closing price (the one we will just receive if we run the code in real time).

3. And finally, let's slightly modify the `retrieve_bars()` function so it adds data points to all three sliding windows (`high`, `low`, and `close`) and calculates the values of the stochastic indicator:

```
def retrieve_bars():
    while True:
        data_point = datastream.get()
        close.add(data_point["close"])
        high.add(data_point["high"])
        low.add(data_point["low"])
        ma = moving_average(close.data)
        stoch = stochastic(high.data, low.data,
                           close.data)
        print(close.data[-1], ma, stoch)
```

If we run our code now, we will get something similar to the following:

```
(1.12949, 0.22589800000000002, 0.9999911465250112)
(1.12941, 0.45178, 0.9998406501473985)
(1.12965, 0.67771, 0.9999557404620697)
(1.12883, 0.9034760000000001, 0.9992298840400107)
(1.12894, 1.129264, 0.1914893617022131)
(1.12925, 1.129216, 0.5212765957448215)
(1.12937, 1.129208, 0.6489361702128061)
```

Again, as always, we should disregard the first *N-1* values, so reasonable readings start from *line 5*.

Summary

Well, it's been a long and – I hope – interesting trip, so it's time now to summarize what we learned.

Technical analysis assumes that price includes everything in itself and attempts to find repeating patterns of behavior, suggesting that the price action following a similar pattern will also be similar to what already happened in the past.

There are just four major classes of technical studies, despite their visual diversity at first glance: market speed or momentum, digital filters, range, and volatility. Each type of study can be used to detect a certain situation in the market, but none of them can produce a ready profitable trading strategy on its own.

The cornerstone of all technical studies is the sliding window, and the bane of technical trading is peeking ahead during development and testing. Using queues to emulate incoming data streams and to organize sliding windows solves the problem of peeking ahead once and for all.

Besides that, this approach makes your application scalable, flexible, and modular with the ability to connect to a live data source after testing without rewriting your trading code.

Now that we have plenty of data points, we definitely want to visualize all of them to be able to quickly check the results or even trade live. So, let's move on to the next chapter.

8

Data Visualization in FX Trading with Python

In previous chapters, we learned how to receive and store market data, how to process it, and how to calculate various technical indicators. However, working with large amounts of time series data frequently leads to errors typically caused by sad mistakes – for example, using incorrect data feed or wrong timestamps. Besides that, when working with TA indicators, it's really wise to check the result of the calculations visually – for example, you want to use a large period moving average to determine long-term price movements, but you make a mistake, enter a small period value, and then find yourself lost in debugging because no real long-term trend can be found. Making your research visual helps identify various mistakes very quickly and saves a lot of time.

In this chapter, we will learn how to visualize data using one of the industry standard libraries, `matplotlib`, and then go on to plotting bar and candlestick charts with the `mplfinance` library, and we will see how it's possible to create charts with live updates and use additional graphics with price charts.

In this chapter, the following topics will be covered:

- Charting and plotting basics – how to use graphical libraries with Python
- Quick plotting using scripts or an interactive console
- Visualizing historical market data
- Creating bar and candlestick charts
- Visualizing live market data
- Adding other objects to price charts

Technical requirements

To run the practical examples in this chapter, you only require Python 3.9 or above.

The basics of charting with Python

There are many libraries that implement charting with Python but at the time of writing, two of them are industry standards – `matplotlib` and `plotly`:

- **Matplotlib** is the oldest charting library (in heavy use since 2003), which was created in order to bring the well-developed charting facilities of Matlab to Python. It can create charts based on any array-like objects, including native Python lists and `numpy` arrays, support numerous types of charts, including financial ones (which is what we need!), provides full control over chart objects, features almost unlimited chart customizations, and can be used with different backends.

- **plotly** is a relatively young competitor (released in 2014). It offers pretty much the same charting facilities as `matplotlib` so the choice between the two is not obvious. Plotly definitely wins when it comes to interactivity and working with chart objects via an API but loses the competition in speed and abilities for customization.

Which one do we choose? Generally speaking, if you do not plan to develop a commercial-grade GUI application, then `matplotlib` is the obvious choice because it's easy to use, is very well documented, and has decent community support.

Before we start, let's quickly look at how `matplotlib` (and similar charting libraries in general) work and clearly decide what we are going to do, and especially what we are *not* going to do. We will learn about different backends, consider the peculiarities of plotting real-time and static data, and get familiar with the internal organization of graphical engines and their interaction with the *outer world* (your code).

Graphical backends

Any charting package used with Python has various **backends** – the very engines that render graphics on screen. Out of the box, we have a choice of four backends: Agg, **PS** (**postscript**), PDF (yes, the standard PDF format used for documents), and SVG (the standard for vector graphics).

Backends have **bindings** – in simple terms, wrappers that facilitate calls to backends from Python. Some backends offer interactive tools and controls out of the box; in this case, you only need to draw a chart and then you can pan and zoom in using built-in controls provided by the backend. Using other backends requires full implementation of the user interface, which is great if you want to customize and polish your app to a commercial-grade level but is pretty annoying if you only want to quickly look at some piece of data.

We are going to use the standard **Agg** backend with **Tk** bindings, which support some interactivity, such as the zooming and panning of plots, out of the box. It is the default backend for `matplotlib`, so you don't need to use any special commands in your code.

Static versus real-time data and related issues

It is important to note the key difference between visualizing static data and dynamic data. By **static data**, we mean any data that is read only once, received, calculated, and so on, and is not modified in real time. Typically, it is used during the research phase when you develop, test, and optimize your trading strategy. In this case, we work with historical data saved on the disk or retrieved via an API from our broker – but in any case, it is not being modified live. This means that both charting libraries work just perfectly without any serious efforts from the developer's side; once the dataset is formed, it can be plotted with a single command.

However, once we switch to real-time data visualization, we encounter problems because we need to update the chart(s) either periodically or upon an event – for example, upon receipt of a new tick. And here, we can encounter issues related to multithreading. To better understand these issues, let's do a quick recap.

Do you remember the concept of multithreading that we covered in *Chapter 5, Retrieving and Handling Market Data with Python*? Running several processes in parallel and connecting them using queues makes our trading apps universal, in the sense that we can develop all logic only once and then switch between data sources in order to go from research and development to production.

However, when we add graphics to our applications, we can sometimes encounter issues, and these issues are rooted in the fact that graphics are also running in a separate thread. This thread is controlled by a separate mechanism, not the one that we use to organize data-receiving and processing threads.

Therefore, adding charting in yet another thread to keep it completely separate from the main thread is tricky, to say the least. So, we will sacrifice the universality of our application in favor of keeping the usage of the graphics simple.

> **Important note about threads, loops, and process termination**
>
> The problem with multithreading is the termination of a thread. If you start a thread and don't add any check on whether to keep it running or terminate, then it will run virtually forever. To keep your code correct, you may want to always add an exit condition to any thread and/or the entire program (which is also a thread). However, when using `matplotlib`, you don't have explicit control over the thread that renders graphics, so you may want to use callbacks from the operating system. Therefore, despite the risk of being criticized by programming purists, I personally use keyboard termination from inside an IDE to stop the graphics loop – keeping in mind that, in production, we won't have to do that, as we never include charting in the production code. It's up to you to choose how you handle this issue, but in my opinion, the simpler, the better.

So, what we *are* going to do is to integrate some basic charting as part of the main thread of the main module. It will serve the only purpose of quick visualization without any intent to be used as a universal charting software, and will be disabled or removed before switching from development mode to production.

What we *are not* going to do is to write complex code that would provide our app with a sophisticated GUI that would fully imitate commercial applications, such as MetaTrader or MultiCharts.

Enough talk – let's get coding.

Installing Matplotlib

Unless you use a clean Python installation, chances are that you already have `matplotlib` installed, so check before trying to install it. Just type `import matplotlib` in the console and watch the result.

If you don't have `matplotlib` installed, you can use the standard installation:

```
python -m pip install -U pip
python -m pip install -U matplotlib
```

If you use Conda packages, then you can install `matplotlib` using the following command:

```
conda install matplotlib
```

Generally speaking, all major third-party Python distributions such as Anaconda, ActiveState, ActivePython, and WinPython have `matplotlib` as part of them.

Using Matplotlib in your code

`matplotlib` is quite a large library and we actually need only a part of it – the very module that does the plotting. As always, I strongly recommend using `import` rather than `from ... import` – to keep namespaces separate:

```
import matplotlib.pyplot as plt
```

This imports the `pyplot` module that actually creates and handles plots. Let's create our first plot:

```
y = range(10)
plt.plot(y)
plt.show()
```

The result will look like the following figure:

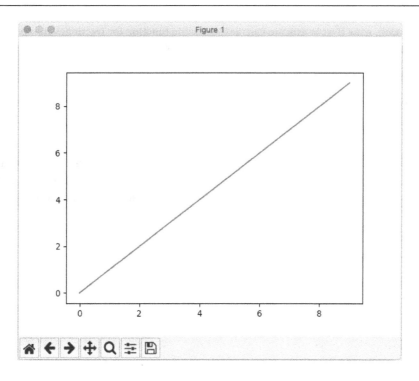

Figure 8.1 – A basic Matplotlib plot

Let's see what actually happened:

1. The graphics library created a figure – the very **canvas** on which all the following charting should be made.

2. Then, **axes** were created in the figure – the rectangle box with scales from 0 to 10, in our case.

3. Then, a graph object was added to the axes – in our case, it's the diagonal line.

4. And finally, `plt.show()` was called – the method that actually displays the chart on screen.

Multithreading: revisited

When you run this code, you will now see a separate process. This process is created by the `plt.show()` method and its name is `python`. Don't confuse it with the Python interpreter! This new process handles only the figure that is currently being displayed on screen. If you kill it, the `matplotlib` main loop is terminated and the figure disappears, but other threads will keep running! So, a better idea is to stop the execution of your code from the IDE, to kill all threads along with this `python` process.

As you can see, we had 10 elements in the `y` list, and the horizontal axis is graduated accordingly, 0 to 10. It's clear that the current plot displays the `y = x` linear function, where arguments are integer numbers. However, what if we wanted to calculate the same function for fractional arguments – say, the same 10 points, but taken between 0 and 1, not 0 and 10?

Let's give it a try:

1. First, as always, we import `pyplot`:

   ```
   import matplotlib.pyplot as plt
   ```

2. Then, we import `numpy` – the universal mathematical library for Python that adds support for vectors and matrices, along with myriads of math functions. We're going to use `arange`, which is somewhat similar to the native Python range but supports fractional steps:

   ```
   import numpy as np
   ```

3. Next, we form the range to display:

   ```
   y = np.arange(0, 1, 0.1)
   ```

4. The rest of the code is unchanged – just creating a plot and displaying it on screen:

   ```
   plt.plot(y)
   plt.show()
   ```

   Then, you should see a figure similar to the following:

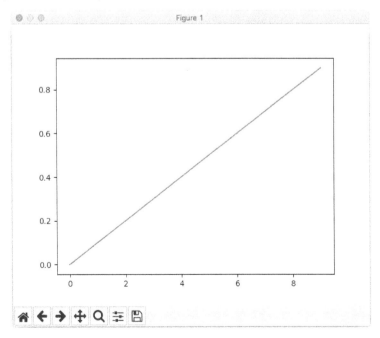

Figure 8.2 – The plot of the linear function in the range between 0 and 1 – the incorrect X-axis scale

But wait! There's something wrong with our chart. Yes, the *Y* axis has now graduated from 0 to 1 with a step of 0.1, but the *X* axis has still graduated from 0 to 10. This happened because we plotted the new array but did nothing to tell the `plt.plot()` method about the new scale by the *X* axis – and by default, this method assumes that we plot any array versus indices of its elements, which is always an array of integers.

5. Let's fix this mistake by adding the correct X-axis data:

    ```
    x = np.arange(0, 1, 0.1)
    ```

    Let's also modify the call of the `plot()` method:

    ```
    plt.plot(x, y)
    ```

    Now, we will see the correct plot, shown in the following figure:

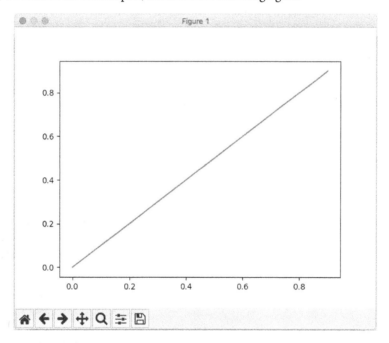

Figure 8.3 – The plot of the linear function in the range between 0 and 1 – now the correct X-axis scale

Now that we know a bit about how the `plot()` method works, let's plot some actual market data.

Simple plots of market data

In the following examples, we will use historical data only. We will learn how to plot live data received from a broker later in this chapter.

There are many ways to read and handle market data, some of which were considered in *Chapter 5, Retrieving and Handling Market Data with Python*. Now, we are going to learn some alternative approaches so that you can best choose what suits your current research and development needs.

Let's start with the most straightforward approach, which uses only native Python data structures. As we saw in *Chapter 5*, the preferred way of storing and manipulating market data is a dictionary because of its full compatibility with the JSON standard and the ability to extract the necessary data by keywords. We will start with dictionaries as well:

1. First, we still need to do some imports:

    ```
    import matplotlib.pyplot as plt
    import csv
    ```

    The `csv` module contains very convenient methods to read and parse **comma-separated value (CSV)** files, which is the de facto standard for storing historical market data.

2. Now, let's open a data file and create a `DictReader()` object:

    ```
    f = open("/Volumes/Storage HDD/Data/LMAX EUR_USD 1
    Minute.txt")
    csvFile = csv.DictReader(f)
    ```

    The `DictReader()` method parses the CSV file into a dictionary or set of dictionaries and returns a `DictReader` object. It uses the first line of the file as the source for keywords, so make sure you have it in your source data. In the sample file I'm using, the header (the first line) looks like the following:

    ```
    Date,Time,Open,High,Low,Close,UpVolume,DownVolume,
    TotalVolume,UpTicks,DownTicks,TotalTicks
    ```

    So, these are the very keywords that will appear in the dictionaries when I have read the file and parsed it with `DictReader()`.

3. Now, we need to convert this object into a list:

    ```
    all_data = list(csvFile)
    ```

If we now look at the last three elements in the list by entering `print (all_data[-3:])`, we will see something like the following:

```
[{'Date': '11/12/2020', 'Time': '17:45:00', 'Open':
'1.18136', 'High': '1.18143', 'Low': '1.18125', 'Close':
'1.18140', 'UpVolume': '249', 'DownVolume': '494',
'TotalVolume': '743', 'UpTicks': '7', 'DownTicks': '5',
'TotalTicks': '12'}, {'Date': '11/12/2020', 'Time':
'17:46:00', 'Open': '1.18140', 'High': '1.18156', 'Low':
'1.18138', 'Close': '1.18154', 'UpVolume': '399',
'DownVolume': '299', 'TotalVolume': '698', 'UpTicks':
'8', 'DownTicks': '4', 'TotalTicks': '12'}, {'Date':
'11/12/2020', 'Time': '17:47:00', 'Open': '1.18154',
'High': '1.18156', 'Low': '1.18145', 'Close': '1.18155',
'UpVolume': '500', 'DownVolume': '650', 'TotalVolume':
'1150', 'UpTicks': '5', 'DownTicks': '6', 'TotalTicks':
'11'}]
```

So, we indeed now have 1-minute data in the form of OHLC bars, along with some information about the volume and the number of ticks per interval (1 minute). Each bar is represented by a separate dictionary, and dictionaries are collected in a list.

4. Now, we need to extract only the data we want to plot – say, closing prices. In order to avoid possible issues by plotting too much data, let's plot just the last 100 data points. There are many ways to do this; we will use list comprehensions:

```
close = [float(bar['Close']) for bar in all_data[-100:]]
```

The rest of the code is the same:

```
plt.plot(close)
plt.show()
```

If you did everything correctly, you should see a chart similar to the one shown in the following screenshot:

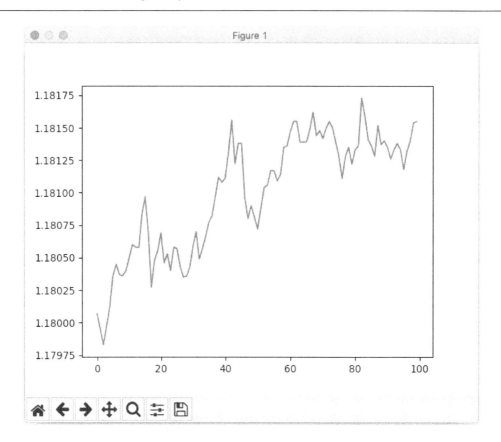

Figure 8.4 – A simple line chart of closing prices

5.   Great, but what about the *X*-axis labels? Oh, it again just counts the data points, 0 to 100, but we want to see something more meaningful here. Let's recall that the plot () method actually plots one iterable versus another, so we'll create labels from the timestamps:

```
time = [bar['Time'] for bar in all_data[-100:]]
plt.plot(time, close)
```

Now, we can see that the numbers along the *X* axis were indeed replaced with something, but this something is really hard to read and understand:

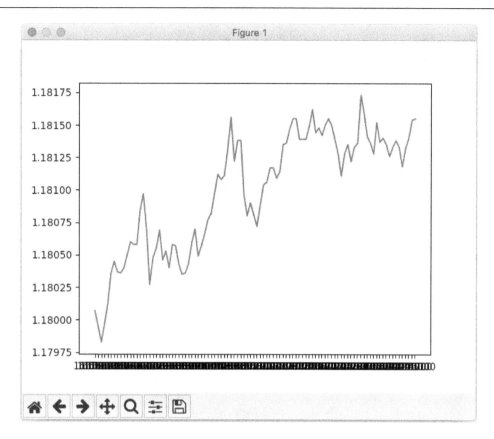

Figure 8.5 – Using timestamps as X-axis labels without proper formatting gets erratic results

Unsurprisingly, the labels (the timestamps) are rather long, there are too many of them, and they are displayed one over another, making the result unusable. So, we want to format them somehow, printing labels only every 10, 20, or 100 ticks and rotating them to save screen space.

In order to do that, we should recall the sequence of events that is triggered by the call to the plot () method, which is explained in the *Using matplotlib in your code* section in this chapter. First, a *figure* (a blank canvas) is created, an *axis* (rectangle box with axes) is added, and then the actual *plot* is drawn. All three objects were created automatically by a single call to the plot () method. However, in order to be able to modify the visual representation of the plot, we need to get access to the axes object directly. We now want to rewrite the entire code responsible for plotting in order to separate the three aforementioned objects.

6. So, after we formed the `time` list and before the `plot ()` call, we add the following:

    ```
    fig = plt.figure()
    ```

7. This creates a new empty figure object and returns a handle to the `fig` variable. Then, we add the following:

    ```
    ax = fig.add_subplot()
    ```

8. This one creates a new subplot, or axis – the very rectangle that we want to customize. Great – now we can access it using the `ax` variable. So, let's limit the number of tick labels printed along the *X* axis:

    ```
    ax.set_xticks(np.arange(0, len(time) + 1, 15))
    ```

    The `set_xticks ()` method uses only one argument here – an iterable that specifies indices of only those elements in the `time` list that we want to plot. In our example, we use a numpy `arange` that contains integer numbers with a step of 15 to plot every 15th timestamp.

9. Finally, to make our plot even more readable, let's turn the labels by 45° and plot the result:

    ```
    plt.xticks(rotation=45)
    plt.plot(time, close)
    plt.show()
    ```

    If you did everything correctly, you should see a chart like the following:

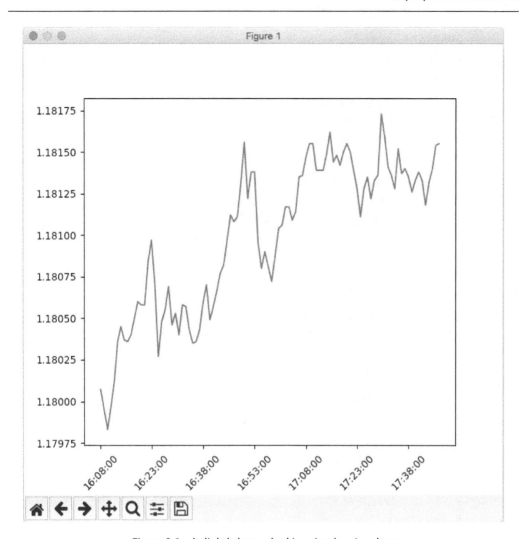

Figure 8.6 – A slightly better-looking simple price chart

So far, we have plotted charts only for the last 100 data points, but what if we want to plot the market data of a certain day in the past?

10. Let's rewrite the entire code now to keep everything that we've learned so far together:

```
import csv
import matplotlib.pyplot as plt
import numpy as np
f = open("/Volumes/Storage HDD/Data/LMAX EUR_USD 1
```

```
Minute.txt")
csvFile = csv.DictReader(f)
all_data = list(csvFile)
```

So far, there's no difference; we just import the necessary modules and read the data file. Now, we want to plot 100 bars, starting from midnight of December 12, 2019. So, we find the position of the dictionary with the relevant value of the Date keyword in the all_data list of dictionaries:

```
starting_bar_number = 0
for bar in all_data:
    if bar['Date'] == '12/12/2019':
        break
    starting_bar_number += 1
```

11. Then, we extract the required data for plotting:

```
close = [float(bar['Close']) for bar in all_
data[starting_bar_number:starting_bar_number + 100]]
time = [bar['Time'] for bar in all_data[starting_bar_
number:starting_bar_number + 100]]
```

Then, we actually plot using some nice formatting:

```
fig = plt.figure()
ax = fig.add_subplot()
ax.set_xticks(np.arange(0, len(time) + 1, 15))
plt.xticks(rotation=45)
plt.plot(time, close)
plt.show()
```

That's it! Now, we can enjoy our chart:

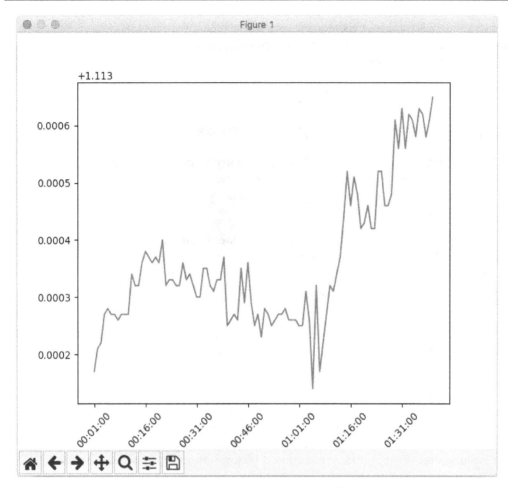

Figure 8.7 – A simple price chart of data from a specified date and time

Here, we omit all the capabilities of matplotlib, including the formatting of titles, using colors, multiple subplots, and much more – at the end of the day, this book is not a matplotlib tutorial. If you're interested in learning more about this reliable charting package, I'd recommend starting with its official website (https://matplotlib.org), where you'll find a lot of examples, tutorials, and general documentation.

Alright, now we know how to plot basic price charts – simple line charts of closing (or any other) prices versus timestamps. However, we all know that the most common format for charting in the financial world is a bar chart or candlestick chart. How do we plot such a chart with matplotlib?

Well, a few years ago, matplotlib itself used to have a finance module that supported the charts in question. However, now it's deprecated. So, we have only two options – either building financial charts bar by bar using matplotlib's bar() method or opting for a relatively new but advanced package, mplfinance. This package offers very simplistic and straightforward methods to plot price charts, but it won't plot data stored in native Python structures, such as lists or dictionaries. Instead, it uses **pandas** to handle market data.

So, what is pandas and how can we use it?

Visualizing static market data with pandas

pandas is *"a fast, powerful, flexible, and easy to use open source data analysis and manipulation tool, built on top of the Python programming language"*, as declared on its official web page at https://pandas.pydata.org. It was originally developed exactly for the purpose of manipulating time series data, especially market prices.

Instead of native Python lists or NumPy arrays, pandas uses **DataFrames** as a core data object. You can think of a DataFrame as a table, where columns represent various named time series (or any other series) and rows contain actual data, with the first row always containing the names of the series. Pretty much the same as with the historical market data file that we've used so far? Yes, and this makes the learning curve with pandas really steep.

pandas offers methods to add, delete, and rearrange columns, create and modify indices, slice and create subsets, merge and reshape DataFrames, and even handle missing data.

> **Note**
>
> pandas is quite a comprehensive package that offers various methods to handle data to suit very different needs. This book is in no way a pandas tutorial; we are going to use only those methods that are required to accomplish the task of plotting market data. If you are interested in learning more about pandas, I'd recommend starting with a simple tutorial at https://www.w3schools.com/python/pandas/default.asp.

Installing pandas

The official pandas website recommends installing Anaconda, which comes with pandas on board, and refers to other installation methods as *advanced*. However, there's nothing really advanced about them. You can use the standard PyPI installation:

```
pip install pandas
```

Alternatively, you can use Conda:

```
conda install pandas
```

Reading data from CSV files with pandas

pandas offers a straightforward method to read data from a CSV file. Let's try the following code:

```
import mplfinance as mpf # this is for future use with charting
import pandas
file_name = "/Volumes/Storage HDD/Data/LMAX EUR_USD 1 Minute.
txt"
source_data = pandas.read_csv(file_name)
print(source_data)
```

Of course, as always, you want to replace the value of file_name with the actual path to the locally stored historical data CSV file.

If you did everything correctly, you will see output like the following:

	Date	Time	Open	...	UpTicks	DownTicks
TotalTicks						
0	1/27/2015	13:29:00	1.12942	...	3	2
8						
1	1/27/2015	13:30:00	1.12947	...	4	7
12						
2	1/27/2015	13:31:00	1.12953	...	9	4
14						
3	1/27/2015	13:32:00	1.12944	...	2	10
13						
4	1/27/2015	13:33:00	1.12876	...	5	4
12						
...	...	...	...	...	...	...
...						
2136274	11/12/2020	17:43:00	1.18134	...	4	7
11						
2136275	11/12/2020	17:44:00	1.18124	...	7	4
11						
2136276	11/12/2020	17:45:00	1.18136	...	7	5
12						
2136277	11/12/2020	17:46:00	1.18140	...	8	4
12						
2136278	11/12/2020	17:47:00	1.18154	...	5	6

```
            11

[2136279 rows x 12 columns]
```

You can see that the first row was used to create column names and the rest formed the actual data.

Note that in front of the data read from the file, there's an additional column without a name, and it contains just integer numbers from 0 to 2,136,278 (in the example with my file). This is the **DataFrame index**. We can retrieve any specific records by referring to them using these numbers – again, pretty much as we would do if we used lists. Of course, it's very inconvenient, as we want to be able to retrieve any piece of historical data by referring to a particular date or time range. Fortunately, pandas offers a way to build a custom index for a DataFrame, so let's continue with our code.

Setting index for a dataframe

First, let's form the timestamps from the `date` and `time` fields:

```
source_data['Timestamp'] = pandas.to_datetime(source_
data['Date']) + pandas.to_timedelta(source_data['Time'])
```

Here, we use built-in methods, `to_datetime()` and `to_timedelta()`, which convert string values into a single `Timestamp` object.

> **Referencing columns in pandas**
>
> In the preceding code, you can see how pandas allows you to reference a certain column by its name. This is very similar to finding values by keywords in a dictionary, but in pandas, the entire column is returned, not a scalar value.

Assignment to a column with a non-existent name (`Timestamp`, in our case) effectively creates a new column with this name.

Having created the new column, let's set it as the index:

```
source_data.set_index(source_data['Timestamp'], inplace=True)
```

If we now check the contents of `source_data`, we will see that the new index was generated and added to the DataFrame:

```
                          Date        Time   ...   TotalTicks
            Timestamp
Timestamp                                     ...
2015-01-27 13:29:00   1/27/2015   13:29:00   ...            8
2015-01-27 13:29:00
```

```
2015-01-27 13:30:00    1/27/2015  13:30:00  ...           12
2015-01-27 13:30:00
2015-01-27 13:31:00    1/27/2015  13:31:00  ...           14
2015-01-27 13:31:00
2015-01-27 13:32:00    1/27/2015  13:32:00  ...           13
2015-01-27 13:32:00
2015-01-27 13:33:00    1/27/2015  13:33:00  ...           12
2015-01-27 13:33:00
       ...                  ...       ...     ...          ...

                       ...
2020-11-12 17:43:00   11/12/2020  17:43:00  ...           11
2020-11-12 17:43:00
2020-11-12 17:44:00   11/12/2020  17:44:00  ...           11
2020-11-12 17:44:00
2020-11-12 17:45:00   11/12/2020  17:45:00  ...           12
2020-11-12 17:45:00
2020-11-12 17:46:00   11/12/2020  17:46:00  ...           12
2020-11-12 17:46:00
2020-11-12 17:47:00   11/12/2020  17:47:00  ...           11
2020-11-12 17:47:00


[2136279 rows x 13 columns]
```

Great! Now we have indexed all our data points (minute bars) by timestamps. Let's now create a simple bar chart for the same 1-minute historical data that we used earlier.

Creating simple bar charts using pandas and mplfinance

Of course, we don't want to plot all data in one chart. The data file I'm using in this chapter contains about 5 years' worth of 1-minute bars, or more than 2 million records, so creating a chart with more than 2 million bars in it would simply freeze rendering forever. Let's create a chart for just a piece of history, specifying the date, the starting, and the ending time:

```
sample_date = '23-03-2020'
start_time = '00:01:00'
day_close_time = '23:00:00'
```

The data in my file is in the GMT+1 time zone, so 23:00 here equals 17:00 in New York time, which is the bank settlement time for the FX market (see the *Trading the FX market – what and how* section in *Chapter 3, FX Market Overview from a Developer's Standpoint*). Also, note that the first timestamp for the day (the `start_time` variable) is 1 minute past midnight; for bars, timestamps mean the time of the last tick or the closing price of the interval (see the *Universal data connector* section in *Chapter 5*, *Retrieving and Handling Market Data with Python*, for a detailed explanation of data compression and timestamps).

Making slices and subsets in pandas

The most heavily used method to extract a subset from a DataFrame is `.loc()`. Its usage is again very intuitive, as it's very similar to making slices of native Python lists; you only need to specify the start and end indexes for the new sub-DataFrame, as shown in this pseudocode:

```
sub_dataframe = original_dataframe[start : end]
```

In our actual code, it will look like the following:

```
all_day_sample = source_data.loc[sample_date + " " + start_
time: sample_date + " " + day_close_time]
```

Finally, we want to strip away all unnecessary data and keep only `Open`, `High`, `Low`, and `Close`. Again, with pandas, it can be done in the same straightforward way by just specifying the columns to retain in a list – and the rest will be thrown away:

```
OHLC_data = all_day_sample[['Open', 'High', 'Low', 'Close']]
```

Note the double brackets; the outer pair means that we create a sub-DataFrame based on the specified set of columns, and the inner pair actually specifies the columns in a list. That's all done – now, it's time to create our first bar chart.

Plotting market charts with mplfinance

All charts created by `mplfinance` are, by default, bar charts, so let's start with the most simplistic one:

```
mpf.plot(OHLC_data)
```

If you did everything correctly, you should see a figure like the following:

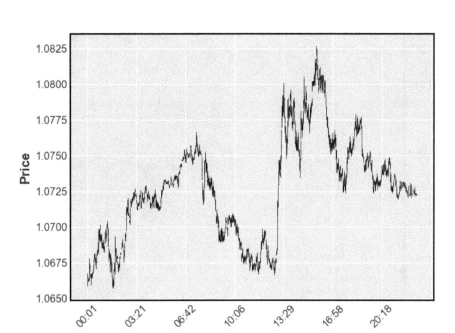

Figure 8.8 – A default bar chart plotted with mplfinance

At first glance, it looks like the same line chart, but this is because we have a few too many bars on a relatively small canvas. Here, we can benefit from the fact that the TkAgg backend used by default in matplotlib (and mplfinance is built on top of matplotlib) is interactive; you can click the magnifying glass icon and zoom in to any part of the chart – say, the spike in the middle of the day:

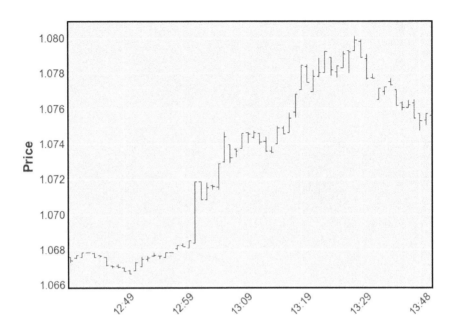

Figure 8.9 – Using the interactivity of the TkAgg backend to zoom in and out

There are several options to customize the mplfinance charts. For example, we can plot a candlestick chart instead of a bar chart and even add a number of moving averages to it:

```
mpf.plot(OHLC_data, type = 'candle', mav = (20, 50, 200))
```

Here, mav means **moving averages**, and their periods are specified in a tuple. The result is shown in the following figure:

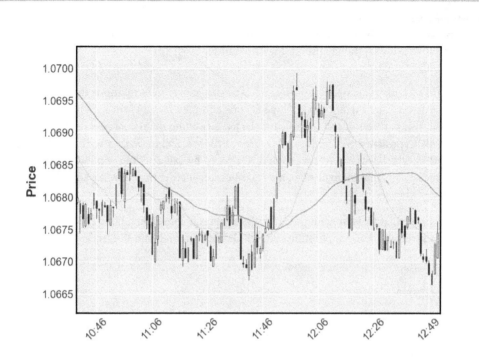

Figure 8.10 – A candlestick chart with moving averages plotted with mplfinance

Now, we can use both Matplotlib's `pyplot` and `mplfinance` to create price charts in the form of simple line charts or nice-looking bar or candlestick charts. However, so far, we have worked only with saved data that is static and not updated in real time. But what do we do with data being received live from a broker or a data vendor? Let's see how we can solve this problem using the universal data connector approach.

Visualizing live market data

Before we move on, I strongly recommend you reread the *Working with saved and live data – keep your app universal* section in *Chapter 5, Retrieving and Handling Market Data with Python*, and the *Sliding windows* section in *Chapter 7, Technical Analysis and Its Implementation in Python*. We are going to use the same architecture to create live plots of market data.

> **Important reminder**
>
> Whatever data we receive from a live data source should go into a queue. This should be done in a separate thread. Then, data is read from the queue into a sliding window that controls the actual amount of data – for any processing or plotting.

When we worked with static historical data, we used very convenient methods that allowed us to read an entire dataset into memory in one line of code and then navigate through it. Of course, any convenience is always paid for, and in this case, the fee is running the risk of peeking ahead (see the *Trading logic – this is where a small mistake may cost a fortune* section in *Chapter 4, Trading Application – What's Inside?*), which was efficiently solved in *Chapter 7* by using sliding windows and threading and feeding data points into them one by one, regardless of whether they were saved locally or being received from the broker.

So, in other words, what we were doing so far in this chapter is convenient, but it contradicts the idea of building a universal trading application suitable for both research and live trading.

Why, therefore, did we do all that, you may ask?

There are two reasons.

First, don't forget that we use charts only to *either* visually confirm an idea during the research phase *or* to check the consistency of live ordering in production. When we work on the development of a trading idea, it is infinitely more convenient to be able to immediately visualize a certain piece of historical data, especially if you work in an interactive environment such as IPython. That's where using pandas with `mplfinance` may be the right choice.

Second, visualization is used not only to plot market data but also (and probably even more intensively) to plot the results of a backtest, running simulated trades over historical data. And since a backtest is by definition something *carved in stone* – that is, not updated live – then using the approaches that we considered earlier in this chapter will serve our purpose just fine.

All in all, we want to visualize live market data in order to check its correctness, see various indicators, and/or track the order execution. Let's see how it's done.

Plotting live tick data

As always, we start with several imports:

```
import json
import threading
import queue
import matplotlib.pyplot as plt
```

The `json` module will help us parse the response from the data server; we are already familiar with the other modules

Then, we import a method to establish WebSocket connections from the `websocket` library:

```
from websocket import create_connection
```

Next, we create a class that implements the sliding window (see the *Sliding windows* section in *Chapter 6, Basics of Fundamental Analysis and Its Possible Use in FX Trading*):

```
class sliding_window:
    def __init__(self, length):
        self.data = ([0]*length)
    def add(self, element):
        self.data.append(element)
        self.data.pop(0)
```

Then, we add a function that creates and maintains the WebSocket connection with the market data server. This function has three arguments:

- The URL to connect
- The message we send to the server to subscribe to market data
- The queue in which we place incoming ticks

You can also implement the function as a class method if you plan to build a complex application with multiple connections:

```
def LMAX_connect(url, subscription_msg, ticks_queue):
```

Create the connection:

```
    ws = create_connection(url)
```

Then, send the subscription message, which we will specify later, outside the function code (if you implement the function as a `class` method, you may want to pass the subscription message as a parameter or have it as a `class` attribute):

```
    ws.send(subscription_msg)
```

Upon successful subscription, the function awaits incoming ticks and places them into a queue:

```
    while True:
        tick = json.loads(ws.recv())
        ticks_queue.put(tick)
        print(tick)
```

The `print(tick)` statement is added only for debugging purposes. All preparations are done, so now, let's proceed:

```
url = "wss://public-data-api.london-demo.lmax.com/v1/web-
socket"
subscription_msg = '{"type": "SUBSCRIBE","channels": [{"name":
"ORDER_BOOK","instruments": ["eur-usd"]}]}'
```

Here, we specify the server to connect to and the message we will send to subscribe to market data. Please refer to *Chapter 5, Retrieving and Handling Market Data with Python*, for a detailed description of the LMAX data structure and the *Retrieving data – garbage in – garbage out* section in *Chapter 4, Trading Application – What's Inside?*, to refresh your memory on important issues regarding receiving and processing data.

Next, we'll create the queue to store the incoming ticks:

```
pipe = queue.Queue()
```

We will also create a thread to retrieve data:

```
data_receiver_thread = threading.Thread(target = LMAX_connect,
args = (url, subscription_msg, pipe))
data_receiver_thread.start()
```

If you did everything correctly and ran the code, you will see the order book data coming from the WebSocket:

```
{'type': 'ORDER_BOOK', 'instrument_id': 'eur-usd',
'timestamp': '2022-10-28T09:12:26.000Z', 'status': 'OPEN',
'bids': [{'price': '0.995350', 'quantity': '1000000.0000'},
{'price': '0.995340', 'quantity': '2000000.0000'},
{'price': '0.995330', 'quantity': '500000.0000'}, {'price':
'0.995320', 'quantity': '500000.0000'}, {'price': '0.995310',
'quantity': '1500000.0000'}, {'price': '0.987800',
'quantity': '1000000.0000'}, {'price': '0.985000',
'quantity': '13000000.0000'}, {'price': '0.980000',
'quantity': '13000000.0000'}], 'asks': [{'price': '0.995410',
'quantity': '500000.0000'}, {'price': '0.995420', 'quantity':
'1000000.0000'}, {'price': '0.995430', 'quantity':
'1500000.0000'}, {'price': '0.995440', 'quantity':
'2000000.0000'}, {'price': '0.995450', 'quantity':
'3000000.0000'}, {'price': '0.995810', 'quantity':
'410000.0000'}]}
```

We want to plot only the top of the book – that is, the current best bid and best ask – so let's add another function that will parse incoming ticks and send `bid` and `ask` values to the respective sliding windows. We implement this function without arguments because it shares data structures (bid and ask sliding windows) with the charting part of the code:

```
def get_ticks(ticks_queue):
    while True:
        tick = ticks_queue.get()
        if 'bids' in tick.keys():
            bid = float(tick['bids'][0]['price'])
            ask = float(tick['asks'][0]['price'])
            bids.add(bid)
            asks.add(ask)
            print(bid, ask)
```

This function gets ticks from the queue, extracts bids and asks, and sends them to the respective sliding windows (`bids` and `asks`). Let's create them – first, we specify the length of the sliding window (let's set it to 60, which will display about 1 minute's worth of data, given that LMAX sends an update at a rate of about 1 tick per second):

```
window_size = 60
```

Then, add two windows, for `bids` and `asks` respectively:

```
bids = sliding_window(window_size)
asks = sliding_window(window_size)
```

Now, we wrap the processing function into a thread:

```
trading_algo_thread = threading.Thread(target = get_ticks, args
= (pipe,))
trading_algo_thread.start()
```

If we now run the code we have developed so far, we will see pairs of bids and asks updated about every 1 second:

```
0.99626 0.99631
0.99626 0.99629
0.99624 0.9963
0.99624 0.9963
0.99624 0.99629
```

Great job! Now, we want to plot this live data in a chart.

At this point, the most natural course of action would be to create the third thread and do all the plotting inside it, to keep all three processes (retrieving data, processing, and plotting) separate from each other and the main thread.

Alas, with `matplotlib` (and many other charting suites), to do this is very complex (although not impossible). So, unfortunately, we have to live with the fact that charting is (easily) available only in the main thread.

First, let's wait till the entire data in the sliding windows is filled with meaningful values:

```
while bids.data[0] == 0:
    pass
```

Then, we create the figure and the axes separately (as we did earlier in this chapter when we customized the axis labels):

```
fig = plt.figure()
ax = fig.add_subplot()
```

Next, we add two lines for our two data series (the bids and asks):

```
line1, = ax.plot(bids.data)
line2, = ax.plot(asks.data)
```

Finally, we start the main charting loop, which will draw the lines and refresh the figure once every second:

```
while True:
    line1.set_ydata(bids.data)
    line2.set_ydata(asks.data)
```

The following command adds small margins above and below the plots, just to improve the visual perception:

```
    plt.ylim(min(bids.data) - 0.0001, max(asks.data) + 0.0001)
```

Then, we actually plot the chart:

```
    fig.canvas.draw()
```

We then wait for 1 second for the graphics to be rendered and appear on screen; otherwise, the loop blocks the rendering we don't let it run during this pause:

```
    plt.pause(1)
```

So simple! If you did everything correctly, you should see a figure similar to the following one updating every second:

> **Note**
>
> It takes time to fill the entire sliding window. In our example, it will be about 60 seconds before the figure appears.

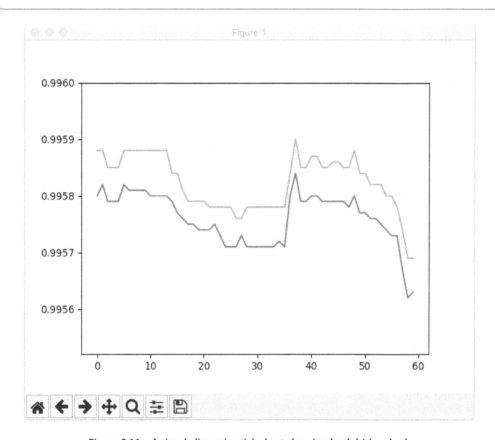

Figure 8.11 – A simple live price tick chart showing both bid and ask

Well, now we can draw live charts of market prices, and it has turned out to be quite simple and straightforward – but only in form of lines for every tick. What if we want to aggregate data and then plot a bar or candlestick chart? Let's find the solution in the next section.

Plotting live bar or candlestick charts

Earlier in this chapter, we worked with bar and candlestick charts, and we know that the most streamlined way of doing that is by using the `mplfinance` library. The idea is to use the `mplfinance.plot()` method in a loop and update, similar to how we just did for line plots of tick data. So, what we want to do now is add a new function that would split the incoming tick data stream into bars according to a certain rule, adds the formed bars to a DataFrame, and sends the resulting DataFrame to the charting loop:

1. Let's start with imports. Some imported modules are the same as in the previous example because we need them to retrieve data from a WebSocket connection again:

   ```
   import json
   import threading
   import queue
   from websocket import create_connection
   ```

2. Then, we import the `datetime` method, as we will convert string timestamps into `datetime` objects:

   ```
   from datetime import datetime
   ```

3. Finally, we have some imports to facilitate charting:

   ```
   import matplotlib.pyplot as plt
   import pandas
   import mplfinance as mpf
   ```

   Then, we will reuse some of the code from the *Plotting live tick data* section – the assignment of the `sliding_window` class, `url`, and `subscription_msg` variables, and the initialization of `pipe`, `window_size`, `bids`, and `asks`. We will also reuse the `LMAX_connect()` function without changes.

4. Now, we will create a new queue into which we will send DataFrames for plotting:

   ```
   data_for_chart = queue.Queue()
   ```

   We will also create a new function that will do the job of splitting the incoming tick data stream into bars:

   ```
   def make_bars():
       bars = pandas.DataFrame(columns=['Timestamp', 'Open',
   'High', 'Low', 'Close'])
       bars.set_index('Timestamp', inplace=True)
   ```

5. We've created an empty DataFrame, set the column titles, and assigned `Timestamp` as the index. Next, we set the time frame (resolution) to 10 seconds and initialize the timestamp:

```
resolution = 10
last_sample_ts = 0
```

Now, as always, if we work with infinite processes in threads, we start the loop, in which we read a tick, extract its timestamp and last bid price (we assume we want to plot bids; if you want to plot any other data from the order book, just choose the appropriate key and value in the dictionary), and if this is the very first tick we received, initialize the `open`, `high`, `low`, and `close` values for the upcoming bar and set `last_sample_ts` to `ts`:

```
while True:
    tick = pipe.get()
    ts = datetime.strptime(tick['timestamp'], "%Y-%m-
%dT%H:%M:%S.%fZ")
    last_bid = float(tick['bids'][0]['price'])
    if last_sample_ts == 0:
        last_sample_ts = ts
        open = high = low = close = last_bid
```

6. Now, we specify the condition with which we will start a new bar. In this case, we do it as soon as the difference between the current time (`ts`) and the time of the previous bar (`last_bar_sample`) becomes greater than the value stored in the `resolution` variable:

```
delta = ts - last_sample_ts
if delta.seconds >= resolution:
    bar = pandas.DataFrame([[open, high, low,
close]], columns = ['Open', 'High', 'Low', 'Close'],
index = [ts])
    bars = pandas.concat([bars, bar])
```

7. So, as soon as a new 10-second interval is started, we create a new DataFrame bar using the `Open`, `High`, `Low`, and `Close` values and the current timestamp, and add it to the main DataFrame bars. The rest of the function's code is pretty apparent; first, we again initialize all four price variables, update the timestamp of the last bar, and put the DataFrame in the queue:

```
last_sample_ts = ts
open = high = low = close = last_bid
data_for_chart.put(bars)
```

Of course, if the condition is not `true` (the time since the bars opened did not exceed the resolution threshold), we just update the price variables:

```
else:
    high = max([high, last_bid])
    low = min([low, last_bid])
    close = last_bid
```

8. The trick is done; now, let's create two threads:

```
data_receiver_thread = threading.Thread(target = LMAX_
connect)
data_receiver_thread.start()
trading_algo_thread = threading.Thread(target = make_
bars)
trading_algo_thread.start()
```

9. Create the figure and get a handle on the axes:

```
fig = mpf.figure()
ax1 = fig.add_subplot(1,1,1)
```

Then, run the plotting loop:

```
while True:
    chart_data = data_for_chart.get()
    ax1.clear()
    mpf.plot(chart_data, ax = ax1, type='candle', block =
False)
    plt.pause(1)
```

The `block = False` optional argument to the `mpf.plot()` method tells the renderer to release the chart after drawing and allow adding or modifying objects in it (so that we can do live updates). Don't forget to add a pause (`plt.pause(1)`); otherwise, the loop will always be busy and won't let the system display the chart on screen.

If you run this code, the first thing you will see is a single huge candlestick because we don't have enough data yet:

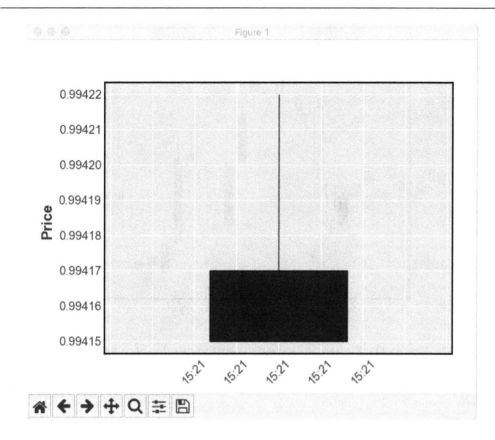

Figure 8.12 – The initial view of the live candlestick chart

Then, the chart will update every 10 seconds, and after 4 minutes, you will see something like what is shown in the following screenshot:

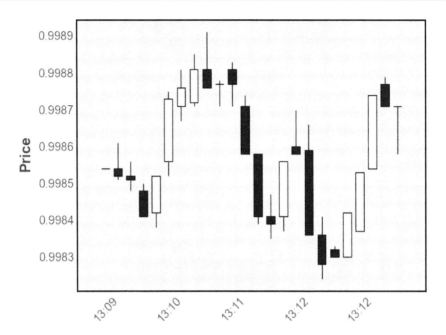

Figure 8.13 – A 10-second candlestick chart made with live price data

10. As we receive more and more data, there will be more and more candles on the chart, so at a certain point, it will become unreadable. Therefore, you may want to add a limit and throw away the oldest row from the DataFrame as the newest one comes in, just before we place the DataFrame in the `data_for_chart` queue:

```
if len(bars) > 100:
    bars = bars.iloc[1:, :]
data_for_chart.put(bars)
```

Here, I specified 100 bars to display, and as soon as this limit is reached, older bars will disappear from the screen – pretty much like in MetaTrader, MultiCharts, TradeStation, or any other charting application.

Very frequently, we will need to plot something else along with the price data. It can be a technical indicator, a trendline, just a mark denoting an entry or exit, or anything else. Let's see how we can do that in the next section.

Adding objects to price charts

It is not difficult to add any objects to the chart if we know their coordinates because all `matplotlib` methods always plot one array-like object versus another. So, basically, all we need to do to add any special objects to a chart is to calculate their position in the list, or the array along the X axis and the corresponding value along the Y axis.

Let's consider a simple yet valuable example. In *Chapter 3*, *FX Market Overview from a Developer's Standpoint*, we saw that price takers can only buy at the ask and sell at the bid. We also saw that a large order can move the price a few points (pips) up or down because it consumes the liquidity from several levels in the order book. So, we can assume with a good degree of confidence that if the best bid suddenly became greater than the best ask at the previous tick, then it was possibly a trace of a significant buy order. And it works vice versa – if we observe a plunge of the best ask below the previous best bid, then it may be a footprint of a significant sell order.

Let's visualize these two situations by adding triangle markers, pointing up and down on the tick chart for supposed buys and sells respectively. For this purpose, we will use the code that we wrote to visualize live tick data (see the *Plotting live tick data* section) and just add a few lines:

1. First, we need to add two new objects that will display the markers. We add them just below the lines where we create objects to display bids and asks (`line1` and `line2`):

    ```
    line3, = ax.plot(buy_signals_x, buy_signals_y, 'g^')
    line4, = ax.plot(sell_signals_x, sell_signals_y, 'mv')
    ```

    Special modifiers here denote the color and the style of the graphics – `'g^'` means a green triangle pointing up and `'mv'` means a magenta triangle pointing down. You can find a comprehensive list of the optional parameters of the `pyplot.plot()` method at `https://matplotlib.org/stable/api/_as_gen/matplotlib.pyplot.plot.html#matplotlib.pyplot.plot`.

2. Next, we need to calculate the coordinates (positions) of these markers. We will do it at the very beginning of the main charting loop (immediately after `while True:`). Let's add four respective lists to store the coordinates:

    ```
    while True:
        buy_signals_x = []
        buy_signals_y = []
        sell_signals_x = []
        sell_signals_y = []
    ```

    Then, fill them at all occurrences of the best bid being greater than the previous best ask, or the best ask being lower than the previous best bid:

    ```
    for i in range(1, window_size):
    ```

3. Note that we start counting from 1 and not from 0 because we want to compare a value in the list with the **previous** value, and starting from 0 would compare `bids.data[0]` to `bids.data[-1]`, which is effectively the **last** element in the list, not the **previous** one:

    ```
    if bids.data[i] > asks.data[i - 1]:
        buy_signals_x.append(i)
    ```

```
buy_signals_y.append(bids.data[i] - 0.0001)
if asks.data[i] < bids.data[i - 1]:
    sell_signals_x.append(i)
    sell_signals_y.append(asks.data[i] + 0.0001)
```

We add a margin of 1 pip to the values along the *Y* axis so that the markers will be placed slightly away from the main chart.

4.   The rest is the same as what we did for plotting bids and asks; just add calls to the set_xdata() and set_ydata() methods:

```
line3.set_xdata(buy_signals_x)
line3.set_ydata(buy_signals_y)
line4.set_xdata(sell_signals_x)
line4.set_ydata(sell_signals_y)
```

That's it! If we run our script now, we will see green and magenta markers pointing to the exact places where supposedly big buys or sells happened:

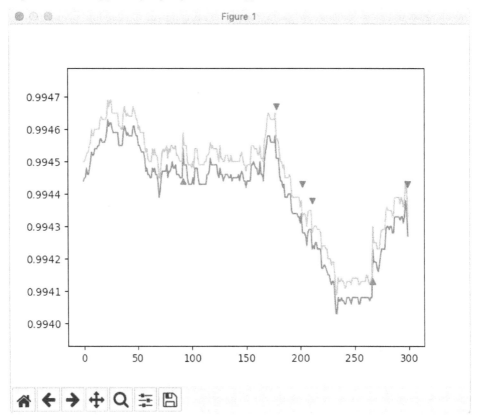

Figure 8.14 – A tick chart with spread-crossing marks added

Wow! Does the chart show the exact points to buy or sell? Looks like we've found an excellent trading strategy. Now, is the only thing left to do to automate it and look for a bank with reliable safe deposit boxes to store the earned cash?

Of course not. Just look at the following screenshot, and you will see that sometimes chasing *big money* can be quite a disappointing experience:

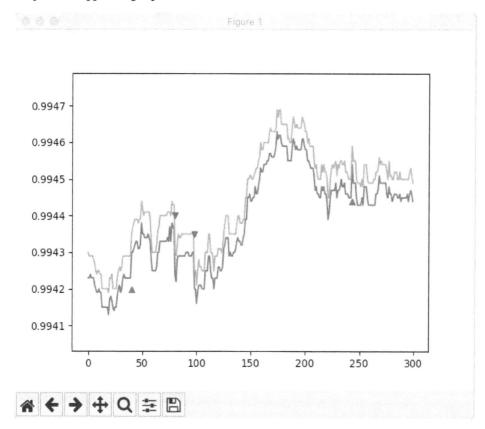

Figure 8.15 – Another illustration of spread-crossing – the price reverses and goes in the opposite direction

So, as I have maintained throughout the book, there is no free lunch and there is no Holy Grail in trading, which means that it is impossible to make money consistently for a reasonably long period of time by using only one magical trading rule. Instead, we need to develop a trading strategy, something that will incorporate trading logic (when we enter and exit the market and why, which normally consists of plenty of rules), money management (how much we trade), and risk management (what we do if things go wrong or, preferably, how to anticipate that and avoid trading). And this is what we are going to consider in the remaining part of this book.

Summary

In this chapter, we learned about the general principles of handling charts with Python. Now, we can quickly find the required part of historical data and plot it as line or candlestick charts. We also learned how to plot live market data and update the charts in real time. Finally, we learned how to add custom graphics to a price chart and discovered that crossing the spread can indeed be a potentially valuable trading signal. We are prepared to visualize any data, be it market prices or the performance of our trading algorithm, so it's high time we step into the domain of trading strategies to understand how and why they work, and to make the right choice for further development. This is what we are going to consider in the next chapter.

Part 3:
Orders, Trading Strategies, and Their Performance

In previous parts, we learned about the FX markets, understood how they operate, and discovered how to avoid the intrinsic risks. We also considered the essential components of most trading algorithms, which aim at addressing the peculiarities of the subject domain.

Part 3 moves forward by explaining the ideas behind most trading strategies, including all-time classics such as trend following, momentum, and mean reversion, along with more advanced arbitrage and stat arbitrage, market making, and high-frequency trading. We will also learn about the most common types of orders, typical issues with their execution, and ways to mitigate the associated risks. Finally, we will build our first trading app, test it, and learn about one of the most common mistakes among quant traders.

This part comprises the following chapters:

- *Chapter 9, Trading Strategies and Their Core Elements*
- *Chapter 10, Types of Orders and Their Simulation in Python*
- *Chapter 11, Backtesting and Theoretical Performance*

9

Trading Strategies and Their Core Elements

In previous chapters, we considered **algorithmic (algo)** and systematic trading from two standpoints: we learned about the market itself, its participants, the way it operates, and how all this is reflected in the pricing; on the other hand, we did some preparation work in programming, so now we can retrieve and process market data, build technical indicators, and do some charts and plots. In other words, we have the heart and the bones of the body of our future trading application, and now it's time to add brains and limbs: the trading logic that generates orders, and the order execution control mechanism that finally connects the app with the final destination – an exchange, a broker, or an **electronic communication network (ECN)**.

In this chapter, we will consider the most important classes of trading strategies that are typically used to trade the FX markets. We will learn about the sources of profit generation, consider typical trading ideas and their practical implementations, and understand their technical requirements.

Note that we are not going to develop actual codes implementing strategies of all these types. Some of them may be available only to institutional traders while others require sophisticated and expensive infrastructure, such as the colocation of trading servers directly with the exchange or ECN servers, special hardware such as **field programmable gate arrays (FPGAs)**, and so on. There are two reasons why we mention them in this book. First, it's definitely useful to know alternative approaches to algo trading. Second, you never know where you will find yourself in the future: for example, as a bank dealer or researcher at a hedge fund, and, in that case, this knowledge, even quite surface-level, will be very helpful.

In this chapter, you will learn about the following topics:

- Alpha and beta as sources of profit generation
- Options pricing – the most science-consuming risk models
- Alpha classics – trend-following, mean reversion, and breakout

- Arbitrage – let's earn from others' mistakes

- Statistical arbitrage

- Event-driven trading strategies

- Market making – profiting from liquidity provision and associated risks

- High frequency, low latency – where Python fails

Alpha and beta – widely used, widely confused

If you have ever read any article or book on algo or systematic trading or just ever listened to CNBC, most likely you have already heard about **alpha**- and **beta**-generating programs (strategies, systems, funds, you name it). And as is quite often the case with heavily used terms, not everyone who uses them really understand their meaning. Let's shed some light on this terminology, as understanding it will really help sort out the kaleidoscopic variety of trading strategies.

Alpha – earn from changes in price

According to the general definition of alpha (which you can find, for example, at InvestmentU – `https://investmentu.com/what-is-alpha-investing/`), **alpha** (α) *"is a specific measurement of the worth of an investment based on its performance relative to the market. Specifically, alpha measures the ability of an investment to beat market returns."*

Sounds familiar? Most likely yes if you are interested in markets and trading (otherwise, why would you be reading this book?)

But is it clear and understandable? No, as this *definition* replaces one unknown term (*alpha*) with another (*beat the market*, which is often also called **edge**).

The article goes on with *"Alpha is synonymous with abnormal rate of return."* Why *abnormal*? Because the efficient market theory claims that there is no way to systematically outperform the market, thus any excess return can be considered *abnormal*. This makes much more sense, as now we understand that alpha is a metric that compares the return of a strategy, portfolio, or investment to a benchmark (referred to as **broad market** in the preceding article).

In simpler words, there is a benchmark and there's the return of a trading strategy. If the latter is greater than the former, then the strategy generates alpha.

Simple? Yes, but we have to make two important remarks.

First, it is essential to note here that by *beating the market*, the alpha approach only considers the manipulation of underlying assets, such as selling short, exiting positions and re-entering at different prices, changing the proportion of assets in a portfolio, and so on.

> **Note**
>
> In other words, generating alpha normally means the active manipulation of the assets themselves, without the use of derivatives or sell-side activities, such as market making.

Second, there is a problem that is frequently overlooked: we do need that very benchmark against which we're going to compare the returns of a trading strategy.

When we talk about investment, the benchmark is obvious: a stock index. One of the most popular benchmarks of this kind is the S&P 500 – the index of 500 large-capitalization US companies. You can buy shares from all these companies and follow the index by holding them, for example, for 1 year. Alternatively, you can buy only some shares in a proportion other than in the index, buy different shares, sell some shares and replace them with others, or make any other active investment – but when you compare your returns with the return of the index at the end of that very year, and *if you did better than the index itself by manipulating the market exposure, then you can say that you generated alpha.*

Why does this approach make sense in equities investing?

If we look at the entire history of the S&P 500 index, we can immediately see that the US stock markets always grow over time. Yes, there are recessions, and there was even the Great Depression, but in the very long run, if you buy shares from all companies from this index and wait for over 30 years, then you will almost for sure make a profit.

Don't take my words for granted: check any source for S&P 500 historical data and you will see it yourself. The following is a chart by Yahoo! Finance in semi-log scale (check it out yourself at `https://yhoo.it/3U6I5rm`):

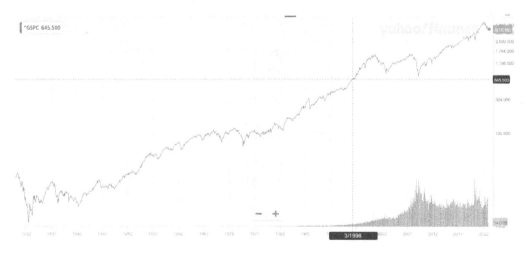

Figure 9.1 – Historical data of the S&P 500 index shows that the US
stock markets have a strong tendency to grow over time

With FX trading, it's more complex and confusing because currencies are not normally used as long-term investment vehicles – at least as widely as equities. The reason is that currencies feature interest rates, something that makes them radically different from traditional investment assets (see the *Economic news* section in *Chapter 6, Basics of Fundamental Analysis and Its Possible Use in FX Trading*, for a discussion on *carry trading*) and these interest rates change over time based on central banks' decisions. So, when you buy and hold a stock, it normally brings you dividends, or in the worst case, you just don't receive anything if the board decides not to pay dividends this year. However, if you buy and hold a currency, it's quite possible that you pay for the luxury of having this currency in your portfolio – if the difference in the interest rates between the two currencies in a pair is negative.

> **Using and abusing S&P 500 as a benchmark**
>
> Because of the enormous popularity of the S&P 500 index, it is frequently used as a benchmark for everything, not only investing in stocks. I have even witnessed a comparison of this index to the performance of a high-frequency trading fund. Of course, this has nothing in common with the traditional meaning of alpha, beta, and other metrics.

So, it's clear that we need a benchmark that is adequate for the specifics of the FX market. What can we use as such a benchmark then?

The simplest benchmark for FX trading strategies could be the currency itself.

Using currency rates as a benchmark

We can use exactly the same approach as with a stock index: compare the return of the trading strategy to the return in the currency itself for the same given period of time. For example, if we look at the historical rates of EURUSD from January 2021 to January 2022, we can see that they declined from about 1.2240 to about 1.1290, which is down 8%. So, if you bought the euro at the beginning of 2021 and held it until the end of the same year, then your *"investment"* would have made about -8% (and in reality, even worse because of the difference in the interest rates). But if you actively managed your investment by closing long positions and opening short positions when the rates were going down, you would probably have made, say, only -5%. Technically, you could even say that you *beat the market*, although, from a practical standpoint, such an investment would hardly make sense.

The good news in FX trading is that you can easily buy and sell currencies – quite unlike stocks where selling short a stock that you don't own (to profit from falling prices) may be problematic. So, the most reasonable way to generate alpha in FX trading is to change the direction of your positions according to the direction of the market price movements.

But what to do in case you trade not just one currency pair but a portfolio of currencies? Are there benchmarks that could be used to evaluate the alpha in such a case?

Yes, and one of the most acknowledged benchmarks of this kind is the **US Dollar Index (USDX)**.

Common FX benchmarks – the USDX

The USDX (ticker DXY) is *"a live measure of the performance of the US dollar against a basket of other currencies"* (see Forex.com, `https://www.forex.com/en-us/news-and-analysis/what-is-the-dollar-index/`). If we are to interpret it in terms of investment, then it is quite similar to stock investment, but instead of stocks, you buy or sell the US dollar versus a basket of currencies (which at the moment consists of the euro, the British pound, the Swiss franc, the Canadian dollar, the Japanese yen, and the Swedish krona).

For example, if the DXY's value was 100 at the beginning of a year, and at the end of the year, its value was 110, that would equate to a gain of 10%. If you had bought dollars for this basket of currencies at the beginning of the year, then you would have had a gain of 10% for your investment – again, in terms of that same basket of foreign currencies.

The USDX is useful for the evaluation of FX trading strategies and portfolios because it's already cleared of the interest rates and we may say that it presents the potential alpha in the FX market in its purest form.

If we look at the historical values of the USDX in the following chart, we can see that quite unlike the S&P 500, it cannot be used as a long-term investment – the same as is the case with any single currency:

Figure 9.2 – Historical chart of the USDX (chart by TradingView)

Generally speaking, if you outperform this index by manipulating the currencies in it (buying, selling, or adjusting proportions in the basket), you generate alpha relative to this index.

The USDX is not the only FX index. Many large institutions offer their own indices that aim to evaluate various segments of the FX markets or even various trading or investment approaches. Let's have a look at a few indices provided by the most important international banks, as these indices are frequently used as benchmarks not only for passive investment but also for active trading.

Bank indices – more details, more confusion

These indices sometimes only serve indicative purposes; others are tradable instruments. For example, Deutsche Bank lists (`https://index.db.com/dbiqweb2/home.do?redirect=productpagelist&region=All&regionHidden=All&assetClass=FX&assetClassHidden=FX&returnStream=ALL&returnStreamHidden=ALL`) plenty of FX indices. Some of them represent classical buy and hold while others track Deutsche Bank's own active investment. So, if you develop an alpha-generating strategy, then it makes more sense to compare its performance against one of these indices. Let's consider an example.

Suppose you develop a basket trading strategy that buys undervalued currencies and sells overvalued ones. Then, it makes sense to compare the performance of your strategy to the Deutsche Bank FX Momentum USD Index (`https://index.db.com/dbiqweb2/servlet/indexsummary?redirect=benchmarkIndexSummary&indexid=99800323&currencyreturntype=USD-Local&rebalperiod=2&pricegroup=STD&history=4&reportingfrequency=1&returncategory=ER&indexStartDate=20191103&priceDate=20221103&isnew=true`) and if your strategy delivers greater returns with lower volatility, then great – you make alpha with your strategy:

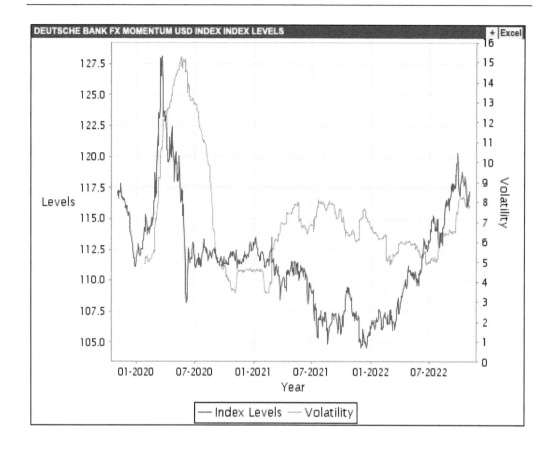

Figure 9.3 – Deutsche Bank FX Momentum USD Index chart

Overall, currency rates do not tend to grow over time perpetually. That's why using their rates for a single currency or a basket of currencies as a benchmark does not make as much sense as using a stock index as a benchmark for investing.

Let's summarize all of this. In the world of FX trading, by generating alpha, we assume that we will outperform any of the relevant FX indices – including the buy-and-hold return for a single currency – by actively manipulating the currencies in a portfolio. In this sense almost all *buy-side* strategies fall into this category (see *Chapter 1, Developing Trading Strategies – Why They Are Different*, to refresh your memory on buy-side and sell-side market participants). This is the very kind of strategy we're going to consider further in this book.

> **Key takeaway**
>
> In the simplest terms, by alpha in FX trading, we mean making profits when the price goes anywhere, up or down. So, for alpha-generating strategies, the worst market is the one where the price doesn't move sufficiently.

But is this really a problem? Do these markets exist – those where prices don't change substantially?

Of course they do. Any FX market may become more or less volatile, mostly thanks to changes in liquidity and sometimes special conditions imposed by central banks. For example, let's look at the chart of the euro versus the Swiss franc from April to September 2012, the time when the **Swiss National Bank (SNB)** decided to artificially peg the rate of the Swiss franc to the euro:

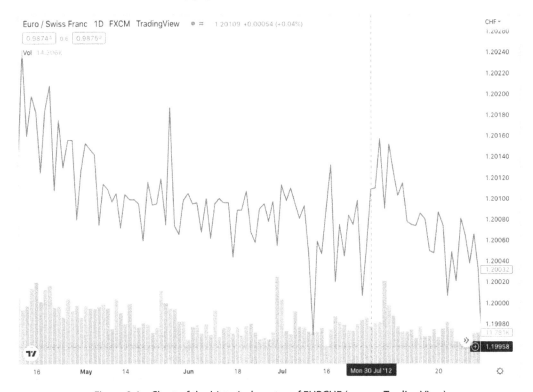

Figure 9.4 – Chart of the historical quotes of EURCHF (source: TradingView)

We can see that this currency pair had traded within a narrow range of only 26 pips for almost 5 months! Just to compare, the average daily range of the same currency pair as of November 2022 is 60 pips. Clearly, it was virtually impossible to generate any alpha in such a *stable* market.

But is there a way to still generate profits when the price doesn't go anywhere?

The answer is yes, and now enter the second character of the play: beta.

Beta – earn on volatility

The concept of beta also originates in stock investment. It refers to the volatility of the returns achieved by the portfolio – and as in the case with alpha, again, versus a benchmark. Sure, in the case of stock trading, this is also usually a stock index, with the S&P 500 again being the most common example.

We already discussed market volatility in the *Volatility indicators* section of *Chapter 7, Technical Analysis and Its Implementation in Python*. The volatility of returns from an investment or a trading strategy can be studied in a more or less similar way. In investment and trading, beta is a measure of the risk of how much you can potentially afford to lose in order to achieve the expected profit.

To better understand the volatility of returns, let's consider the example of traveling. Say, you want to get from London to New York. The most straightforward way to get from the starting point to your target is to take a direct plane. This route will be our benchmark. You can also enjoy a two-week trip by sea, which will be much slower and less straightforward. Otherwise, you can travel by car to France, then by train and bus to Norway, then by ship to Iceland, then by plane to Canada, and from there to New York by car, train, or bus.

See the difference? In all three cases, you get from the starting point to your target, but the volatility of your path will differ dramatically.

It's the same with returns: let's chart the hypothetical returns for two trading strategies (or investment portfolios, it doesn't matter) over time. One of them would be less volatile and the other one more so:

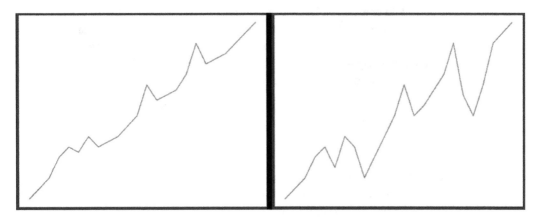

Figure 9.5 – Same start and destination, different volatility of a road trip or an investment

It's clear that the volatility of returns for the right-hand chart is greater than in the left-hand one, and any normal investor or trader would prefer the latter. In the language of risk metrics, we say that *the beta in the right-hand chart is greater than the beta in the left-hand one.*

If we now look at the FX markets from the same standpoint as in the previous section, we can see that as is the case with alpha, it's difficult to assess an *investment versus a benchmark* because no one invests in currencies like in stocks. So in FX trading, the beta could be interpreted as volatility of the market itself, and if a strategy profits from this volatility, then we say that this is a beta-generating strategy.

How can we earn on volatility rather than price movements?

It is possible by using one of the most complex yet powerful financial instruments – options.

Options – stable income with unlimited risk

This subheading sounds ridiculous, doesn't it? How can stable income go hand in hand with unlimited risk?

To understand it, let's first understand what an option is and how it's possible to trade them.

An **option** is a derivative (see *Chapter 1, Developing Trading Strategies – Why They Are Different*, for a brief explanation of the underlying and derivatives) that gives its holder the right but not the obligation to buy or sell the underlying asset at a certain price in the future.

I know that it's really hard to understand at first, so let's consider an example. Say, it's October and a kilo of apples costs $1 at the moment. I think that its price will grow to $2 by December, but another market participant thinks that even if it grows, it won't exceed $1.5. So, this market participant writes an option to buy apples at $1.5 in December and sells this option to me for a premium.

Now, if I am wrong and a kilo of apples in December indeed costs less than $1.5, then I will lose the amount of money I paid to my counterparty as the premium and the counterparty will make a profit (this very premium), but if I am right and a kilo of apples costs $2 or higher, then I realize my right to buy apples at $1.5 and immediately sell them at $2, thus making a profit. And this profit is obviously covered by my counterparty who sold me such a right.

As you can see, *the option writer earns purely on volatility*: for them, it really doesn't matter where the price goes; they earn if the volatility doesn't exceed a certain level.

Can you see the problem here?

For option sellers or writers, the profit is always fixed and equal to the premium, but the potential loss is unlimited. In our example, what if apples traded at $20 rather than $2? Such an unexpected and sharp growth in price could hurt the option writer significantly.

To illustrate how it is possible to earn selling options, let's go back to the example of EURCHF from the previous section. If a market trades in a narrow range, it is possible to write options to buy above this range (they are called **call options**) and options to sell below this range (they are called **put options**) and collect a premium, which works as a stable income.

But we all know that there's no trade without risk, and if the market suddenly goes outside of the range (and quite frankly, it's not a matter of *if* but of *when*), option writers may suffer from severe losses.

Let's see how it actually happened with that same EURCHF. The SNB maintained the rate of the franc pegged to the euro and this caused this market trade within a narrow range, as we saw previously. But one day – on January 15, 2015 – SNB decided to unpeg the franc from the euro. As the result, EURCHF plunged by over 20 figures (a figure is 100 pips) or almost 20% in a moment, and option writers who sold put options (and a put option is the right to sell at a certain price) suffered from unbelievable losses because there was no opportunity to liquidate their massively losing positions. *Figure 9.6* illustrates this price jump (or, rather, an asteroid downfall) and you can see how volatility exceeded any imaginable and believable limits in a few minutes:

Figure 9.6 – Sharp fall of EURCHF on the decision of the SNB to unpeg the franc from the euro

All in all, although not risk-free, it is possible to trade on volatility regardless of the actual direction of price movements, and strategies of this kind are referred to as beta-generating strategies.

Typically, option traders use various volatility models that help calculate *safe* price levels and adequate premiums for writing options. This approach is called **options pricing** and it is one of the most science-consuming domains in algo trading. We are not going to consider it in this book because it requires quite advanced knowledge in specific areas of mathematics.

Now that we are familiar with the idea of generating alpha and beta, let's consider some of the most popular alpha-generating strategies.

Alpha classics – trend-following, mean reversion, breakout, and momentum

Let's quickly recap the idea of generating alpha: we want to beat the market or perform better than an index (or just the rate itself in FX trading) by actively managing the position in the market. This means we try to buy when we expect the price to go up and we try to sell when we expect the price to go down.

Therefore, in order to successfully generate alpha, we basically have only two options: either we suppose that the price will continue moving in an already established direction, or we anticipate a change. In the former case, we make an attempt to buy when prices go higher and sell when they go down. In the latter case, we try to buy when prices go down and sell when they go up.

> **Note for nerds**
>
> In all the discussions and examples here, I intentionally don't go deep into mathematics. We are focusing on the qualitative side of these phenomena to better understand their nature, and we will consider some of the specific mathematical models that describe these phenomena later in this book. I have also intentionally left some of the market models and trading strategies without practical implementations because they are too complex to consider within one chapter.

Now that we understand our (somewhat limited) options, we will consider each option in detail. Let's start with a classical strategy that attempts to join the already established price movement and stay with it.

Trend following

This is probably the most well-known trading strategy ever. It was born in stock markets and as we already know, stock markets tend to perpetually grow over time. So, when trading stocks, it indeed makes sense to buy and hold the position following the overall upside trend.

Funnily enough, a trend in trading is one of those terms that does not have a strict formal definition. Some authors define a trend as a sequence of higher highs and higher lows or vice versa – lower highs and lower lows in the market price, but such a definition is ambiguous because it misses the volatility (see the example about traveling from London to New York in the *Beta – earn from volatility* section). We can say that the market is in trend if the following applies for a given period of time:

- Prices change substantially (that is, the difference in price between the start and the end of the observed interval is greater by absolute value than the average)

- The market has low beta – that is, the volatility is less than the change in prices

- The observed time interval is substantial: its duration is several orders of magnitude greater than the duration of a single sample (for example, if the data resolution is 1 day, then we can consider a trend on a timespan of 50-200 days)

Let's look at a couple of examples. These charts illustrate trending (in the right-hand chart) and non-trending (in the left-hand chart) markets:

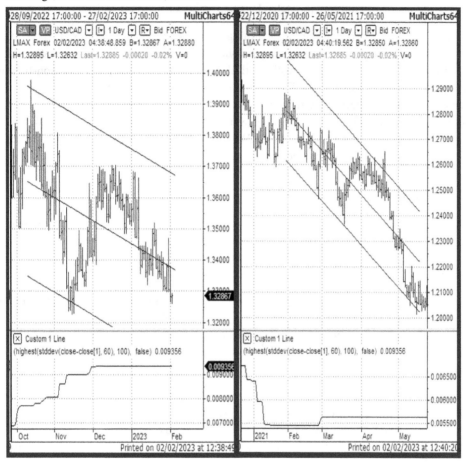

Figure 9.7 – Trending (right) and non-trending (left) markets according
to a beta-based definition (charts by Multicharts)

This figure clearly shows the inconsistency of the classical definition of a trend (higher highs and higher lows or lower highs and lower lows). In both charts, there is a certain downward trend in the price. In both charts, we can see a sequence of lower highs and lower lows. However, considering beta makes it clear that the left-hand chart represents a non-trending market and the right one depicts a trending market.

If we calculate the volatility as standard deviation and plot it above and below the regression line in the middle, we can see that the width of the resulting regression channel is greater in the left chart while the price itself has a greater absolute value of change in the right chart. To simplify the analysis, we added an indicator below each chart that plots the maximum value of the standard deviation for the period in consideration – thus, the line represents the latest actual value of volatility. You can see that in the right-hand chart, the alpha is greater and the beta is lower than in the left one, so we can say that according to our definition, the right chart represents a true trend.

If we can identify a trend, preferably at the beginning, join this long-term price movement, and exit before it reverses, then we can potentially generate alpha. Of course, since we are in systematic trading, we need a *technical trading setup*, a set of mathematical formulae that qualify trending or non-trending markets with a certain degree of probability. I intentionally won't go into math now; the purpose of this chapter is just to familiarize you with the concepts. There are a few classical technical setups for identifying trends, mostly based on moving averages (see *Chapter 7, Technical Analysis and Its Implementation in Python*) and linear regression. We will see the implementation of such a technique in *Chapter 12, Sample Strategy – Trend-Following*.

Mean reversion

The idea behind this type of trading strategy was originally born again in stock trading. Despite the fact that in the long term, markets always tends to grow, in the shorter term, we can always see rises and falls in the market price. Therefore, we can assume that there is a certain mean price that grows over time and consider deviations as temporary, so the price will eventually go back to that mean value.

From this standpoint, even the Great Depression was only a deviation, and indeed, if you were bold enough to buy US stocks in the 1930s and lived long enough to hold them until 1950, then you could have easily doubled or tripled your fortune, at least its notional value (if you didn't consider inflation, then you may be quite surprised to discover that you cannot buy three times as many goods with your tripled amount of money).

The point in **mean reversion** is thus the observed time interval. If we consider a short time span, say, 1 year or less, we can see any type of market effects there: trending up (or a **bullish market**), ranges, flattening, or trending down (or a **bearish market**). However, from a long-term perspective, it appears that almost all bearish markets are only temporary pullbacks from a hypothetical mean value that is constantly growing.

As we already know, currency markets do not exhibit the same long-term upside bias as stock markets, so it's impossible to just buy every significant pullback and be on the positive side in 10-20 years. Instead, we have an advantage: we can buy and sell any currency versus any other equally easily. Therefore, the concept of mean reversion in currency markets is slightly different: if we can identify the current price as being too far from the theoretical mean value, then we enter the market in the direction toward this mean, that is, opposite to the current direction of the price movement.

Mean reversion is also frequently referred to as **counter-trend trading** (or, to be more precise, counter-trend trading is a variation of mean reversion) because with counter-trend trading, we don't just buy or sell and then hold the position for a long time, but rather enter the market for a relatively short time against the direction of the main price movement. The following figure illustrates possible counter-trend trades placed inside quite an established trend:

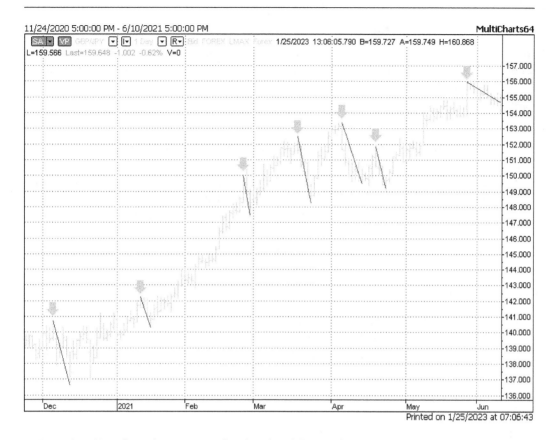

Figure 9.8 – Hypothetical counter-trend trades placed during a long-term trend (chart by Multicharts)

In this figure, big grey down arrows mark potential entries against the trend (that is, when we would be able to sell the British pound and buy the Japanese yen) and thin black lines mark the potential profit that could be achieved if we stayed in a counter-trend position for that amount of time (assuming we exit at the end of each line). As you can see, counter-trend trades are way shorter in time than trend-following and they are much more frequent.

You may ask: why place counter-trend trades if we could just buy GBPJPY in September 2020 and sell in May 2021?

There are two serious reasons for that.

First, trends in the currency markets are quite infrequent. A trend-following strategy may place only 4-6 trades in 3 years, and there's no guarantee that all of them will be profitable (as with any systematic trades).

Second, the longer we stay in a position, the greater risk that the market will eventually go against us. Besides that, the volatility of returns from a trend-following position (beta of returns) will be high because it will replicate the volatility of the market itself. So, placing multiple counter-trend trades that stay in the market for a considerably shorter period could possibly improve the beta of the overall strategy performance.

Currency markets also have quite an interesting feature: the shorter the timeframe, the more mean-reverting the market. Using daily data, it is possible to find really long-term trends, although not many. If you consider sampling market data at 4-hour intervals (you can refresh your memory about market data sampling in the *Data compression – keep the amounts to the reasonable minimum* section in *Chapter 5, Retrieving and Handling Market Data with Python*), it will already become problematic to identify tradable trends: methods that work on daily data will yield a lot of *false* trends. And if you go down in data compression to 1 hour, 1 minute, or less, you will see that the proportion of duration of trending to non-trending market phases will degrade so much that mean reversion becomes almost the only trading technique that can be successfully used.

Why does it happen this way?

One of the key factors that destroys trend-following in shorter timeframes in currency markets is that all of them exhibit strong intraday periodicity. This periodicity is explained by the nature of this market: it is open 24 hours, 5 days a week, but the activity of market participants is quite different during different hours of the day.

Midday (from here on assuming we are in the GMT time zone) features greater liquidity and greater trading volume, and equally, important economic news are released during London and New York work hours. Night always has lower liquidity and lower trading volumes, and there is no important economic news, with the exception of the Asia Pacific region. So, intraday price volatility inevitably exhibits strong periodicity, thus making identifying tradable intraday trends quite problematic. In *Figure 9.9*, you can see one of the simplest representations of volatility (just the range of each bar, that is, the difference between the bar's high and low) and it's clear that intraday periodicity is really strong in the FX markets:

Figure 9.9 – Intraday (1 minute) price chart and volatility (chart by Multicharts)

In this figure, we can clearly see first (left to right) something that looks like a trend, but it lasts for only 2 days and after that, turns into a sideways (range) market. At the same time, volatility (plotted as simply the difference between the high and the low for each bar below the price chart) maintains this strong periodicity, and if you look carefully at the figure, you can see that every day, with no exception, we have periods of slowly changing prices and fast-changing prices. So, this factor significantly contributes to the overall intraday price behavior of currency markets, being more mean-reverting than trending.

As with trend-following, we are not going into a discussion of particular trading setups for trading mean reversion. Normally, technical indicators such as the RSI or a stochastic oscillator are used to determine the direction of the price movement and *overbought* and *oversold* zones, and then a trade is placed against the movement once the price is in such a zone. In *Chapter 14, Where to Go Now?*, I will provide links to a few resources on these technical setups, which you can use in your own strategies.

The prominent intraday periodicity in the market activity should make us think: isn't there a way to systematically trade this periodical process? The answer is yes, although not directly and not in all markets. Let's look at the breakout trading technique.

Breakouts

Both trend-following and mean reversion are attempts to trade the changes in price itself. **Breakouts** are a different beast: it's an attempt to trade changes in volatility.

The idea behind the breakout is based on the assumption that periods when market is trading in a narrow range and periods when it bursts into sharp price movements interleave with one another. In the language of volatility, this means that low-volatility periods eventually turn into periods of high volatility. Thus, the breakout market model assumes that the price movements consist only of these two phases: low and high volatility, and if we can identify the former, then we can possibly enter the market as soon as it leaves its *"comfort zone"* and join the freshly establishing price movement. With breakout trading, we don't care about trends, mean reversion, or any other factors; we focus only on the relatively short-term process of changing the volatility from low to high.

The following figure illustrates a typical breakout setup. We can see that from 11:30 until about 13:30, GBPJPY traded in a narrow range (shown by two horizontal lines on the price chart) and the volatility was also low (below the average shown as the horizontal line on the volatility chart below). Then, something happened; the price left the range and steadily went up for a distance three times the width of the original range. Volatility also increased and remained above average during the entire movement.

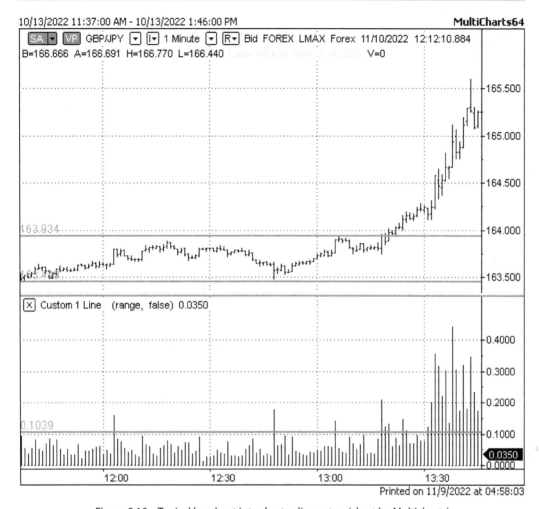

Figure 9.10 – Typical breakout intraday trading setup (chart by Multicharts)

Although breakout trading looks very attractive and quite natural for FX trading given the intrinsic alternation of low and high volatility periods intraday, it's not a Holy Grail of trading – as with any trading technique. I intentionally presented you with an *ideal* breakout chart, but in reality, situations such as this are quite infrequent in all FX markets. Besides that, the definition of a breakout setup is very vague and has many degrees of freedom.

Indeed, we say that price should first trade *in a narrow range*, but how do we define *narrow*? Then, we say that the price should leave this range and volatility should also exceed its mean, but even in this idealistic example, we can see a number of *false breakouts* – when volatility exceeded the average, but the price didn't go anywhere.

So, in order to take advantage of breakouts, we need to have a robust formal mathematical description of what a *narrow range* is, what *the price leaving the range* means, and how we consider volatility to be *greater than average*.

Now, we have been acquainted with the most popular alpha-generating trading strategies and these are what we will explore further. Unfortunately, it is impossible to consider all kinds of trading strategies in equal detail in one book (otherwise it would become a multi-volume encyclopedia!), but we will take a quick look at them so you know that the world of systematic and algo trading is enormously wide and diverse. Maybe it will ignite your interest in other applications of algo trading, or – who knows? – maybe it will help you make a career in finance.

Arbitrage – let's earn from others' mistakes

Arbitrage in financial markets means taking advantage of situations when the same asset is priced differently at different trading venues. Such a situation is usually called **mispricing** (there are other meanings of this term, and we will get back to it in the very next section about statistical arbitrage). Due to the colossal fragmentation of the FX market (see *Chapter 3, FX Market Overview from a Developer's Standpoint*) mispricing there is not infrequent, so an arbitrage strategy looks pretty straightforward: as soon as we see that, say, EURUSD is priced at 1.00012 at LMAX and 1.00013 at IS Prime, then we simultaneously buy at LMAX and sell at IS Prime, pocketing one-tenth of a pip.

I think you can clearly see some problems with arbitrage, which directly follow from its description.

First, the potential profit from a single trade is ridiculously small, so you have to make lots of trades in order to be consistently profitable. And don't forget about trading costs: commissions, trading server maintenance fees, and so on. Your trade should cover them all; otherwise, you will only achieve what traders refer to as **paper profit**.

The second (and main problem) with classical arbitrage is the number of arbitrageurs – they act so quickly that the price may change before your order is executed. Then, you have two options: either wait in hope that the price returns to a level where trade is profitable or liquidate your position with a loss. In this sense, the type of risk in arbitrage is somewhat similar to that of market making (see the *Market makers – comfortable, sophisticated, expensive* section *Chapter 3, FX Market Overview from a Developer's Standpoint*) although the former is an alpha-generating buy-side trading activity, and the latter is a beta-earning sell-side trading activity.

FX markets also feature a unique form of arbitrage, which is called **triangle arbitrage**. This kind of arbitrage exists only because we don't buy and sell assets for currency, but trade currencies against each other. So, we can search for opportunities for mispricing in so-called synthetic currency pairs. Let's consider an example.

Let's suppose that the EURUSD is traded at 0.99745. At the same time, the USDJPY is traded at 146.336. If we calculate the rate of the euro versus the Japanese yen using these two rates, we will get the rate of EURJPY at 145.963, but when we look at the real market, we find that the actual rate of EURJPY at a particular trading venue is 145.972. The difference between the real currency pair (EURJPY) and our synthetically calculated rate is 0.9 pips. So, we immediately sell USDJPY (thus, we have JPY and have sold USD) and EURUSD (thus we have USD and have sold EUR), which efficiently creates a short position in EURJPY. At the same time, we buy EURJPY, from where it's traded at a mispriced rate and makes a profit of 0.9 pips.

Of course, triangle arbitrage is prone to the same diseases as *plain* arbitrage: speed is crucial, and potential losses are always much greater than potential profits. Therefore, normally, arbitrage is the realm of financial institutions, and we have considered it here briefly only so that you knew how it works (and let me repeat again, who knows where you will find yourself working next year?)

Statistical arbitrage

As we saw in the previous section, arbitrage is based on the idea of mispricing: a situation in which an asset is priced incorrectly. But to say whether something is priced incorrectly or correctly, we need a reference that is known to be priced correctly, don't we?

In classical arbitrage, such a reference is the asset price itself, and we take advantage of mispricing across different trading venues trading the same asset. **Statistical arbitrage (stat arb)** uses the concept of fair value to determine whether the asset is mispriced. In simple terms, with classical arbitrage, we compare the price of the asset versus another price of the asset that exists at the same moment in time. With stat arb, we compare the price of the asset to a theoretical fair value to which we expect the price to revert in the future.

In a certain sense, stat arb is a modification or extension of the concept of mean reversion. Indeed, a successful mean reversion strategy is based on the statistical analysis of various price-volume-volatility setups, with the assumption that if the price is too far from a certain mean value, then it will return to it sooner or later. Stat arb replaces the mean value with a fair value, which can be derived from multiple factors, from money flows to political situations.

One of the most popular applications of stat arb is **derivatives trading**. We already quickly mentioned derivatives in the *Trade mechanics – again some terminology* section of *Chapter 3, FX Market Overview from a Developer's Standpoint*. Let's get a bit deeper into this complex yet very interesting domain.

In simple terms, a derivative is a financial instrument that gives its owner either a right to buy or sell an asset or the obligation to buy or sell an asset at a certain price on a certain date. Note these two mandatory attributes of a derivate: *at a certain price on a certain date*. This makes derivatives priced differently from the asset (which is called the **underlying**) – because they all have an **expiration**, a date on which the final settlement should be made.

It indeed sounds sophisticated if you're not familiar with derivatives, but in fact, it's quite simple. Let's consider an example.

Suppose that today is January 1 and the current price of EURUSD is 1.00000. I think that the price will grow by the third Friday of March to 1.02000. You think that it will not exceed 1.01000. So, you sell a **future contract**, which is an obligation to sell the euro at 1.01000, and I buy this contract, which for me, means an obligation to buy the euro from you on the same date – the third Friday of March. This date is called the expiration date of the future contract, and the process of mutual buying and selling on expiration is called **settlement**.

I think it's clear what may happen with our positions on the expiration date. If I am right and the price of the euro has indeed raised to 1.02000, then I buy the euro from you at 1.01000 and immediately sell at 1.02000, which means I made a profit of 100 pips. Subsequently, you have to sell the euro to me at 1.01000, and given its market price is now 1.02000, you suffer a loss of 100 pips.

The expiration date significantly affects the price of the future contract. Typically, the more distant the expiration date, the greater the difference in the price of the respective future contract compared to today's price, or the spot price. The following figure illustrates this difference:

MONTH	OPTIONS	CHART	LAST	CHANGE	PRIOR SETTLE	OPEN	HIGH	LOW	VOLUME	UPDATED
NOV 2022 6EX2	OPT	.il	1.01255	+0.01225 (+1.22%)	1.0003	1.0022	1.0137	0.9940	1,143	08:00:28 CT 10 Nov 2022
DEC 2022 6EZ2	OPT	.il	1.01455	+0.01165 (+1.16%)	1.0029	1.00415	1.01875	0.9962	169,910	08:01:09 CT 10 Nov 2022
JAN 2023 6EF3	OPT	.il	1.02135	+0.01545 (+1.54%)	1.0059	1.0083	1.02135	0.9994	192	07:48:40 CT 10 Nov 2022
FEB 2023 6EG3	OPT	.il	-	-	1.0079	-	-	-	0	07:31:01 CT 10 Nov 2022
MAR 2023 6EH3	OPT	.il	1.02185	+0.0119 (+1.18%)	1.00995	1.0123	1.0255	1.0033	1,356	08:01:05 CT 10 Nov 2022
APR 2023 6EJ3	OPT	.il	-	-	0.0000	-	-	-	0	07:31:01 CT 10 Nov 2022
JUN 2023 6EM3	OPT	.il	1.0300	+0.01325 (+1.30%)	1.01675	1.0150	1.0300	1.0150	81	07:47:24 CT 10 Nov 2022

Figure 9.11 – Prices of CME FX euro futures with various expiration dates (source: CME)

You can see that the more distant the expiration date, the greater the price of the respective future contract. This means that the overall sentiment in the market at the moment of this snapshot is bullish – most traders think the euro will grow over time.

Of course, this sentiment can't be traded as is – because the price of the underlying can go down and then the prices of future contracts will also decrease. However, differences in prices open doors to stat arb between them: we can assume that eventually – by the expiration date – the price of the future should revert to the *fair value*, which will be the spot price of the euro itself. Thus, buying contracts with earlier expiration dates and selling those that expire later, or vice versa, could be a kind of stat arb between the derivatives markets.

Normally, a stat arb setup includes hundreds of markets, and sometimes thousands, looking for statistically confirmed potential mispricing (potential – because they do not exist in a single moment of time, but may be realized in the future). We are not going to consider stat arb in detail, as this domain is so large that it deserves a separate book.

However unlike classical arbitrage, stat arb is surely available to any trader (with sufficient funding to afford to have dozens of concurrently open positions), so if you are interested in learning more about it, I'd recommend starting with some mathematics, namely, learning about correlation (`https://en.wikipedia.org/wiki/Correlation`) and cointegration (`https://en.wikipedia.org/wiki/Cointegration`), and then reading a short but quite informative article by Sabir Jana, CFA (`https://medium.com/analytics-vidhya/statistical-arbitrage-with-pairs-trading-and-backtesting-ec657b25a368`), in which the author explains the basics of building a stat arb setup using stocks – but the same approach can be applied to currencies and their derivatives.

So far, we have considered alpha-generating strategies that base their entries on various setups in terms of price, volume, and volatility. However, there is a class of strategies that do not consider this market information at all, or at least partly. These are event-driven strategies – and don't confuse them with the event-driven architecture of applications!

Event-driven trading strategies

An **event-driven strategy** mostly relies on non-market data such as economic or political news. We already considered the impact of these events on the market price (see *Chapter 6*, *Basics of Fundamental Analysis and Its Possible Use in FX Trading*). So, an event-driven strategy can attempt to enter when significant news hits the market and exit soon after.

The problem with strategies of this kind was also considered in detail in the same chapter: due to insufficient liquidity around the time of a news release, the price may jump in virtually any direction at an arbitrary distance, so you have no chance to place a trade at the desired price. At the same time, the return of liquidity may drive the price in the opposite direction, completely eliminating the potential for a profit in a few minutes (see *Chapter 6* again for an example with the British pound and the release of the UK's GDP figures).

I can confirm that profitable news traders used to exist in the early 2000s, but it has been really hard to make this trading consistent after 2010. So, we are not going to use non-price information in our strategies for any purpose other than, probably, stopping the execution of the strategy before potentially high-impact news.

Market-making – profiting on liquidity provision and associated risks

We already considered market-making in detail in the *Market makers – comfortable, sophisticated, expensive* section in *Chapter 3, FX Market Overview from a Developer's Standpoint*, so there's no need to repeat ourselves here. We will mention market-making here only for consistency as an example of a sell-side trading strategy. If we want to classify market-making as pertaining to alpha- or beta-generating strategies, probably we could qualify it as beta-generating. However, at the same time, high values of beta are harmful to market-making. In general, market making requires the trader not only to be sufficiently funded but also to meet various regulatory requirements, which makes this activity available mostly to institutions.

This is no surprise that market making requires not only direct access to the order book, with the ability to update the best bid and ask there, but also assumes that you are able to send your own bids and asks and match client orders faster than others. In this way, we are entering the realm of low-latency and **high-frequency trading** (**HFT**).

High frequency, low latency – where Python fails

Our overview would be incomplete without mentioning HFT. Its roots are in the financial crisis of 2008 when liquidity became the main issue in most, if not all, developed markets. Exchanges started to offer an incentive to those who provided liquidity, waiving many restrictions that previously required liquidity providers to be regulated. As a result, many market participants started to offer liquidity, or, rather, demonstrated this liquidity in the order book – because they sent an order only to withdraw it from the book some milliseconds later. In other words, they started to bluff creating an illusion of liquidity.

Of course, to be successful here, you need to be able to process thousands of transactions per second and reduce the latency (that is, the time between the order is sent to the exchange and the time it appears in the order book) to the absolute minimum. That's why HFT requires very expensive computers located at very expensive data centers as close to the exchange servers as possible.

HFT was heavily criticized, especially after two events known as **flash crashes**: situations in which the price drops a significant amount (over 10%) without any visible reason. It is quite possible that if an HFT trader sent a large order, then a buy-side market participant decided to trade against this order, and the HFT trader withdrew the order a fraction of a millisecond before the trade, then the buy-side order would swipe the order book, moving the price to levels that, of course, were neither expected nor desirable (see the *Exchange and order book* section in *Chapter 3, FX Market Overview from a Developer's Standpoint*).

So, it's clear that HFT is a domain in which Python will fail because of its speed. Most HFT algos are written in C++ or sometimes in C, with the most critical parts sometimes in Assembler. It's worth mentioning again that compilers such as Numba or Cython may dramatically increase the speed of Python code; however, they cannot achieve the speed of compiled C or C++ code. Besides that, all Python-based solutions have very limited support for FPGAs, so sometimes professional algo traders say that Python is suitable only for *slow HFT* algorithms (which work in milliseconds not microseconds).

With all these considerations in mind, there's no wonder that we are not going to consider HFT trading strategies in this book. Just be aware when you see a nice order in the order book, you cannot always grasp it for your profit!

Summary

In this chapter, we learned about the key terms and concepts of systematic and algo trading. We familiarized ourselves with alpha and beta as risk metrics in investment and at the same time, as different methods for profit generation in algo trading. We considered a few popular alpha-generating trading strategies and learned about their advantages, shortcomings, and associated risks. We also touched on the complex domain of options trading as the primary method to earn on market beta and gave a quick look at other trading strategies, such as arbitrage and stat arb, market-making, and HFT.

Now that we know the conditions under which a certain strategy may enter or exit the market, the last obstacle on our way to a first trading application is the mechanism that generates orders according to the strategy rules, sends them to the market, and controls their execution. Recalling the analogy at the beginning of this chapter, now we have added the brains to our trading app, and it's time to add the limbs with which it will be able to move. This is what we are going to develop in the very next chapter.

10

Types of Orders and Their Simulation in Python

In the previous chapter, we considered a number of classical trading strategies usually employed in FX trading. All of them can be automated – that is, the decision to place a trade can be made based on quantitative data only, and placing a trade in the market can be done by an algorithm. So, we need now to find a proper way to place trades and control their execution.

We already mentioned (see *Chapter 1*, *Developing Trading Strategies – Why They Are Different*) that any trade, manual or automated, can be placed in the market by using an order: an instruction to the broker (or any other intermediary) to buy or sell. What could be simpler? However, the reality is always more complex. You may want to trade at a certain price, no worse than a certain price, no more than a specified amount of pips (points) from a certain price, and so on. Besides that, in the real market, there is real liquidity, which is always very far from infinite, so you may have your orders rejected, filled partially, or executed at the *wrong* prices, and many more unexpected and undesired things may happen if you are not prepared.

Now, it's time we learn about the main types of orders typically supported by most FX liquidity pools, consider the difference in execution depending on the order type, understand the choice of order types depending on the goal, and get prepared to outline the architecture of an order simulation engine, which imitates possible execution issues and, along with the trade logic, helps you test and improve your strategy to fit the real-life conditions before putting real money at stake.

In this chapter, we will cover the following topics:

- Order ticket – what you send is what you get
- Market orders – the way to get maximum control over transactional risk
- Limit orders – guaranteed price, but not execution
- Time in force – better control over execution
- Stop orders – maximum uncontrolled risk
- Compound orders

Order ticket – what you send is what you get

Let's start with drafting a prototype of a general order ticket – something that is sent to a trading venue.

Normally, orders are sent either as FIX messages (see *Chapter 4, Trading Application – What's Inside?*) or in JSON format according to the venue's specifications. As we also noted in *Chapter 4*, every venue has its own data and ordering interfaces, but the core properties of an order always remain the same.

Actually, the list of these properties is quite logical. Let's prepare an empty form and fill in its fields one by one.

First, each order should go out with an ID. Otherwise, how do we or the trading venue refer to it? If we trade live, then the trading venue will generate an order ID that we receive, but if we run a backtest and want to modify orders that had been sent earlier, we need an internally generated order ID. Anyway, number one in our order form is **Order ID**:

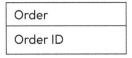

Figure 10.1 – The first attribute of an order is Order ID

Next, we need to let the venue know which market we want to trade in. As always, please keep in mind that every trading venue has its own specification. For example, EURUSD can be sent as *EURUSD*, *EUR/USD*, *eur-usd*, and so on. So, check the venue's documentation before actually sending orders. Let's add the second record to the order ticket – **Instrument ID**:

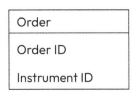

Figure 10.2 – Instrument ID added

We also need to specify the amount we want to trade or the trading size. The trading size can be specified in lots (again, refer to the venue's documentation regarding how much one lot is) or just in money.

For example, with LMAX, an order to buy 1 lot of EUR USD would mean buying 1,000 euros and selling the respective amount of the US dollars, and with Interactive Brokers, an order to sell 100,000 USD JPY would mean actually selling 100,000 USD and buying the respective amount of the Japanese yen. Be careful when specifying the order size! Now, our order ticket consists of three records:

Figure 10.3 – Trading size specified in the order

And of course, we should specify the side of the trade: whether we want to buy or sell. Some venues just use *BUY* and *SELL* specifiers, while others suggest using *BID* and *ASK* to denote the side, so as you can see, the advice to consult the venue's documentation is the only stable thing in algo trading. All in all, now we have four records in the order ticket:

Figure 10.4 – Specifying the side of the trade

Are we ready to go? Seems so, but not really. The trading venue expects a few other parameters of our trade to be specified: we should say *how* we want the order to be executed, *at which price*, and *when*. The first of these three extra parameters is called the order type, and we normally distinguish between *market orders*, *limit orders*, and *stop orders*. There are also so-called **compound** or **conditional orders**, which essentially are combinations of these basic three order types, but they are not supported by all venues. So we will consider in detail only the three main types of orders.

Market orders – the way to get maximum control over transactional risk

Let's start with the most simplistic (at least at first glance) type of order: the market order. A **market order** is an order to buy or sell a certain amount of an asset at a **market price**. By market price, we normally assume the best bid or the best ask (see *Chapter 3, FX Market Overview from a Developer's Standpoint,* for the explanation of the best bid and ask), and most trading strategy developers test their ideas using only the best bid/ask historical data. So, we can add another record to our order ticket prototype, and this record represents the order type:

Order
Order ID
Instrument ID
Trading size
Side
Type: Market

Figure 10.5 – Specifying the order type

We already saw (see again *Chapter 3, FX Market Overview from a Developer's Standpoint*) that liquidity may have a substantial impact on how orders are executed in reality and it is considered quite a frequent situation when a single large order may move the best bid or ask during its execution. So, it's important to make sure that the order will be executed at a price closest to the last best bid or best ask seen in the order book immediately before sending the order to the market.

Using this order type makes sure that if the order is executed, then you get the exact amount of the traded asset specified in the order. At the same time, it doesn't guarantee that the average execution price will be the same as the top of the book because this kind of execution method allows buying or selling up to the entire amount currently present in the order book.

For example, let's have a look back at the example of an order book shown in *Chapter 3* (*Figure 3.1* in the *Exchange and order book* section). Imagine that we send a market order to buy 1,000 contracts. Will it be executed? Yes, because there are more than 1,000 contracts in the order book. But at which price will it be filled?

The order book at the moment of sending the order had 155 contracts at the best ask price (2,149.25), then 306 contracts at 2,149.50, then 291 contracts at 2,149.75, and 532 contracts at 2,150.0. So our order will consume all liquidity from the first 3 price levels and 248 contracts from the 4th. The resulting average execution price can be calculated using the standard weighted average formula:

$$\bar{P} = \frac{\Sigma(pq)}{\Sigma q}$$

Here, P means the weighted average price, p denotes the price in the order book, and q means the quantity, the number of contracts traded at the price, p. In our example, it will be about 2,149.658, which is quite far from 2,145.25, which used to be the best ask at the moment we fired our order.

The phenomenon of an order being executed at a worse market price or the process of filling the order in parts according to the present liquidity is called **slippage**.

So, market orders can be useful when we need to fill the exact trading size, but this also may lead to filling at a price worse than expected. Why then did we say that market orders are *the way to get maximum control over transactional risk* in the very title of this section?

The reason is that by using market orders, you can be as granular and as precise with the ordering as possible. Indeed, nothing prevents us from developing an algorithm that would first check the liquidity in the order book and then send orders only of the amount that would not destroy it. In case you need to fill an order with a large size (for example, you work for a financial institution), you can split this order into parts and send multiple market orders in sequence until the entire amount is filled – again, without disturbing the order book too much.

Another *benefit*, if I may say so, of using market orders is that this is the only type of order that is accepted by all trading venues without a single exception. Although we are going to consider orders of other types, such as limit and stop, remember that they are not always supported by the venue with which you plan to work.

Possible execution issues

Besides the liquidity and average price fills just discussed, the main issue with market orders is that such an order (if sent without a time-in-force specifier – see later in this chapter) will be executed at whatever price is currently present in the market. Yes, 99% of the time, it doesn't cause real issues as the liquidity is quite sufficient, especially if you trade major currency pairs (those that constitute the US dollar index, see *Chapter 9, Trading Strategies and Their Core Elements*, the *Common FX benchmarks – US dollar index* section), but do you remember what happens around the time important economic news is released? Just have a quick look back at *Figure 6.2* and *Figure 6.4* in *Chapter 6, Basics of Fundamental Analysis and its Possible Use in FX Trading*, and refresh the US **non-farm payroll (NFP)** and UK GDP cases: the gaps or the distance in price between just adjacent ticks during such an event may reach dozens of pips.

So, if we consider the US NFP case, and assume that you wanted to sell at 1.0230 with a market order a second before the NFP was released, so the order most likely would have been executed at the first tick after the news release, which was at 1.0210 – 20 pips away from the desired price!

Alright, seems like it's more or less clear with market orders: we say *buy* or *sell* and get filled immediately (with or without liquidity-related issues). But what to do if we want to buy or sell *at a certain price*, or, to be even more precise, to get our order executed at no worse than a certain price? Well, here comes the limit order.

Limit orders – guaranteed price, but not execution

In general and brief, a **limit order** is an order to buy or sell the specified amount of the asset at the specified price or better.

What does *better* mean here?

This means that if I send a limit order to *buy* EURUSD at 1.0100, then any price *below* 1.0100 will match my order. On the contrary, if I send a limit order to *sell* EURUSD at 1.0100, then any price *above* this level will match. In other words, by using a limit order, I say that *I am ready to buy or sell at any price no worse than the one specified in the order.*

What happens if you send a limit order at a price that is better than the current market price? For example, a *buy limit* order at a price that is *below* the current ask? Well, it depends on the particular implementation of limit orders used by your broker or execution venue. If you trade at an exchange (for example, if you trade currency futures), then your order will be routed directly into the order book.

If you trade spot or forward contracts, then most likely, such an order will reside in the trading venue's system until the market price touches the order level and then the order will be converted into a market order. If the market price never reaches the order level, the order may be canceled or may reside in the broker's order book virtually forever (actually not forever, of course, every broker has their own rules on what to do with *forgotten* limit orders).

What happens if we send a limit buy order at a price that is worse than the current market price – for example, a *buy limit* order at a price that is *above* the current ask? In this case, the order will be executed immediately, and it will start absorbing the liquidity from the order book level by level, pushing the price higher and higher, but *this process will stop as soon as the limit price is hit.* Thus, a limit order sent at a price worse than the market can be considered a *market order with protection.*

Now we know that besides market orders, we can use limit orders, and in case we use them, we should specify a new field in our order ticket prototype: *order price.*

Figure 10.6 – Price attribute added for stop and limit orders

So far, it looks like limit orders are the best to use in all situations, but is it really true? Of course, as there's neither a free lunch nor a Holy Grail in trading, limit orders are no panacea to execution issues. Let's take a deep dive into this domain, as execution issues with limit orders are far less obvious than those of market orders.

Possible execution issues

While the main execution issue with market orders is that they guarantee the execution itself but do not guarantee the execution price, the main issue with limit orders is exactly the opposite: a limit order guarantees the execution price (just by its definition) but does not guarantee the execution as such.

Indeed, let's carefully consider both cases: if we send a limit order to be executed at a *better price* (that is, a *lower than the current price* for a *buy limit* and a *higher than the current price* for a *sell limit*) to an exchange, and if we send such an order to a broker or an ECN.

If we work with an exchange, limit orders go straight into the order book (well, actually not really straight: first they pass the broker's risk management systems that check whether you have sufficient margin to send such an order, but it doesn't matter in the current context). However, we should remember that the order book is, in reality, two-dimensional (see *Figure 3.2* in *Chapter 3*, *FX Market Overview from Developer's Standpoint*, in the *Exchange and order book* section) and that our order will always be put at the end of the current order queue at the same price level. So, when the market price touches the order level, that is, someone actually traded at the order price, there is no guarantee that the size of that trade was sufficient to match all orders from the same price level – including ours.

> **Note**
>
> One of the most common mistakes during the research and development phase of an algo trading project is assuming that all limit orders are executed, even if their prices were touched by a single tick. This erroneous assumption often leads to the creation of various *Holy Grails* of trading that work only on paper.

If we trade with an FX broker or an ECN, then most likely, our limit order won't go into any order book and no one will see it except for that same broker – until the market price reaches the order level. At this moment, the limit order is transformed into a market order and actually sent to the market. With this approach, we may suffer from the same disease as when trading with market orders – potentially, it could be executed at a price that is worse than the limit order price, which sounds exactly the opposite of the very definition of a limit order.

There are several workarounds for this issue, and most of these workarounds are implemented by execution venues. Most of them check the liquidity in the order book before actually sending the market order: if the order size exceeds the liquidity at the best bid/ask, then the order is executed only partially, up to the actual available amount. This way, the traditional behavior of a classical exchange order book is imitated.

Sounds disappointing?

Well, in fact, some (not all, unfortunately) execution venues allow for somewhat greater control over the order execution. Checking the liquidity in the order book prior to sending an order is a good practice, but with some trading technology providers, we can also use special conditions, or specifiers, to control the order's time in force.

Time in force – better control over execution

The specifiers mentioned previously are normally called **time in force** conditions, although, as you will see a bit later in this chapter, for some of them, it is not really obvious or intuitive.

> **Important disambiguation**
>
> More often than not, these execution method specifiers are referred to as the **type of order**. This can be found not only in some brokers' documentation but also in books on trading, and even academic research. So, be very careful when you encounter *type of order* or *time in force* in any documentation, and make sure you understand what exactly the author had in mind: the type of order as such (market, limit, stop, etc.), the time during which it is valid, or how the order should be executed liquidity-wise!

In the following subsections, we will consider different order specifiers in detail.

Immediate or cancel

An **Immediate-or-Cancel (IOC)** instruction attached to a market order means: I want to buy or sell *at most* X euros, dollars, lots, contracts, whatever, at the market price (that is, current best bid/ask), but no worse than this price, and *I don't care if I do not get the entire X euros, dollars, and so on, but only a smaller amount*. If there's not sufficient liquidity to fill my order, then fill in what is available and cancel the rest.

In other words, *with IOC, I prioritize price over size*.

For example, I send an IOC market order to buy 1,000,000 EUR USD. The current ask price is 1.01234 and the currently available amount at ask is 500,000. Then, I will get 500,000 EURUSD bought at 1.01234 and the rest of my order (another 500,000) will be canceled.

Using IOC orders is probably the best way to prevent execution at an unwanted price, but you should remember that using it may lead to partial fills – so, your trading algorithm should somehow account for situations of this sort.

Fill or kill

A **fill-or-kill (FOK)** instruction means: I want to buy or sell *exactly X* euros, dollars, lots, contracts, and so on *at the market price*, but if there is insufficient liquidity at the best bid/ask to fill the entire order, then do not execute this order at all (or *kill* the order).

In other words, *with FOK, I prioritize the integrity of the order over its execution*.

In the same example, if I send a market buy FOK order for 1,000,000 EURUSD but there's only 500,000 at the best ask, then the entire order will be killed (canceled) and no partial fill will be executed.

You may wonder why both IOC and FOK are considered time-in-force specifiers: both assume immediate, instant execution of the order. Well, the answer is probably in the question: with IOC or FOK, we specify that the order should be executed *as quickly as possible*; this way, we specify its time in force.

Most execution venues support IOC or FOK only for market orders, but there are some that allow adding IOC or FOK to limit orders as well. This makes sense because some execution venues just convert a limit order into a market one when the limit order's price is touched by the market, so the market order's time-in-force specifiers become absolutely valid in such a scenario.

Of course, there are other time-in-force specifiers that give an order a much longer life than IOC or FOK. The most common are **good for a day** and **good till canceled**.

Good for a day (GTD) and good till canceled (GTC)

Both specifiers assume that the order can be filled in parts and set the time frame during which it can be filled.

A GTD order tries to fill what is available at the best bid/ask and the remaining will reside in the venue's order book till the end of the day (that is, 5 P.M. New York time in most cases). Any moment the price returns to the order level, another portion of the order is executed.

A GTC order behaves in a similar way, but there's no explicitly specified time until which the order remains actual. The trader should take care of all GTC orders, manually or automatically.

In reality, both specifiers are used with limit orders and simply mean the time during which such an order will remain in force, because if we take all appropriate measures by checking the liquidity, then in most cases, a limit order will be executed instantly.

Now that we are familiar with time-in-force specifiers, it's time to update our proposed order ticket structure:

Figure 10.7 – Time in force attribute added

So far, we have discussed market (*I buy now*) and limit (*I buy at this price or better*) orders. But it would be quite logical to suppose that if we have an *at this price or better* order, then there should exist an *at this price or worse* order, wouldn't it? Yes, such an order type does exist, and it's called the stop order.

Stop orders – maximum uncontrolled risk

Essentially, a **stop order** is an order to buy or sell the specified amount of the asset *at the specified price or worse*.

You may ask at this point: why on Earth would I want to buy or sell at a price worse than I'd like to?

The answer is very simple: both *better* and *worse* are just references to where the order price is relative to the current market price.

For example, if the current price of EURUSD is 0.99673 and I send a buy-stop order at 0.9989, then my order will be executed at any price equal to or greater than 0.9989. Similar to limit orders, a stop order will reside in the broker's order book until the market price touches the order price and then converted into a market order. Note that, unlike limit orders, stop orders are never sent to the order book immediately, even if you trade with an exchange. This is quite natural, in fact: if I send a limit order to the order book, then I improve the liquidity in the market as others may become my counterparties and then I become a liquidity provider to them in a certain sense. But if a stop order had been sent to an order book, it would just immediately match one of the limit orders there and move the price immediately by an unpredictable distance.

Indeed, let's consider an example. Say we have an order book for EURUSD and the current market price (best bid/ask) is 1.00000/1.00005. There are some limit orders to buy at 0.99999, 0.99998, and so on, and some limit orders to sell at 1.00006, 1.00007, and so on. Now, imagine someone sends a stop order to buy at 1.0020 and this order is sent to the order book. Of course, sellers (those on the *ask* side) will be more than happy to sell at 1.0020 and not at 1.0010 or 1.00008. So, a stop order sent to the order book would trigger the order book level that is the most distant from the current best bid/ask, which is strictly opposite to the very idea of an order book.

> **Note**
> Not all execution venues support stop orders. Many institutional liquidity pools support only market and limit orders (and some of them only market orders). So it's always a good idea to emulate stop orders locally.

So, going back to the question about the reason why we may want to use a stop order, now we understand that we can use it when we want to do one of these two actions:

- Enter the market at a price that is greater than current if we want to buy, and at a price that is less than current if we want to sell.

- Exit a position when the price goes against it – that is, with a loss. It happens if the current price is less than the entry price for a long position (buy) or the current price is greater than the entry price for a short position (sell).

If we use a stop order to exit from a losing position, then it is called a **stop-loss order**.

Note

Quite frequently, stop orders are confused with stop-loss orders. However, stop orders can be used to both enter and exit the market, while stop-loss orders are always used only to exit from a losing position. In other words, *stop order* is a term with a more broad sense that pertains to general trading, and *stop-loss* is a narrow term pertaining to just trade logic. From the trading venue's standpoint, there is no difference between a stop order used to open a position or to close it, so *stop-loss* orders may be mentioned only in a particular broker's documentation, not that of a trading venue.

Now that we know that stop orders are somewhat *artificial* and actually executed as conditional market orders, we can understand the typical issues with their execution.

Possible execution issues

Of course, the main execution issue with stop orders is similar to that of market orders: the slippage with stop orders is potentially unlimited. If we send a buy-stop order, then it will be executed at any price equal to or greater than the order price. It is similar to a sell-stop order: it will be executed at any price equal to or less than the order price.

Stop orders guarantee execution but do not guarantee the price – and in this sense, they are somewhat similar to market orders. Let's go back again to *Figure 6.2* in *Chapter 6, Basics of Fundamental Analysis and its Possible Use in FX Trading*, which illustrates the sequence of ticks (trades) around the publication of US NFP data. Imagine we have a long position before the news and we set a protective stop (stop-loss) order at 1.02250. With the very first tick after the news release, this stop order will be executed – but not at 1.02250. It will be executed at the first available price, which would be 1.02100 or worse (lower).

Always remember that even if you placed a stop-loss order, it doesn't mean that you limited your losses by the order's price level. It can be executed way beyond the requested price, thus increasing the losses.

It's worth mentioning that some market makers offer *guaranteed stop-loss execution*. This means that during an event such as US NFP or a similar situation when the price may jump beyond the stop order price in one tick, they would still execute the order at the requested price, not the market price. Only market makers can do that as it is they who quote the market for you as the price taker. Of course, there's no free lunch here either, so market makers ask for a premium for this service. Such a premium typically means a wider spread or a greater commission.

Does it make sense to use *guaranteed* stop-loss orders? Well, it depends on the trade logic of your model and its statistics. If you use stop orders as a regular means of exiting the position even in a *calm* market, then the answer is probably no because you will lose more in spreads and commissions. If you use them only as a protective measure against an unexpected disastrous market price movement, then the answer is probably yes, as such a disastrous movement can ruin your account in one tick – just recall the case of the Swiss National Bank unpegging the rate of CHF from the euro described in *Chapter 9, Trading Strategies and Their Core Elements*, in *Figure 9.6*.

With all that in mind, stop orders kept at the broker are mostly used as protective stop-loss orders, which exit from a losing position and cut running losses. If your strategy logic assumes entering the market along with the price movement, which is typical for a breakout strategy, for example, then it's always a better idea to emulate such a stop order locally and send it to the market as a market or even a limit order to prevent bad execution.

Now, we can suggest the final draft of our general order ticket, which would support all three main types of orders (market, limit, and stop) and all the essential attributes required to send the order to a broker:

Figure 10.8 – All types of orders are now supported in the order ticket

Similar to limit orders, IOC and FOK are not used with stop orders, but GTD and GTC are. Besides that, some execution venues offer an additional condition to trigger a stop order, which is to convert a stop order into a market order: whether it's triggered when the bid or the ask price hits the order level. However, this specifier is not common.

Market, limit, and stop orders are de facto standard orders accepted by almost any trading venue. However, some venues offer other types of orders that are frequently referred to as compound orders, which we will explore in the next section. They are not common and not essential, but it's worth at least knowing that they exist and how they work in very general terms.

Compound orders

Compound orders are those that assume a certain logical chain in their execution. That's why they are also referred to as **conditional orders**. Strictly speaking, such an order is not a single order: it's a sequence of orders that are triggered one by another.

As the most common example, let's consider a **stop-limit order**. Unlike stop or limit orders, it requires two prices to be specified: stop and limit. If such an order is sent to the execution venue, first, the venue's matching engine waits till the stop price of the order is touched by the market (best bid/ask) price. After that, the order is executed using its limit price exactly like when executing a limit order. So, a stop limit order is a combination of both.

For example, if the current price of EUR USD is 1.01015 and I want to buy it at 1.0102, I can use a stop order to enter the market – but I remember that during the execution of a stop order, I can get a potentially unlimited slippage. Therefore, I send a stop limit order with two prices: a stop price of 1.0102 and a limit price of 1.01025. Then, as soon as 1.0102 is touched by the market (this means that either ask or bid becomes equal or greater than 1.0102; see the explanation on special execution conditions for stop orders in the previous section), a limit-buy order at 1.01025 is actually executed. So, I will buy EURUSD at any price between 1.0102 (the stop price) and 1.01025 (the limit price).

It's worth mentioning that stop-limit orders are used only to enter the market and never used as stop-loss orders. A stop-loss order must ensure the entire order size is filled, but a stop-limit order, like any limit order, cannot guarantee the execution of the entire order size.

Summary

Now, we are familiar with orders of the three main types, and we know in which cases we prefer to use market, stop and limit orders, and in which cases we'd rather avoid using them. Besides that, from previous chapters, we remember how to receive and handle market data, and how to use technical analysis, and we remember the key risks and have at least some ideas on how to mitigate them. So, we are ready for the final, ultimate job of any algo trader in the research and development phase: we are about to start drafting a trading application, something that will receive data, process it, generate trading signals, convert them into orders, send the order to the broker, process the broker's response, and collect the trading statistics, which can ultimately prove or disprove the trading idea. This is what we are going to do in the next chapter.

11
Backtesting and Theoretical Performance

It's been a long and, hopefully, interesting – although difficult at times – journey. It took us ten chapters to get familiar with all the essentials of market structure and the key concepts that create the foundation of systematic and algo trading. Now, we have approached the conclusion of this entire book. It's time to bring all the pieces together and start developing our first trading application that can be used in both research and production.

We are going to develop a universal prototype that you will be able to use and reuse by just re-writing some parts without modifying the entire structure. We will trace all the paths from receiving a tick to placing an order – while checking the consistency of all our actions. We will learn how to keep parts of the trading application synchronized and see why it's so important to do so. And finally, we will collect some very basic statistics of a sample trading strategy and calculate its theoretical performance – the most essential logical point in the entire research and development process.

In this chapter, we will cover the following topics:

- Trading app architecture – revised and improved
- Multithreading – convenient but full of surprises
- Trading application with a live data feed
- Backtesting – speed up the research

Trading app architecture – revised and improved

In *Chapter 1, Developing Trading Strategies – Why They Are Different*, we proposed a generalized architecture of a trading application. In brief, it consists of the following components:

- **Data receiver**: Something that retrieves live data from the market or historical data stored locally; see *Chapter 5, Retrieving and Handling Market Data with Python*

- **Data cleanup**: A component that eliminates non-market prices; see *Chapter 1, Developing Trading Strategies – Why They Are Different*

- **Trading logic**: The *brains* of the trading app that make trading decisions (see *Chapter 6, Basics of Fundamental Analysis and Its Possible Use in FX Trading, Chapter 7, Technical Analysis and Its Implementation in Python*, and *Chapter 9, Trading Strategies and Their Core Elements*), frequently with integrated pre-trade risk management

- **Ordering interface**: A component that receives trading signals from the trading logic, converts them into orders, and keeps track of their execution; see *Chapter 10, Types of Orders and Their Simulation in Python*

- **Post-trade risk management** and **open positions management**, such as keeping track of the running loss and liquidating losing positions or all positions

Anyway, this simplified architecture lists the essential components but does not say anything about how they communicate with each other. Of course, it is possible to use a linear architecture where all the components are implemented as dependent pieces of code executed one after another in sequence. Such a solution is simple, but has significant drawbacks:

- You won't be able to add more trading logic components to run multiple strategies in parallel

- You won't be able to send orders to multiple trading venues

- You won't be able to receive information about the actual consolidated market position in the trading logic

- You won't be able to reuse the same code (at least in parts) for both development and production

Let's stop for a while at these four disadvantages.

Regarding the first two points, you may probably say that you're not going to run multiple strategies and trade at multiple trading venues as we're only making our first steps into algo trading, and doing that cross-venue and cross-trading logic is more of an institutional activity. I could argue that, in reality, it's more than normal for private traders to do all that, but these two points are less important than the remaining two.

To understand the importance of the third point, we have to introduce a new term: **consolidated market position**.

Imagine that you have several strategies and all of them trade in the same market – say, EURUSD. The first one bought 100,000 euros, the second one sold 80,000, and the third one bought 50,000. Why has this happened? It's quite a common situation: for example, you run a short-term mean reversion strategy, longer-term breakout, and long-term trend following strategies (see *Chapter 9, Trading Strategies and Their Core Elements*); they generate trading signals independently, but so long as they all trade the same market, they all contribute to the amount of the asset currently traded. This amount is called the consolidated market position.

In our example, the individual positions per strategy are 100,000 long, 80,000 short, and another 50,000 long, so the consolidated position is *70,000 long*. This is your real market exposure and all position sizing calculations should rely on this figure.

But what about the entry price for such a consolidated position?

In *Chapter 10, Types of Orders and Their Simulation in Python*, we explored the average execution price for an order that was executed in parts. The same approach can be used to calculate the average entry price for the consolidated market position. Let's do this simple math for our example with three open positions.

Suppose that the first (100,000 long) position was opened at 1.0552, the second (80,000 short) at 1.0598, and the third (50,000 long) at 1.0471. First, we calculate the sum of these prices multiplied by the respective trading size. Don't forget that short positions (which effectively reduce the consolidated market position) should be accounted for as negative numbers:

```
S = 100000 * 1.0552 - 80000 * 1.0598 + 50000 * 1.0471 = 73091
```

Now, we divide the sum, S, by the actual consolidated market position, MP, which equals *70,000*, and we get the average entry price:

$$\bar{P} = \frac{S}{MP}$$

In our example, the consolidated average price is approximately 1.0442. At first glance, it looks ridiculous as it is way lower than the lowest of the actual traded prices. But it's really easy to make sure it's correct.

Imagine that the current market price is 1.0523. Let's calculate the running **profit or loss** (typically referred to as running **PnL** or running **P/L**; see *Chapter 3, FX Market Overview from a Developer's Standpoint*, the *Trade mechanics – again some terminology* section) for each position: it's just the distance between the current price and the entry price multiplied by the trading size. The first position running PnL at 1.0523 equals (1.0523 – 1.0552) * 100,000 = -$290, the second position running PnL equals (1.0523 – 1.0598) * -80,000 = $600, and the third position running PnL equals (1.0523 – 1.0471) * 50,000 = $260. Thus, for the consolidated market position, the running PnL equals $570.

Now, let's do the same math with the price and the size of only one consolidated market position. Given it was *opened* at 1.0442 and the current market price is 1.0523, its running PnL is (1.0523 – 1.0442) * 70,000 = $567, which is not exactly equal to $570 only because we rounded the average price to the 4th digit. So, we can indeed use the average price and the resulting trading size of the consolidated market position instead of calculating the PnL for each position separately.

> **Note for nerds**
>
> Such a consolidated position calculated as the average of all orders with their respective trade volume is often called the **Volume Weighted Average Price** (**VWAP**). However, the VWAP is normally only used to evaluate a position that was accumulated by multiple entries to the same direction, and so long as we are discussing the net position as the result of trades taken to both sides, I prefer using *consolidated*, although it's not a regular term.

A consolidated market position is extremely important to correctly implement risk management. If you don't know this position, you have no idea about your running profit or loss, so you don't know when to liquidate a losing position – which may end up with a disastrous loss. Moreover, you may not know even how much to liquidate, and open a new position instead of only covering a loss.

Even if you run only one strategy in one market, it is no less important to know the exact market position as it exists in the real market: don't forget that a certain order may not be executed or executed at a price different as expected due to several reasons (see *Chapter 10*, *Types of Orders and Their Simulation in Python*). So, if you don't let your code provide feedback from the broker to the trading logic, you may have a hard time managing your positions.

The fourth disadvantage is hopefully more evident: if we can suggest an architecture that is flexible, modular, and reusable, then it has an advantage over something that should be modified entirely every time you want just to switch a data source.

So, with all these considerations in mind, what can we suggest to make the architecture of our trading app meet all the requirements mentioned?

We already know the solution, and we used it quite successfully in *Chapter 5*, *Retrieving and Handling Market Data with Python*. This solution is to use *threads* and *queues* to make the components of the app work independently. I strongly recommend that you refresh your memory regarding threads and queues by referring to the *Working with saved and live data – keep your app universal* section of that chapter.

Now, let's redraw the app architecture diagram, this time at a bit lower level, closer to the transport layer, not just business logic.

As always, we will start from the beginning: receiving live (tick) market data.

Market data component

This component should be able to receive ticks from virtually any source, clean it up, translate them into the single format used throughout our app, and put them into the data queue:

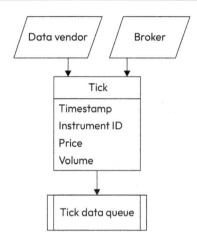

Figure 11.1 – Tick data receiving component

The beauty of this approach is that as soon as the tick is sent to the tick queue, we can forget about it. This process is now isolated from the rest of the app, and should we need to change the data vendor or the broker, we can do that by rewriting the respective module without making a single change in the rest of the code.

Many strategies require tick data. For example, arbitrage strategies (see *Chapter 9, Trading Strategies and Their Core Elements*) can work using *only* tick data. However, the majority of trading strategies use logic based on compressed data, not ticks. So, we need to add a component that can aggregate ticks into bars (see *Chapter 5, Retrieving and Handling Market Data with Python*, the *Data compression – keep the amounts to the reasonable minimum* section).

Data aggregation component

This module should be able to not only aggregate live tick data into bars. When we develop a strategy, we normally use historical market data stored locally already in a compressed form, so there's no need to waste time aggregating ticks during a test run. Thus, we must add the following part to our app architecture:

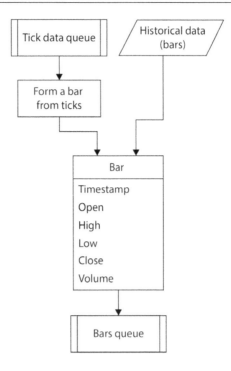

Figure 11.2 – Reading bars from storage or forming bars from ticks

Again, as in the previous case, this process is isolated from the rest of the application, so we can implement it once and forget about it until we need to modify something in the way we aggregate ticks into bars.

Next, we should implement the trading logic.

Trading logic component

This component may use both tick and bar data as input and produce orders as output. This output should go into the order execution control component of our trading app, so it's quite natural to use another queue again: the ordering queue that would isolate the order execution component from the rest of the application.

However, besides just sending orders out, we need another connection between the trading logic and the order execution components. This connection should provide feedback from the execution of the order to the trading logic. How do we establish such a connection?

The first idea that probably comes to mind at this point is to use yet another queue. However, in this case, it's not convenient. Queues are great when you want to trigger a certain process as soon as data is in the queue – in other words, they are ideal for event-driven processes. But market position or equity values do not trigger any process by themselves: they are only used by various components of the trading app as auxiliary values. Therefore, instead of a queue, we will create an object that will store all the required data about the implemented trading strategy and share this object across all components of our trading app.

This object can contain any strategy metadata, such as market position, equity time series (see below), running PnL, realized profit or loss, various statistical metrics, and so on:

Trading strategy params
Market position
Last price
Equity
Equity timeseries
Initial capital
Leverage

Figure 11.3 – Prototype of an object that stores trading strategy metadata

Last price means the quote received with the previous tick (or bar) and it serves to calculate the running PnL between two ticks (or bars): if the position is *long* and the price has *increased*, then the running PnL has also *increased*, if the position is *short* and the price has *decreased*, then the running PnL nevertheless *increased*, and so on. If we sum all changes in the running PnL on every tick or bar from the moment when the strategy started until the present, then we will get the overall profit and loss, which is frequently referred to by traders as **equity**. This is a bit of professional slang because formally, the equity is the value attributable to the owners of a business (see, for example, https://corporatefinanceinstitute.com/resources/valuation/equity/ for details), but in algo trading, *equity* frequently means just the realized profit and loss, plus the value of the open position.

We can also save the equity value on each tick or bar, thus creating a time series. This time series is normally referred to as the equity curve and works as the most common illustration of the trading strategy's performance: the way the strategy behaved in the past and when and how much money it made (or lost). This information can also be used by the trading logic, along with market price data and market position.

We also included two money management-related parameters: **initial capital** and **leverage**. These values can be used to check if we have sufficient funds to trade and also to determine the actual trading size for our orders.

Now that we've added such a universal object that transfers strategy metadata between the trading logic and the order execution component, we can add the trading logic component to our architectural diagram:

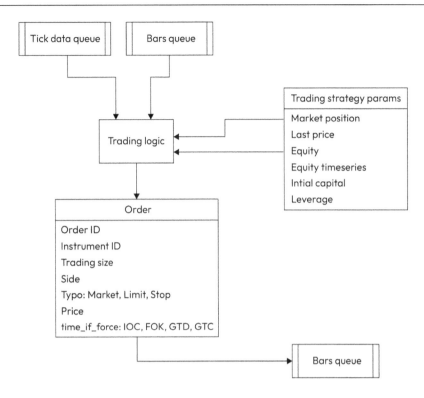

Figure 11.4 – Trading logic and common trading strategy parameters container

The last mandatory component to be added is the order execution component.

Order execution component

This component not only implements an ordering interface with the broker or emulates the execution of orders locally. It will also do some basic analysis of the strategy's performance – for the needs of the trading logic. It should process the order, send it to a broker or emulate it locally, receive the execution status, process this status (for example, if the order was rejected, decide what to do: cancel or submit again), calculate the running PnL, and build the equity curve. Let's add it to our diagram:

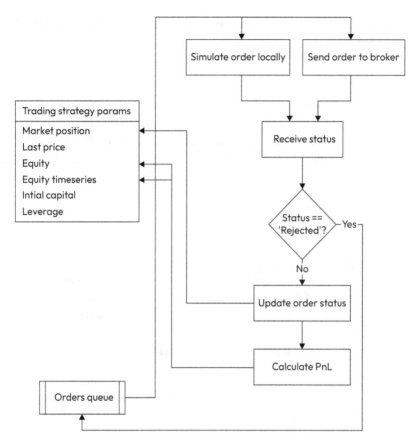

Figure 11.5 – Order execution control module and its interaction
with the trading strategy properties object

Let's see how it works. First, we receive an order or orders from the order queue. These orders were generated and put into the queue by the trading logic. Then, we send an order to the broker or emulate its execution locally and receive the order status. If the order was executed, then we update the PnL and add another data point to the equity time series. If the order was rejected, we return it to the order queue and the whole process starts over automatically.

Note that the strategy metadata (market position, equity, and so on) is updated with every processed order. This ensures the ultimate precision in making trading decisions and controlling the actual market exposure.

Great! We now have a general view of the entire trading app architecture. And the most pleasant thing is that it is split into small, relatively simple components. We know how these components should communicate with each other, we know the data formats, and we know the sequence in which they should operate, so it seems we know everything we need to implement a trading application.

But before we start coding, I'd like to emphasize two advantages of the suggested architecture that are very hard to overvalue.

Advantages of the modular architecture

First of all, this architecture makes sure that **your trading app will never peek ahead** during the research phase (while using historical data). At this point, I recommend that you refresh your memory regarding peeking ahead, which was considered in detail in *Chapter 4*, *Trading Application – What's Inside?*, in the *Trading logic – this is where a small mistake may cost a fortune* section – I am sure you will appreciate the suggested architecture of our trading app.

Second, this architecture provides for a flexible modular code that conforms to the concept of a universal trading application: you can quickly switch data sources and trading venues and use the same application both for research and production.

It seems like we have covered everything we need to start coding our first trading application. However, there is one point of extreme importance that is surprisingly too frequently missed by so many developers: the problem of thread synchronization. To understand this problem and find out the right solutions to it, let's do a brief **lyrical digression** about multithreading.

Multithreading – convenient but full of surprises

We already worked with multithreading (see *Chapter 5*, *Retrieving and Handling Market Data with Python*, the *Universal data connector* section), and we found that using multiple threads makes life way easier when we develop modular scalable applications. However, we never explored how multithreading is implemented in Python.

Two concepts are frequently confused: **multiprocessing** and **multithreading**. The difference between them is that the former uses the concept of isolated processes, each of them having a **global interpreter lock (GIL)**, thus enabling parallel execution using separate physical or logical processors or processor cores (so-called **true parallelism**), whereas the latter runs a single process that doesn't care about the number of processors or cores: it executes threads in small portions, allowing each thread to run for several milliseconds and then switching to another one. Of course, from a human perspective, it does look like processes are running in parallel. In most cases, we don't even think about which thread is executed at which moment. But when implementing event-driven processes, it becomes critical to know what happens first: for example, if we try to generate an order before market data is received, it may end with an error in the best case.

To learn how real multithreading works, let's write some simple code with three threads emulating the respective components of our trading application:

```python
from threading import Thread
import time
def t1(): # A thread that emulates data receiving
```

```
    while True:
        print('Receive data')
        time.sleep(1)
def t2(): # A thread that emulates trading logic
    while True:
        print('Trading logic')
        time.sleep(1)
def t3(): # A thread that emulates order execution
    while True:
        print('Processing orders')
        time.sleep(1)

thread1 = Thread(target=t1)
thread2 = Thread(target=t2)
thread3 = Thread(target=t3)
thread1.start()
thread2.start()
thread3.start()
```

Since we start the threads one by one (1, 2, and then 3), we may expect to see messages stating Receive data, Trading logic, and Processing orders and repeating in this same order. However, when we run the code, we will see something different:

```
Receive data
Trading logic
Processing orders
Receive dataProcessing orders
Trading logic

Processing ordersReceive data

Trading logic
Processing orders
Receive data
Trading logic
Trading logic
Processing orders
```

```
Receive data
Trading logicProcessing orders
Receive data

Processing ordersReceive data
Trading logic
```

We can see that while on average the number of messages of each kind is more or less the same, the order in which they appear is almost random, making the output chaotic. This happens because, by default, no thread has any priority and each runs a small portion as soon as it can.

Of course, such a behavior is not suitable for a trading app: we want to make sure that we first receive a tick, then process it, then generate an order, and finally send it for execution – in this very order and not any other!

There are several solutions to this problem. We will use two: using data streams as events for synching and using `threading.Event()` objects to switch between threads. We will consider each approach in detail in the upcoming sections.

Let's start by implementing a version of the trading app that works with live tick data, and then see how we can easily transform it into a powerful backtesting tool (if you don't clearly remember the meaning of backtesting, just jump back to *Chapter 2*, *Using Python for Trading Strategies*, the *What is paper trading and backtesting?* section).

Trading application with live data feed

As always, we start by doing some imports:

```
import json
import threading
import queue
from datetime import datetime
from websocket import create_connection
```

Next, we create a class that contains the strategy metadata (see the *Trading logic component* section):

```
class tradingSystemMetadata:
    def __init__(self):
        self.initial_capital = 10000
        self.leverage = 30
        self.market_position = 0
        self.equity = 0
```

```
        self.last_price = 0
        self.equity_timeseries = []
```

Now, we prepare three (!) tick data queues:

```
tick_feed_0 = queue.Queue()
tick_feed_1 = queue.Queue()
tick_feed_2 = queue.Queue()
```

Why three? This is one of the solutions to the thread synching problem explained in the *Multithreading – convenient but full of surprises* section.

The first queue (`tick_feed_0`) connects the market data receiver with the ticks aggregation component, which forms bars. This component is activated every time a new tick is in the first queue. After the component has finished, it puts the same tick into the second queue (`tick_feed_1`).

`tick_feed_1` connects the ticks aggregator with the trading logic, and the trading logic is invoked only when there's a new tick in `tick_feed_1`. But it may enter this queue only after the first component has finished working! So, trading logic cannot be invoked earlier than a new tick is processed. Then, similarly, the trading logic components put the same tick into the third queue (`tick_feed_2`).

`tick_feed_2` connects the trading logic with the order execution component, and this component is invoked no earlier than there's a new tick in `tick_feed_2`. So, using three queues to connect components one to another ensures the correct sequence of operations.

> **Important note**
>
> This method of synching threads would work only if the interval between ticks is greater than the round trip time for all threads triggered by it to finish working. This is valid for most data feeds as normally, we receive no more than 10 ticks per second, and the round trip processing time is typically around 0.0001 seconds. This approach won't work with heavy load exchange market data received via the ITCH protocol, which sometimes receives over 10,000 ticks per second. However, this is specific to institutional trading and we don't consider solutions of this kind in this book.

Next, we must add a queue to process aggregated market data (`bar_feed`), a queue to store orders (`orders_stream`), create an instance of the system metadata class, and specify the parameters required to connect to a data feed (in our example, we use LMAX as the source of market data):

```
bar_feed = queue.Queue()
orders_stream = queue.Queue()
System = tradingSystemMetadata()
url = "wss://public-data-api.london-demo.lmax.com/v1/web-
socket"
```

```
subscription_msg = '{"type": "SUBSCRIBE","channels": [{"name":
"ORDER_BOOK","instruments": ["eur-usd"]}]}'
```

Now, we can reuse the code that we developed in *Chapter 8, Data Visualization in FX Trading with Python*, in the *Plotting live tick data* section:

```
def LMAX_connect(url, subscription_msg):
    ws = create_connection(url)
    ws.send(subscription_msg)
    while True:
        tick = json.loads(ws.recv())
```

Now, we have to put the tick into the first tick queue. But before we do that, we have to check the consistency of the received market data. We discussed non-market prices in *Chapter 1, Developing Trading Strategies – Why They Are Different*, so let's just quickly refresh it: a non-market price is *too far* from the market. Of course, sometimes, it's difficult to judge whether it is *too far* or *not so far*, but in essence, we can at least filter out ticks in which the difference between the bid and ask (also known as spread) is several times greater than normal. Events of this sort are quite infrequent, but I was lucky to capture one of these moments while plotting tick charts (see *Chapter 8, Data Visualization in FX Trading with Python*). The following figure illustrates such a *bad tick* in which the bid is way lower than it should be:

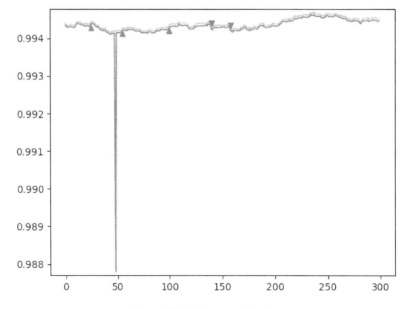

Figure 11.6 – Non-market price

To filter out at least bad ticks of this sort, let's add a simple check: if the spread is greater than 10 pips, then skip this tick:

```
if 'instrument_id' in tick.keys():
    bid = float(tick['bids'][0]['price'])
    ask = float(tick['asks'][0]['price'])
    if ask - bid < 0.001:
tick_feed_0.put(tick)
```

Next, we need to implement the ticks aggregator. In our example, let's form 10-second bars so that we can test our app and check if everything works correctly faster (without waiting for 1 minute or 1-hour bars to complete).

We will use only bid data to form bars for simplicity. Why is this possible? Because most of the time (except for the time around important news releases, bank settlement time, and the end/beginning of the week), the spread (the difference between the bid and ask) is more or less constant. So, if we want to emulate the real execution of orders, then we can use real bid and ask in the tick data stream, but for the trade logic, we can use bars built with only one price. Of course, for strategies of a certain kind, such as arbitrage, both bid and ask data are essential (and sometimes last trade along with the two), but now, we're building a prototype that you will be able to customize the way you want when you are familiar with the approach in general.

For aggregating ticks into bars, we used almost the same code from *Chapter 8, Data Visualization in FX Trading with Python*, in the *Plotting live tick data* section, so not much commenting is required here:

```
data_resolution = 10
def getBarRealtime(resolution):
    last_sample_ts = datetime.now()
    bar = {'Open': 0, 'High': 0, 'Low': 0, 'Close': 0}
    while True:
        tick = tick_feed_0.get(block=True)
        if 'instrument_id' in tick.keys():
            ts = datetime.strptime(tick['timestamp'], "%Y-%m-
%dT%H:%M:%S.%fZ")
            bid = float(tick['bids'][0]['price'])
            delta = ts - last_sample_ts
            bar['High'] = max([bar['High'], bid])
            bar['Low'] = min([bar['Low'], bid])
            bar['Close'] = bid
```

We created a bar, received a tick, and updated the bar's high, low, and close values. Now, as soon as the time since the bar's open is greater than or equal to 10 seconds, we start a new bar:

```
if delta.seconds >= resolution - 1:
    if bar['Open'] != 0:
        bar_feed.put(bar)
        last_sample_ts = ts
        bar = {'Open': bid, 'High': bid, 'Low': bid,
'Close': bid}
    tick_feed_1.put(tick)
```

Note the last line of this function. It puts the same tick that's received into `tick_feed_1`. This is done to trigger the next component, the trading logic:

```
def tradeLogic():
    while True:
        tick = tick_feed_1.get()
        try:
            bar = bar_feed.get(block=False)
            print('Got bar: ', bar)
```

Now, it's time to add some trading logic.

> **Note**
>
> For testing purposes, we don't care whether our test strategy is profitable or not – we only want to generate as many orders as possible to watch the emulated execution.

So, let's implement the following simple logic:

- If the bar closes up (`close > open`), then sell
- If the bar closes down (`close < open`), then buy

With this *"strategy"*, we may expect many orders to be generated quickly, so we will be able to test our app without waiting for too long:

```
####################################
#       trade logic starts here      #
####################################
open = bar['Open']
close = bar['Close']
if close > open and System.market_position >= 0:
```

Here, we are checking that the bar's closing price is greater than Open and also that the current consolidated market position is positive. We're doing this because we don't want to open multiple positions in the same direction. In other words, if we are already long in the market, we only wait for a short position to open, and vice versa:

```
order = {}
order['Type'] = 'Market'
order['Price'] = close
order['Side'] = 'Sell'
```

The following if...else statement checks whether we are opening the position for the first time. If we are, then we don't have any current market position at the time of order generation, so in our example, the trading size is 10,000. But if there is already an open position and we want to open a new position in the opposite direction, then *we should first close the existing position* and *then open the new one*, which effectively requires twice the trading size. We have to use 10000 to close and 10000 to open a new position, which means a trading size of 2 * 10,000 = 20,000:

```
if System.market_position == 0:
    order['Size'] = 10000
else:
    order['Size'] = 20000
```

Finally, we must put the order into the order queue:

```
orders_stream.put(order)
print(order) # added for testing
```

Now, we must do exactly the opposite for the buy order:

```
if close < open and System.market_position <= 0:
    order = {}
    order['Type'] = 'Market'
    order['Price'] = close
    order['Side'] = 'Buy'
    if System.market_position == 0:
        order['Size'] = 10000
    else:
        order['Size'] = 20000
    orders_stream.put(order)
    print(order)
#################################
```

```
        #       trade logic ends here      #
        ####################################
    except:
        pass
    tick_feed_2.put(tick)
```

Why do we use 10,000 base currency as the trading size?

If we trade EURUSD, a currency pair quoted with 4 or 5 digits, then buying or selling 10,000 euro (see *Chapter 3, FX Market Overview from a Developer's Standpoint*, the *Naming conventions* section) would mean that 1 pip costs $1. Therefore, we can interpret the results of our tests both as in money and in pips. Since the FX market is highly leveraged (see the same in the *Trade mechanics – again some terminology* section in *Chapter 3, FX Market Overview from a Developer's Standpoint*), it's more convenient to calculate all PnL in pips and then scale it using leverage.

Note that this function uses a `try...except` statement. The reason is that we use two queues: `tick_feed_1` to receive ticks and `bar_feed` to receive actual bars. However, ticks are only used in this function to trigger its execution (see the detailed explanation at the very beginning of this section), while bars are used to make actual trading decisions. The problem is that bars normally arrive far less frequently than ticks, so we can't wait until there's a bar in the `bar_feed` queue; otherwise, the normal execution of our app would be interrupted. That's why we use the `block = False` attribute when reading from the `bar_feed` queue. However, if there's a new tick in `tick_feed_1`, but there's no bar in `bar_feed`, then the attempt to read from there would raise an exception. Therefore, we catch this exception and – in our current implementation – just do nothing, waiting for a new bar to arrive in the queue.

The final component of our trading app is order execution. We invoke this function by a tick received in `tick_feed_2`, where it's put by `tradeLogic()`:

```
def processOrders():
    while True:
        tick = tick_feed_2.get(block = True)
        current_price = float(tick['bids'][0]['price'])
```

With every received tick, we update the equity value of the trading system. Remember that *equity* in traders' slang means the sum of all PnL values calculated on each tick or bar. If we have a long position and the current price is greater than the previous price, then the equity value increases on this tick/bar. The opposite is also true: if we have a short position and the current price is less than the previous price, then the equity value also increases on this tick/bar.

I believe you've got it: if we're long and the price decreases or if we're short and the price increases, then the equity decreases on this tick or bar. To calculate the actual equity value on the current tick, we multiply the difference in price between the current and the previous ticks by the market position value:

```
System.equity += (current_price - System.last_price) *
System.market_position
System.equity_timeseries.append(System.equity)
System.last_price = current_price
print(tick['timestamp'], current_price, System.equity)
# for testing purposes
```

Now, we start scanning the order queue and executing orders as they appear there. Note that we again use the `block = False` attribute, so we never wait for an order in the order queue: if there's no order by the time a new tick is received, we just go ahead and proceed with the main loop:

```
while True:
    try:
        order = orders_stream.get(block = False)
```

After we've received an order, we should do the risk management check: whether we have sufficient funds to execute this order. To calculate the available funds, we should add the current equity (positive or negative) to the initial capital and subtract the margin required for the currently open market position, which is the value of this market position divided by the leverage:

```
available_funds = (System.initial_capital +
System.equity) * System.leverage - System.market_position /
System.leverage
```

> **How to calculate available funds**
>
> The calculation of available funds that we are using in our code is not 100% correct. The problem is that it is possible to have a huge position in the market with some positive running PnL. In this case, our formula would say we have sufficient funds, but in reality, until this huge position is closed, we may not have enough money in the trading account. So, to be perfectly precise with this calculation, we should have introduced yet another variable to the system metadata that would account only for realized PnL (calculated by closed positions). However, we are not going to do this now, again for simplicity and transparency's sake.

Now, if the order size is less than the available funds in the trading account, we can execute the order. A bit later, we will write a separate function that emulates the order execution. In production, this function can be replaced by an actual call to the broker's API:

```
if order['Size'] < available_funds:
    emulateBrokerExecution(tick, order)
```

After attempting to execute the order, its status is changed either to `'Executed'` or `'Rejected'` (or any other status returned by your broker), so let's decide what to do with it. Of course, if the order was successfully executed, we only update the strategy metadata (and print the result for testing purposes):

```python
if order['Status'] == 'Executed':
    System.last_price = order['Executed Price']
    print('Executed at ', str(System.last_
price), 'current price = ', str(current_price), 'order price =
', str(order['Executed Price']))
    if order['Side'] == 'Buy':
        System.market_position = System.market_
position + order['Size']
    if order['Side'] == 'Sell':
        System.market_position = System.market_
position - order['Size']
```

If the order was rejected, we return it to the same order queue:

```python
elif order['Status'] == 'Rejected':
    orders_stream.put(order)
```

Again, let me reiterate that, in reality, you may need more complex order handling, but it will depend on both the type of strategy you're going to run and the types of order statuses provided by your broker.

Finally, we will just add the except clause so that nothing happens if there's no order in the order queue:

```python
except:
    order = 'No order'
    break
```

We're almost there! All we need to add now is the function that emulates the order execution at the broker. For the first version of our emulator, we will implement only the execution of market orders:

```python
def emulateBrokerExecution(tick, order):
    if order['Type'] == 'Market':
        if order['Side'] == 'Buy':
```

It's time for the final preflight check: making sure the market has sufficient liquidity before sending the order!

```python
current_liquidity = float(tick['asks'][0]
['quantity'])
```

Don't confuse bids and asks! If we buy, we check the liquidity at the offer (ask) and execute at the ask price, while if we sell, we use bids:

```
            price = float(tick['asks'][0]['price'])
            if order['Size'] <= current_liquidity:
                order['Executed Price'] = price
                order['Status'] = 'Executed'
            else:
                order['Status'] = 'Rejected'
        if order['Side'] == 'Sell':
            current_liquidity = float(tick['bids'][0]
['quantity'])
            if order['Size'] <= current_liquidity:
                order['Executed Price'] = price
                order['Status'] = 'Executed'
            else:
                order['Status'] = 'Rejected'
```

Now, let's review the components of the trading application we have added so far:

- Strategy metadata object (class `tradingSystemMetadata`)
- Queues for price data and orders (`tick_feed_0`, `tick_feed_1`, `tick_feed_2`, `bar_feed`, and `orders_stream`)
- A function that connects to the data source (`LMAX_connect(url, subscription_msg)`)
- A function that forms bars from ticks (`getBarRealtime()`)
- A function that makes trading decisions (`tradeLogic()`)
- A function that processes orders (`processOrders()`)
- A function that emulates order execution at the broker (`emulateBrokerExecution(tick, order)`)

All we have to add to the very end of our code is a block that initializes and starts all four threads:

```
data_receiver_thread = threading.Thread(target = LMAX_connect,
args = (url, subscription_msg))
incoming_price_thread = threading.Thread(target =
getBarRealtime, args = (data_resolution,))
trading_thread = threading.Thread(target = tradeLogic)
ordering_thread = threading.Thread(target = processOrders)
```

```
data_receiver_thread.start()
incoming_price_thread.start()
trading_thread.start()
```

We have just developed our first trading app! It's time to run it and check if it's doing what we expect. I will run it and wait until the second order is executed (because I want to make sure that I submit correct orders both in case the strategy has an open position in the market and in case there's no open position). If you repeated all these steps correctly, you should see an output like the following:

```
2022-12-12T12:03:20.000Z 1.05658 0.0
... (7 ticks omitted from output to save space)
2022-12-12T12:03:28.000Z 1.05664 0.0
```

We started at 12:03:20, so we received nine ticks (remember, LMAX doesn't send actual ticks, but 1-second snapshots of market data). At the 10th second, we form a bar:

```
Got bar:  {'Open': 1.05658, 'High': 1.05668, 'Low': 1.05658,
'Close': 1.05666}
```

The bar's close is greater than the bar's open, so according to our test strategy logic, it is a signal to sell – and indeed, there's an order that immediately follows the bar:

```
{'Type': 'Market', 'Price': 1.05666, 'Side': 'Sell', 'Size':
10000}
```

Note that the order size is 10000 because we opened the position for the very first time and we don't have open positions in the market yet. We check the 10th tick to make sure that its price equals the closing price of the bar and the order price:

```
2022-12-12T12:03:29.000Z 1.05666 0.0
```

Now, we can see the execution report:

```
Executed at  1.05666 current price =  1.05666 order price
=  1.05666
```

So far, so good. Let's wait for the next bar to form:

```
2022-12-12T12:03:30.000Z 1.05663 0.2999999999997449
... (7 ticks omitted from output to save space)
Got bar:  {'Open': 1.05666, 'High': 1.05666, 'Low': 1.05663,
'Close': 1.05665}
```

We're lucky: the very next bar closed in the opposite direction (close is less than open), so it's time to generate a buy order:

```
{'Type': 'Market', 'Price': 1.05665, 'Side': 'Buy', 'Size':
20000}
```

Note that the order size this time is 20000: we need to close the currently open position of 10000 and then open a new one with the remaining 10000. Let's check the tick price to make sure that the bar's closing price and the order price are correct:

```
2022-12-12T12:03:38.000Z 1.05665 0.09999999999843467
```

Great, everything looks good. Now, let's proceed to order execution...

```
Executed at   1.05672 current price =   1.05665 order price
=   1.05672
```

Stop. What's that? The last tick's price was 1.05665, but the order is executed at 1.05672! Why?

This happens because we form bars using only bid prices and execute orders at actual market prices – bid for sell orders and ask for buy orders. The first order was a sell, so we used the bid price and all prices (bar, tick, order, and execution) coincided. But the second order was a buy, but we still used only the bid price to form a bar – that's why we had the execution price greater than the bar's closing price.

> **The importance of market spread**
>
> This issue perfectly illustrates the importance of taking spread (the difference between the bid and ask prices) into consideration when running tests. So many developers forget about it and run their testing using only bid prices – for simplicity, you know. These tests are not adequate for the real market, and quite frequently generate trade logic that is profitable only when you can buy and sell at the same price, effectively assuming the spread to be zero at all times. Now, you know how to avoid this trap and make sure your tests are always realistic.

Before we move on, let's quickly review our code and see whether it meets the requirements outlined in *Chapter 1, Developing Trading Strategies – Why They Are Different*:

- It filters the incoming tick data feed and excludes non-market prices

- It is event-driven – it generates and executes orders as soon as the trade logic confirms a trade

- It does some basic risk management checks – position size, leverage, and available funds

- It is capable of emulating bad order execution and handling these situations

- And probably the main benefit: this code will never – never! – peek ahead, neither in testing nor in production (see *Chapter 4, Trading Application – What's Inside?*, the *Trading logic – this is where a small mistake may cost a fortune* section)

So, we have developed a robust application suitable for serious production! Of course, it can be improved further, but its core will remain almost unchanged. However, we don't have a tested strategy to run. How can we develop such a strategy?

This is when we can use the concept of backtesting, which we mentioned earlier, almost at the beginning of this book.

Backtesting – speeding up the research

The process of developing a trading strategy (I mean the trading logic, not the application) is an infinite loop:

1. Suggest a hypothesis.

2. Code it.

3. Run a test.

4. If the result is not satisfactory, tweak the parameters and repeat.

5. If nothing helps, look for an alternative hypothesis.

The question is: what kind of application shall we use for testing in *step 3*?

Of course, we could use our existing trading app, draft some strategy logic, and then run it in test mode, as we've just done, collecting orders and analyzing the equity time series. But then a single test may take days, weeks, and even months if we want to test the strategy under different market conditions. Do you think it's a bit too long? I agree. That's why, for research and development purposes, we use backtesting.

We discussed backtesting in *Chapter 2, Using Python for Trading Strategies*, in the *Paper trading, and backtesting – an essential part of systemic trader's risk management* section. In essence, instead of emulating the execution of orders using live data streams, we emulate the data stream itself using pre-saved historical market data. In this case, we can dramatically speed up the testing because computers can process dozens of thousands of ticks or bars per second, compressing months of live testing into minutes or seconds of backtesting. Of course, due to its nature, backtesting cannot guarantee the future performance of a strategy, just because it tests using past data. But regardless, it helps us understand the strategy's behavior under various market conditions. Generally speaking, if a backtest shows that the emulated equity was mostly growing in the past, then we may suppose that it continues growing in the future, and vice versa: if we saw that the emulated equity was only decreasing over time, or oscillating around zero at best, then we should be very cautious with such a strategy as it's hard to imagine why it would suddenly start making money when put to production.

I hope you got the idea: we are going to run our code using saved data, not live, so we can process 1,000 or 10,000, or even more seconds of historical data in 1 second.

Now, I believe you will appreciate the approach we followed when developing our code: if you have pre-saved tick historical data, then *all you need to do is modify the only function* – the one that receives ticks from the data provider – and have it receive data from a local file.

That's it.

Isn't it impressive? Yes, you can use the same code for both research and production, thus reducing the probability of making an error to almost zero.

However, you can't always get hold of historical tick data. Moreover, for strategies that use bars with a higher time frame (such as 1 hour, 4 hours, 1 day, 1 week, and so on), it would be a waste of time waiting until our application forms each bar from ticks. So, we may want to make the following modifications to our code:

- It should now be able to read data from a local file instead of receiving it from a data vendor

- It should be able to process already compressed data (bars) without receiving tick data at all

- It should be able to emulate order execution, which may happen within the duration of a single bar (for example, if the strategy bases its logic on 1-hour bars, then we should be able to emulate order execution between hh:00 and hh:59, where hh stands for the hours' value).

Looking at the architecture of our existing code, it seems like quite a straightforward task. However, there is one caveat.

Do you remember how we used tick data in the existing code? Yes, we aggregated it into bars, but besides that, ticks were served as a system clock that synchronized the components of the entire application. How do we synchronize them in case we don't use tick data at all?

Here, we can use another method of controlling the execution of threads – using events.

Syncing threads using events

Let's quickly jump back to the code that we drafted in the *Multithreading – convenient but full of surprises* section earlier in this chapter. The problem with that code was that each thread was running *when possible*, thus producing output at random to a certain degree. And we want all three threads to work one by one – t1, t2, t3, and then again t1, and so on.

The threading module in Python provides several very efficient methods to solve the problem of controlling threads. One of them is using Event() objects.

A threading.Event() object is placed inside the thread's code and it works like a traffic light. It has two possible states: set or cleared. When the event is set, the thread works as normal. When the event is cleared, the thread stops.

Besides just clearing and setting the events, it is possible to instruct the thread to *wait* until the event is set. In this case, the thread waits for the event and as soon as it's set again, it resumes working.

If we want threads to run in a particular order, then we should stick to the following guidelines:

- We need as many events as there are threads
- An event controlling a specific thread should be cleared *inside* this thread but set *outside* it

Now, let's make some modifications to the code.

First, we need three events:

```
f1, f2, f3 = threading.Event(), threading.Event(), threading.
Event()
```

In our example, f1 will control the t1 thread, f2 will control t2, and f3 will control t3.

Next, to the very end of the t1() function, we do the following actions:

- We clear the f1 event (which controls the first thread)
- We set the f2 event (which gives the green light to the t2 thread)
- We set thread t1 to wait for the f1 event to be set again

The modified code will look like follows:

```
def t1():
    while True:
        print('Receive data')
        time.sleep(1)
        f1.clear()
        f2.set()
        f1.wait()
```

We modify the t2() and t3() functions in the same way (so that each thread controls its next neighbor) and run all three threads:

```
def t2():
    while True:
        print('Trading logic')
        time.sleep(1)
        f2.clear()
        f3.set()
        f2.wait()
```

```
def t3():
    while True:
        print('Processing orders')
        time.sleep(1)
        f3.clear()
        f1.set()
        f3.wait()

thread1 = threading.Thread(target=t1)
thread2 = threading.Thread(target=t2)
thread3 = threading.Thread(target=t3)

thread1.start()
thread2.start()
thread3.start()
```

Now, we can enjoy the output in the perfectly correct order:

```
Trading logic
Processing orders
Receive data
Trading logic
Processing orders
Receive data
Trading logic
Processing orders
Receive data
```

...and so on.

> **Note**
>
> It is possible that for the first two execution loops, the output may still go in an incorrect order: this may happen until two events are cleared and awaited, and only one event is set.

Now that we're familiar with threading.Event() objects, it's time to modify our trading application for backtesting purposes. For clarity and ease of use, I will reproduce its entire code here and point to the exact places where we made any modifications.

Backtesting platform with a historical data feed

As always, we start with several imports:

```
import csv
import threading
import queue
import time
from datetime import datetime
```

Then, we reuse the same `tradingSystemMetadata` class and only add three events to the control threads. We name them `F1`, `F2` and `F3` (flags):

```
class tradingSystemMetadata:
    def __init__(self):
        self.initial_capital = 10000
        self.leverage = 30
        self.market_position = 0
        self.equity = 0
        self.last_price = 0
        self.equity_timeseries = []
        self.F1, self.F2, self.F3 = threading.Event(),
threading.Event(), threading.Event()
```

Next, we need data and order queues. Since we no longer use tick data to sync threads, there's no need to have multiple tick data queues – we only need one queue for bars and another one for orders:

```
bar_feed = queue.Queue()
orders_stream = queue.Queue()
```

Next, we must create an instance of the system metadata object and read the historical data from the file into `all_data`. We must also start the stopwatch (the `time.perf_counter()` method) to keep track of time spent on various operations – just out of curiosity.

Note that we read the data using `csv.DictReader()` so that we receive each bar as a dictionary – this ensures maximum compatibility with the production code that we developed earlier in this chapter:

```
System = tradingSystemMetadata()
start_time = time.perf_counter()
f = open("<your_file_path>/LMAX EUR_USD 1 Minute.txt")
csvFile = csv.DictReader(f)
```

```
all_data = list(csvFile)
end_time = time.perf_counter()
print(f'Data read in {round(end_time - start_time, 0)}
second(s).')
```

Next, we need a modified function that takes bars from the read data one by one, converts necessary fields from `str` into `float`, and puts the bar into the queue. We must also break the execution of this loop after the first 10 bars for debugging purposes:

```
def getBar():
    counter = 0
    for bar in all_data:
        bar['Open'] = float(bar['Open'])
        bar['High'] = float(bar['High'])
        bar['Low'] = float(bar['Low'])
        bar['Close'] = float(bar['Close'])
        bar_feed.put(bar)
        counter += 1
        if counter == 10:
            break
        System.F1.clear()
        System.F2.set()
        System.F1.wait()
    print('Finished reading data')
```

Note the three flags (`System.F1`, `System.F2`, and `System.F3`) at the end of the function: they control the execution of threads and make sure that first, we read a bar, then we generate an order and, finally, we execute – or, rather, emulate – the execution of this order.

Also, note that we do not check data consistency and do not exclude any data points: when we work with saved historical data, we assume this data is already clean.

Next goes the `tradeLogic()` function. The best news here is that its main logical part remains completely unchanged – no modification is required between the `trade logic starts here` and `trade logic ends here` comments in the original code! We only modify this function at its beginning and at its end.

At its beginning, we must add a `try...except` statement that will terminate the respective thread when all the data has been processed. To do that, we must set the timeout attribute of the `get()` method to `1`. This means that `get()` will wait for 1 second for a new bar to appear in the queue, and if no bar is there after 1 second, then an exception is generated. On exception, we just break the loop and effectively terminate the thread:

```
def tradeLogic():
    while True:
        try:
            bar = bar_feed.get(block=True, timeout=1)
        except:
            break
        ####################################
        #      trade logic starts here      #
        ####################################

        ####################################
        #      trade logic ends here        #
        ####################################
        bar_feed.put(bar)
        System.F2.clear()
        System.F3.set()
        System.F2.wait()
```

We omitted the entire trade logic because it is indeed identical to what we used in our first version of the trading app.

Note that at end of the function code, we return the bar into the queue: its data will be required by the orders processing component. And as in the case of the previous function, we set the F3 flag, giving the green light to the next operation (orders processing), clear F2, and stop the trade logic thread until the F2 flag is set.

Next, we must rewrite the order execution emulator quite substantially: the difference between the production and backtesting versions is that while backtesting, we only work with compressed data, so checking order execution on every tick no longer makes sense.

Emulating order execution during backtesting

Let's start by emulating market orders since they're the easiest to implement, and stick to the following guidelines:

- We assume that a market order can be generated by the trade logic only at the bar's closing time
- We emulate the execution of a market order only at the bar's closing price

- We assume that the liquidity in the market is always sufficient and therefore we don't have to check it before executing an order

- We assume that the actual execution price was the same as the requested order price as we don't have real-time tick data to test the execution

With all these considerations in mind, the modified `emulateBrokerExecution` function will now look much simpler:

```
def emulateBrokerExecution(bar, order):
    if order['Type'] == 'Market':
        order['Status'] = 'Executed'
        if order['Side'] == 'Buy':
            order['Executed Price'] = bar['Close']
        if order['Side'] == 'Sell':
            order['Executed Price'] = bar['Close']
```

We do not add any flags here as this function is called from inside the `processOrders` function. Let's add this function: you will see that its logic looks very much like the one we used previously, with live tick data:

```
def processOrders():
    while True:
        try:
            bar = bar_feed.get(block = True, timeout = 1)
        except:
            break
```

We started with a similar `try...except` statement that terminates the execution of the thread when there's no more data in the bars queue. Next, we make the same updates to the system metadata as we did previously; the only difference is that we use the bar's closing price instead of the last tick price:

```
        System.equity += (bar['Close'] - System.last_price) *
System.market_position
        System.equity_timeseries.append(System.equity)
        System.last_price = bar['Close']
```

The orders processing logic is again quite similar to the tick-driven code, with the main difference being the absence of risk management checks (whether we have sufficient funds to trade) and rejected orders handling: during backtesting, we assume that all orders are executed:

```
while True:
    try:
        order = orders_stream.get(block = False)
        emulateBrokerExecution(bar, order)
        if order['Status'] == 'Executed':
            System.last_price = order['Executed Price']
            if order['Side'] == 'Buy':
                System.market_position = System.market_
position + order['Size']
            if order['Side'] == 'Sell':
                System.market_position = System.market_
position - order['Size']
    except:
        order = 'No order'
        break
System.F3.clear()
System.F1.set()
System.F3.wait()
```

At the end of the function's code, we again add the respective flags to control the execution order of the threads.

Well, this is it! All we must do now is check the time spent on the backtest (just for fun) and start the threads:

```
start_time = time.perf_counter()
incoming_price_thread = threading.Thread(target = getBar)
trading_thread = threading.Thread(target = tradeLogic)
ordering_thread = threading.Thread(target = processOrders)

incoming_price_thread.start()
trading_thread.start()
ordering_thread.start()
```

But how do we check that the code produces correct results?

Of course, we could add several print statements, as we did with the live trading application, but the goal of backtesting is different: we want to process as much data as possible within as brief a period as possible, and then analyze the collected data. 5 years' worth of 1-minute bars of historical data makes over 2 million data points, so if we just print the updated equity value on each bar, it would make over 2 million prints – which would take forever because `print()` is one of the slowest instructions. So, how do systematic traders analyze the strategy's performance?

Equity curve and statistics

When running a backtest with the code we've just written, we save some basic statistical data: the equity value updated on every tick or bar. If we plot the equity time series, we get an **equity curve**: a visual representation of the dynamics of the trading system's profits and losses over time. Such a chart is the first thing to check after the backtest is complete:

- If the equity curve shows growth over time, then there is a chance (but not a guarantee!) that the strategy may also perform well in the future

- If the equity curve exhibits steady systematical loss over time, it again may not be really bad: consider inverting the rules of the trade logic

- If the equity curve oscillates around zero, it's probably the worst case as this strategy logic is unlikely to make any money in the future

Let's add code for plotting the equity curve to our code after the backtest is complete. We will use the techniques that we discussed in *Chapter 8, Data Visualization in FX Trading with Python*, so I recommend refreshing your memory about using `matplotlib` at this point.

The `matplotlib` main loop cannot be run in a thread (at least easily), so we must add charting in the main thread (like we did when plotting live bar charts in *Chapter 8, Data Visualization in FX Trading with Python*) and keep an eye on the `incoming_price_feed` thread: while it's alive, we just wait and do nothing, but as soon as it finishes working, we plot the equity curve.

So, we just add `import matplotlib.pyplot as plt` to the `imports` section at the beginning of the code and the following simple infinite loop to its end, once all the threads have been started:

```
while True:
    if incoming_price_thread.is_alive():
        time.sleep(1)
    else:
        end_time = time.perf_counter()
        print(f'Backtest complete in {round(end_time - start_
time, 0)} second(s).')
        plt.plot(System.equity_timeseries)
```

```
plt.show()
break
```

If you did everything correctly and used the same historical data file as I did, you will see a chart like the following:

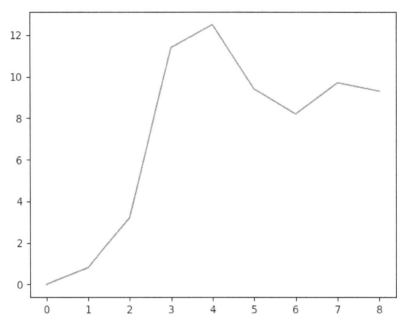

Figure 11.7 – Equity curve of the sample strategy, built on the first 10 bars

This looks great, but how can we make sure that this result is correct? If a backtester emulates the performance incorrectly, we can't rely on the backtesting results.

Fortunately, it's not difficult to check this result. As you may remember, we intentionally used a very simplistic test strategy that generates orders on almost every bar. So, we can rebuild a similar equity curve manually, for example using MS Excel or OpenOffice, and compare it with the chart generated by our backtesting app.

Let's open the data file and remove the unnecessary columns (UpVolume, DownVolume, TotalVolume, UpTicks, DownTicks, and TotalTicks).

	A	B	C	D	E	F
1	Date	Time	Open	High	Low	Close
2	1/27/2015	13:29:00	1.12942	1.1295	1.12942	1.12949
3	1/27/2015	13:30:00	1.12947	1.12959	1.12941	1.12941
4	1/27/2015	13:31:00	1.12953	1.1297	1.12951	1.12965
5	1/27/2015	13:32:00	1.12944	1.12944	1.12883	1.12883
6	1/27/2015	13:33:00	1.12876	1.12907	1.12876	1.12894
7	1/27/2015	13:34:00	1.12902	1.12925	1.12902	1.12925
8	1/27/2015	13:35:00	1.12923	1.12939	1.12919	1.12937
9	1/27/2015	13:36:00	1.12938	1.12939	1.12922	1.12922
10	1/27/2015	13:37:00	1.12921	1.1293	1.12915	1.12918
11	1/27/2015	13:38:00	1.12919	1.12919	1.12873	1.12873

Figure 11.8 – First 10 bars of the source data file

Next, we must reproduce the strategy logic: if the bar closes up (`close > open`), then we buy; if the bar closes down, we sell. We will add a new column that contains the direction of our trade:

	A	B	C	D	E	F	G
1	Date	Time	Open	High	Low	Close	Direction
2	1/27/2015	13:29:00	1.12942	1.1295	1.12942	1.12949	=-SIGN(F2-C2)
3	1/27/2015	13:30:00	1.12947	1.12959	1.12941	1.12941	1
4	1/27/2015	13:31:00	1.12953	1.1297	1.12951	1.12965	-1
5	1/27/2015	13:32:00	1.12944	1.12944	1.12883	1.12883	1
6	1/27/2015	13:33:00	1.12876	1.12907	1.12876	1.12894	-1
7	1/27/2015	13:34:00	1.12902	1.12925	1.12902	1.12925	-1
8	1/27/2015	13:35:00	1.12923	1.12939	1.12919	1.12937	-1
9	1/27/2015	13:36:00	1.12938	1.12939	1.12922	1.12922	1
10	1/27/2015	13:37:00	1.12921	1.1293	1.12915	1.12918	1
11	1/27/2015	13:38:00	1.12919	1.12919	1.12873	1.12873	1

Figure 11.9 – Determining the direction of simulated trade

Then, we must add a column where we calculate the actual PnL per bar by multiplying the difference between the bars' closing prices by the direction and the trading size:

	A	B	C	D	E	F	G	H
1	Date	Time	Open	High	Low	Close	Direction	
2	1/27/2015	13:29:00	1.12942	1.1295	1.12942	1.12949	-1	
3	1/27/2015	13:30:00	1.12947	1.12959	1.12941	1.12941	1	=(F3-F2)*G2*10000
4	1/27/2015	13:31:00	1.12953	1.1297	1.12951	1.12965	-1	2.4
5	1/27/2015	13:32:00	1.12944	1.12944	1.12883	1.12883	1	8.2
6	1/27/2015	13:33:00	1.12876	1.12907	1.12876	1.12894	-1	1.1
7	1/27/2015	13:34:00	1.12902	1.12925	1.12902	1.12925	-1	-3.1
8	1/27/2015	13:35:00	1.12923	1.12939	1.12919	1.12937	-1	-1.2
9	1/27/2015	13:36:00	1.12938	1.12939	1.12922	1.12922	1	1.5
10	1/27/2015	13:37:00	1.12921	1.1293	1.12915	1.12918	1	-0.4
11	1/27/2015	13:38:00	1.12919	1.12919	1.12873	1.12873	1	-4.5

Figure 11.10 – Calculating returns per bar

And finally, we must calculate the cumulative sum of per-bar returns, which is effectively the equity time series:

	A	B	C	D	E	F	G	H	I
1	Date	Time	Open	High	Low	Close	Direction		
2	1/27/2015	13:29:00	1.12942	1.1295	1.12942	1.12949	-1		0
3	1/27/2015	13:30:00	1.12947	1.12959	1.12941	1.12941	1	0.8	0.8
4	1/27/2015	13:31:00	1.12953	1.1297	1.12951	1.12965	-1	2.4	=I3+H4
5	1/27/2015	13:32:00	1.12944	1.12944	1.12883	1.12883	1	8.2	11.4
6	1/27/2015	13:33:00	1.12876	1.12907	1.12876	1.12894	-1	1.1	12.5
7	1/27/2015	13:34:00	1.12902	1.12925	1.12902	1.12925	-1	-3.1	9.4
8	1/27/2015	13:35:00	1.12923	1.12939	1.12919	1.12937	-1	-1.2	8.2
9	1/27/2015	13:36:00	1.12938	1.12939	1.12922	1.12922	1	1.5	9.7
10	1/27/2015	13:37:00	1.12921	1.1293	1.12915	1.12918	1	-0.4	9.3
11	1/27/2015	13:38:00	1.12919	1.12919	1.12873	1.12873	1	-4.5	4.8

Figure 11.11 – Calculating the equity time series

Now, if we plot the equity curve by creating a line chart based on data in column I, we will see the following:

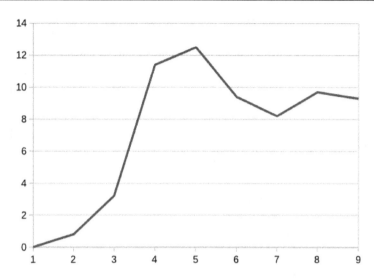

Figure 11.12 – Manual reconstruction of the equity curve in LibreOffice

We can see that the equity curve is identical to what was plotted by our code – and this means that our backtest is reliable! Having checked it only once, we can now trust its results any time we do a test.

I bet you are dying to see a long-term performance report for our great strategy, not limited to just 10 bars. Remember, 1 bar in our source data file is 1 minute, so 10 minutes worth of a backtest is not representative. Let's run the test for the first 1 million bars, which would equate to approximately 32 months' worth of history. We only need to modify one line in the code: replace `10` with `1000000` in `if counter == 1000000:` in the `getBar()` function.

Now, we also can estimate the backtesting speed as per the output in the console. On my (by far not the latest) laptop (Macbook Pro 2012 with a quad-core Core i7 processor, SSD drive, and 16 GB of memory), it took 12 seconds to read the data from the file and 93 seconds to process 1 million bars. Not bad: we can emulate 32 months in less than 2 minutes!

What about the equity curve from such a long-term perspective? Here you are:

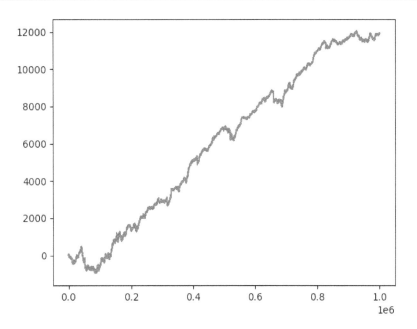

Figure 11.13 – Theoretical performance (equity curve) of the sample
strategy calculated using the first 1,000,000 data points

Wow! Looks like the Holy Grail of trading! Is it possible that such a primitive strategy can indeed generate such steady returns over such a long period?

Generally speaking, every time you get such an optimistic result, focus on finding errors. In our case, it is doubtful that we made an error in the trading logic – it's too primitive and we tested it manually. So, what is it that we probably missed in our backtesting that led to this unrealistically great result? Or maybe this result is indeed realistic?

Of course and unfortunately, it is not.

Let's go back to the `emulateBrokerExecution` function again. We assume that any order is executed on the bar's close – which is fine as we don't have tick data for backtesting. But our code makes no difference between the execution of buy and sell orders: they are both executed at the same price, in our example – bid. But when testing the live trading application earlier in this chapter, we saw that executing orders at actual prices (bid for sell orders and ask for buy orders) may make quite a difference in PnL. So, as we don't have ask prices in our historical data, let's emulate it: we will add a typical spread to the bar's closing price, thus accounting for the difference between the bid and ask:

```
if order['Side'] == 'Buy':
    order['Executed Price'] = bar['Close'] + 0.00005
```

In reality, the spread in EURUSD may vary from as low as 0 to as much as 0.0010 and even greater (usually before the release of important economic news; see *Chapter 6, Basics of Fundamental Analysis and Its Possible Use in FX Trading*), but it's safe to assume that 1/2 pip is more or less adequate to emulate the average spread.

Let's run the backtest again and see the equity curve:

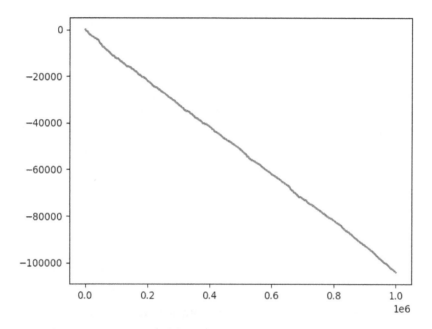

Figure 11.14 – More realistic emulated equity curve of the test strategy

What a radical difference! Now, instead of steadily gaining money, the strategy is steadily losing money, and is doing so very, very quickly: it lost $100,000 in less than 3 years by trading only one so-called mini-lot (10,000 base currency).

How has this happened?

Although the strategy *made money* on paper without accounting for the spread, on average, it produced a ridiculously small amount of paper money *per trade*: it was *less than the spread*. As soon as we correctly emulated the execution of orders at the bid and ask, the Holy Grail vanished into thin air and the sad truth was revealed.

> **Note**
>
> This story should always be kept in mind when you do any market research and develop any strategy. Always make sure that you emulate the real market conditions to the best possible extent – to avoid getting too optimistic theoretical results and quite painful disappointment in production.

The greatest news after all this is that you now have a tool you can rely on: our backtesting platform.

Summary – where do we go now?

Congratulations on getting so far in our studies! I know that this chapter was very long, but hopefully not boring. We covered virtually all aspects of developing live trading applications and backtesters, so now, you are well equipped with powerful tools that should help you develop great trading strategies.

Let's quickly summarize what we learned in this chapter and outline some vistas.

We now fully understand all four essential components of any trading app: receiving data, processing it, generating orders, and controlling their execution.

We are also familiar with the most typical technical issues, such as incorrectly emulating order execution or processing non-market prices, and we also know how to work around them.

Then, we learned how to synchronize multiple threads by using queues and threading event objects, and we know how to make sure that every component of the trading app runs exactly at the expected moment.

Next, we learned how to rebuild parts of strategy performance manually to check the correctness of a test or live orders generation and execution. Now, we can be 100% sure that we can rely on the code we wrote.

We even created our first Holy Grail of trading – and immediately broke it into pieces by critically reviewing the code, thus learning the main lesson of systematic trading: not the tiniest detail can be missed, intentionally or occasionally, and you should check your results twice before going to production to avoid very unpleasant surprises when trading with real money.

Now, let's point out where we can go further in our development.

First, at the moment, our platform only supports market orders. Yes, from the previous chapter, you may remember that in many cases, market orders are preferred and that we can always emulate orders of all other types with market orders only. However, at least for development purposes, it would be great to add emulation for limit and stop orders.

In its present form, the code does not implement any risk management, neither at the position nor the strategy level. It is essential to add at least basic stop-loss orders that will protect the trading account from an unexpected catastrophic scenario.

It would also be great to calculate at least some very basic statistics about the strategy's performance: at the moment, we can only analyze the equity time series, but we want to know more about the average trade value, number of trades, percent of profitable trades, and so on.

And of course, we can complicate the platform further by adding multiple strategies, grouping them into portfolios, and achieving the highest level of sophistication by adding multiple incoming live data streams. Although this is definitely outside the scope of this book, let me encourage you to be bold and curious, as any true researcher should be, and play with the existing code and try improving it –you will see that, in the long run, your efforts will be highly rewarded.

The remaining chapters of this book are dedicated to implementing trading strategies of specific types. We will add a few components to the backtesting platform we created in this chapter, but no significant changes will be made. Instead, we will focus on developing the strategic logic and analyzing its theoretical performance.

Part 4:
Strategies, Performance
Analysis, and Vistas

In previous parts, we gained sufficient knowledge to be able to develop a robust trading platform suitable for both backtesting and – with minimal modifications – live trading. We even coded a dummy strategy and as expected found that it could not make money if not tested properly.

Part 4 explains how to build a profitable trading strategy, from searching for trading ideas to implementing them in code. We will also learn how to generate the most important strategy performance data and analyze it to make the final verdict on whether such a strategy can be used in real life or not. Then, we will see how to correctly implement limit and stop orders and consider another trading strategy, based on a completely different trading idea. Finally, the last chapter suggests a few guidelines for further self-development in algorithm trading, with links to useful and valuable resources.

This part comprises the following chapters:

12

Sample Strategy –
Trend-Following

In the previous chapter, we developed two trading applications: one to use in production and another one to facilitate the testing and research of trading strategies. Better said, these are two versions of the same application, with different data processing modules. We designed them so that the trading logic developed in the backtesting app could be used in the production one without modifications (or with just minimal modifications in complex cases). We also tested the code using a sample *"strategy"* and saw that the code worked correctly, but the *"strategy"* was steadily losing money – fortunately only on paper (and that's why I consistently put this word in "italics").

Now it's time to learn the process of researching and developing one of the most popular classical trading strategies applied to the FX market. We already discussed it earlier in the book, but only from a qualitative, not a quantitative, perspective. Now we will suggest a formal mathematical model and implement it in code. And, of course, we will backtest and check whether the result can be used for live trading.

In this chapter, we will consider trend-following strategies and learn about the following topics:

- Trend-following revisited – trading setup
- Choosing the market and preparing data
- Trend-following strategy – implementation

Trend-following revisited – trading setup

In *Chapter 9, Trading Strategies and Their Core Elements*, we considered trend-following and came to the conclusion that although it is one of the simplest and most intuitive trading strategies, we still need a set of rules that determine the following:

- Whether there is a trend in the market
- Whether the trend goes north or south (up or down, that is)

- When it's time to join the trend (buy or sell respectively)
- When it's time to exit the existing position (so we expect the trend to end and/or reverse)

Let's understand more in the upcoming sections.

Determining a trend, part 1 – market model

If I ask you whether it's sunny or rainy outdoors, I'm sure you won't hesitate with an answer in most cases. You can easily tell one from another because you are very familiar with a number of attributes that help you make the decision. Indeed, it's easy to tell light from darkness, warmth from cold, moisture from dryness, and so on.

Now, say I ask you whether it's slightly rainy or foggy and do so in the middle of the night. I imagine you'd have a really hard time telling one from another. Most likely, you would even go outside, try to feel the air on your skin and smell the air, and finally return with something such as *"well, it seems to be rain."* In this case, you had to do several tests and use their results to make your judgment.

Why were you able to do these tests and use their results?

Because you have a *model* in your mind, a model of the weather. You wouldn't think about it unless it's your profession and, in most cases, you make decisions intuitively and instantly. However, if put under pressure, you can find some more or less formal attributes – such as humidity, temperature, and wind – to decide upon the weather, again within the framework of the weather model.

Let's now develop a model of market trends following the same example with the weather.

First, and above all, we should decide whether trends are something that always exists or occurs only at times. If we compare both models (permanent trends and occasional trends) with our weather example, we will see the following parallels:

Market	Weather
The market is always in an uptrend or downtrend. Trends may be more or less visible.	The wind blows all the time, only sometimes stronger and other times weaker.
The market can be in *trend mode* or *non-trend* mode.	Sometimes the wind blows and other times the wind doesn't blow at all.

Table 12.1 – Drawing parallels between market trends and the weather

Despite looking quite simple, this table perfectly illustrates the fundamental difference in approaches to modeling the process (market or weather). It is up to the model's developer to decide either that the observed process can only be in one state (only in trend; only wind blowing) or that it can be in multiple states (trend or non-trend in the market example; windy or not windy in the weather example).

This said, we come to a very important conclusion.

There is no such thing as a *true* or *false* model. A model only tries to explain the observed phenomena with certain precision and serves the purpose of making decisions.

So, the ability of a model to help make a practical decision is the only criterion of the model's validity. If looking outside the window is enough to know how to dress for the day, then the weather model is valid. If you make decisions whether to take an umbrella with you by consulting sophisticated equipment and still regularly get wet to the skin, most likely, the model used in this sophisticated equipment is not valid.

In the market, the situation is similar. If we can suggest a simplistic market model that nevertheless is able to consistently outperform a benchmark (see *Chapter 9, Trading Strategies and Their Core Elements*), then this is an acceptable model. At the same time, we may have an extremely sophisticated model that uses artificial intelligence and quantum mechanics, but if in the long run it doesn't beat the market, then it may only be interesting from an academic standpoint.

As we're making our first steps in algo trading, let's start with something simple. We can make our model more complicated later if a simplistic model doesn't work.

In our present case, we should make a decision regarding how we model the market from a trending standpoint:

- The market is always in a trend, up or down; it's just the duration of these trends that may be long or short
- The market is in either a trend or non-trend state, and we should distinguish between the two before determining an uptrend or downtrend

Of course, the first model is simpler: we don't need to suggest a method to tell trend from non-trend, focusing now only on technical setups that tell an uptrend from a downtrend. Again, if this approach doesn't work, we can return to this decision point, change our model, and start the research all over.

So, we have decided upon the first point in our checklist: we choose the *always-in-trend* market model for further research.

Now that we have decided upon the market model, let's move on to finding a proper tool to distinguish an uptrend from a downtrend. Again, we start this step with the simplest solution: moving averages.

Determining a trend, part 2 – moving averages

One of the classical technical analysis studies typically used to determine trends is the moving average. In *Chapter 7, Technical Analysis and Its Implementation in Python*, we already considered moving averages and found that they act as digital filters that eliminate higher frequencies (short-term price fluctuations) and keep lower frequencies, which we consider as dominating long-term tendencies in price movements. Let's quickly refresh our knowledge of this by plotting a 20-period moving average (MA20) over a price chart.

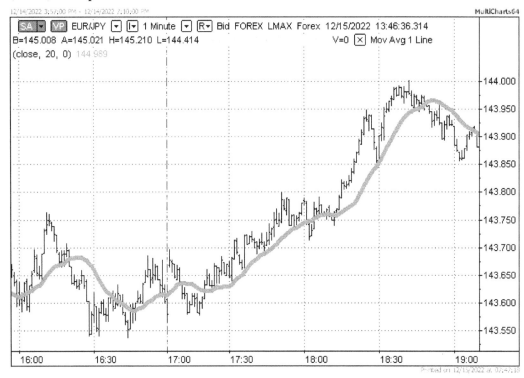

Figure 12.1 – 20-period moving average on top of a 1-minute chart of EURJPY. Chart by Multicharts

We can see that sometimes, the bars' closing prices tend to remain above the MA20, while sometimes they are below it. It is reasonable to suppose that as long as these closing prices remain above the MA20, the market is in an uptrend, and while they remain below it, it is in a downtrend.

The problem with this technical setup is that sometimes prices remain above or below a moving average for too short a period of time. We already agreed that in our model the market is always in trend and we do not separate any special non-trending condition. However, maybe there's a better technical setup, something that would better indicate an uptrend or downtrend without so many *short-term trends*, which we intuitively wouldn't like to even call *trends*.

Yes, there is, and this is one of the oldest classical technical trading setups: we use two moving averages, one with a short period and another one with a long period. Then, we consider an uptrend only when both of the following two conditions are met:

- The price is above the short-period moving average
- The short-period moving average is itself above the long-period moving average

It is similar for downtrends:

- The price is below the short-term moving average

- The short-period moving average is itself below the long-period moving average

Let's see what it may look like on a chart.

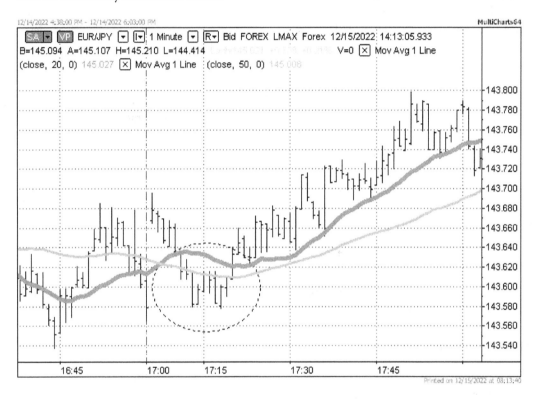

Figure 12.2 – Adding a longer-term moving average helps exclude unwanted situations

In the preceding figure, I added a 50-period moving average (MA50) to the existing MA20 and zoomed the figure in to see more details. The area encompassed by a dotted oval illustrates how adding the second moving average may filter out certain (but, of course, not all) unwanted situations. If we decide whether it's an uptrend or a downtrend only by closing prices being above or below MA20, then during the phase shown in *Figure 12.2*, we would have to decide whether there was a downtrend. However, if we use a setup with both requirements as we suggested previously (that the price should be below MA20 and MA20 should be below MA50), then we can qualify it neither as an uptrend nor as a downtrend. So, in the trade logic, we simply skip this interval – and then we can see that the following price movement develops into a *true* uptrend.

Great, now we have covered two points in our list– we know when there's a trend in the market and know its direction. Now we need to decide when we actually enter and exit a position in the market.

Entry and exit rules

After all the elements of a technical trading setup are determined, the key question remains of when to actually enter and exit a position. In some cases, it may be a non-trivial question and the answer to it may seriously affect the resulting performance of a strategy. However, within our simplistic model, we can assume that we can enter the market as soon as the trend conditions are met. This means that we open a new long position when the following apply:

- The bar's closing price is above the short-period moving average

- The short-period moving average is above the long-period moving average

- Currently, we don't have a long position in the market (so we don't add to an existing position, and we don't buy more if we're already long)

As to exiting from an open position – again, within our market model there's no need to actually exit a position because the model assumes that the market is always in a trend. So, we exit a long position only when we open a short position and vice versa.

In other words, we plan a strategy that is *always in the market* and changes the trade's direction as soon as the change in the trend is detected.

As with the market model, we can change this approach later, if testing the current simplistic model doesn't produce acceptable results.

Money management

Money management means how much you trade with each new order. There are many money management theories and techniques, from very simple to quite sophisticated. Unfortunately, we cannot really cover all of them in one chapter – it would require a separate book! But since we are keeping things simple at the moment and are more interested in learning how the trade logic works in general, let's use the most simplistic money management concept as well: we will use the same constant trading size for all trades, doubling it when we should make a reversal from long to short or from short to long. We already did that in the previous chapter when we developed our backtesting platform.

The rule of thumb is: if your strategy performs acceptably well with a constant trading size, its performance may be improved with money management. If the strategy doesn't perform well with constant trading size then attempts to improve its performance by using various money management rules fail most of the time.

So, we have successfully covered the four key points that we outlined at the beginning of this chapter:

- We know when the market is in trend
- We know the trend's direction
- We know when to enter the market
- We know when to exit it

Plus, we also know how much we have at stake with each trade.

Great, now we can proceed to choose the market we're going to trade using trend-following and prepare the data.

Choosing the market and preparing data

There is one very common misconception regarding systematic trading: it is believed that a technical trading strategy should work in any market. I hope that the previous chapters have already dispelled this myth. Just as an example, let's recall the famous EURCHF market while the Swiss national bank was keeping the rate of the Swiss franc pegged to the euro (see *Chapter 9, Trading Strategies and Their Core Elements*) – go and trade it using trend-following if the price virtually doesn't move at all!

Even if we set aside such extreme examples, anyway, choosing the market can be a non-trivial task. Most of the time, we have to try many markets even if we can make an educated guess about which should perform better with a specific kind of strategy. However, there are some general guidelines that we are going to use now.

First, since we're focused on trend-following, we would like to trade a market that is full of trends (however much it may sound like a truism). If we are in the FX domain, we may want to focus on currency pairs with the greatest difference in the interest rates between the two currencies (see the *Fundamental analysis* section of *Chapter 6, Basics of Fundamental Analysis and Its Possible Use in FX Trading*, for a brief discussion on interest rates and carry trading) because this is one of the very few factors that may lead to forming a more or less long-term trend. So, pairs with currencies such as the Australian dollar or the New Zealand dollar versus the Japanese yen or even the US dollar (especially when the US rates were low) may be good to start with.

Another reason to choose the Australian dollar for trading with a trend-following strategy is that the Australian economy is dependent on gold production, much like the Canadian economy depends on oil (though perhaps to a lesser extent). As a result, the rate of the Australian dollar is prone to corresponding changes in the price of gold and other export commodities. Since commodity prices exhibit cyclic behavior due to manufacturing cycles, we can see this reflected in AUDUSD or AUDJPY. Therefore, with these two considerations in mind, choosing AUDUSD as the first currency pair to try a trend-following strategy seems like a natural choice.

Second, we should decide upon the timeframe or data resolution. Although the previous sample charts with moving averages were made using a resolution of 1 minute, intraday data is not really good for trend-following strategies. The reason is that intraday the FX market exhibits strongly cyclical behavior in volatility patterns (see the *Liquidity and volatility – how one transforms into another* section of *Chapter 3, FX Market Overview from a Developer's Standpoint*). These markets are active during the daytime and slow during the night. This periodicity will produce many *false trends* and make the task of determining a *true trend* significantly more difficult. At the same time, the daily timeframe is free from this feature and we may expect more steady trending behavior with this data resolution (of course, depending on whether the market is prone to trending at all). So, when we have a choice of making our model more complicated by adding a module to the trading logic, which would distinguish between *true* and *false* trends, we'd rather use data with higher resolution to eliminate the problem completely.

Thus, we have decided upon the market (let's start with AUDUSD) and the data resolution (daily). As always, let me note that if we get unsatisfactory results, we can try different markets and timeframes.

Now that we have settled upon all the prerequisites, let's get to coding.

Compressing data to a daily timeframe

Let's start with writing a simple utility that would compress the market data to the required resolution and convert it into the desired format, compatible with our backtesting and live trading code (see *Chapter 11, Backtesting and Theoretical Performance*). We will use the `getBarRealtime()` function from the live version and slightly adapt it as a stand-alone utility.

This utility should do the following:

- Read the source data file (tick or 1-minute bars)
- Aggregate data into any greater timeframe
- Save data to disk using a format compatible with the backtester

As always, we start with imports:

```
import csv
from datetime import datetime
```

We add a sliding window class similar to the one we used in *Chapter 6, Basics of Fundamental Analysis and Its Possible Use in FX Trading*, but we will use it in a bit of a different way: to store values of any parameter (price, time, volume, or whatever) on the current bar and the previous bar. Thus, we add two respective methods to quickly retrieve these values:

```
class slidingWindow:
    def __init__(self, len):
        self.data = [0 for i in range(len)]
```

```
    def add(self, element):
        self.data.pop(0)
        self.data.append(element)
    def last(self):
        return self.data[-1]
    def previous(self):
        return self.data[-2]
```

Then, we specify the source file and the destination file and read the saved data (tick or 1 minute) – pretty much like we did in the previous chapter:

```
source_file = open("LMAX AUD_USD 1 Minute.txt")
dest_file = open("AUDUSD_daily.csv", "w")
csvFile = csv.DictReader(source_file)
all_data = list(csvFile)
```

We immediately write the first line to the destination file – this line will act as a header for further processing the file as a CSV:

```
dest_file.write(("Date,Time,Open,High,Low,Close\n"))
```

Then, we create an instance of the slidingWindow class and initiate the first bar, which we're going to aggregate and then save to the destination file:

```
timestamp = slidingWindow(2)
bar = {'Open': 0, 'High': 0, 'Low': 0, 'Close': 0}
```

Now, we start iterating over all samples in the source file, convert the data, and add the timestamp to the timestamp sliding window:

```
for sample in all_data:
    open = float(sample[' <Open>'])
    high = float(sample[' <High>'])
    low = float(sample[' <Low>'])
    close = float(sample[' <Close>'])
    ts = datetime.strptime(sample['<Date>'] + 'T' + sample['
<Time>'] + 'Z', "%m/%d/%YT%H:%M:%SZ")
    timestamp.add(ts)
```

> **Note**
>
> The header format of the source file may be different. In the files that I use in this book, there are at least two different formats: plain words ('Open', 'High', etc.) and words in triangle brackets (<Open>, etc.). Be careful and don't forget to adapt this piece of code to the source data you're going to use yourself!

If the date of the timestamp is not equal to that of the previous timestamp – meaning that a new day had started – we save the updated daily bar to the destination file and reinitialize the bar:

```
if timestamp.previous() != 0:
        if timestamp.last().date() != timestamp.previous().
date():
            if bar['Open'] != 0:
                dest_file.write(','.join(map(str, [*bar.
values()]))) + "\n")
            bar = {'Date': timestamp.last().date(), 'Time':
timestamp.last().time(), 'Open': open, 'High': high, 'Low':
low, 'Close': close}
```

Finally, we update the currently forming bar:

```
bar['High'] = max([bar['High'], high])
bar['Low'] = min([bar['Low'], low])
bar['Close'] = close
bar['Time'] = timestamp.last().time()
```

Don't forget to close the destination file after the `for` loop has finished:

```
dest_file.close()
```

If you run this code using the same AUDUSD 1-minute historical data as I used (you can find it on GitHub along with the code), you will get a CSV file with daily bars where the 'Time' column features two different times: 17:00 and 23:59. Why is that?

In fact, this is a very important question that deserves an insightful answer.

Be careful with time!

No, this doesn't mean that you should be looking at your watch every other minute. It means that when working with market data, time is the very thing that leads to confusion, especially in cases where you work with data from decentralized markets such as forex.

Working with data from a centralized exchange is somewhat easier: in this case, we always know in which time zone the exchange is located and its working hours. So, in any market data from that exchange, all timestamps will be in the same time zone as the exchange and only between market open and close.

With forex, it's different. We know that there's no single exchange in this market and that it works almost 24 hours, 5 days a week.

Almost, mind you.

First, we must consider time zones. Every FX data vendor and every FX broker may deliver data in any time zone they think is correct. Most frequently used are GMT (UTC) or BST (UTC+1) for London, CET (UTC+1) or CEST (UTC+2) for Frankfurt, and EST (UTC-5) or EDT (UTC-4) for New York. You should check the data source about the time zone used before you do any manipulations with timestamps.

Second, we must consider working hours. Most FX trading venues open on Sunday at around 5 p.m. New York time (New York bank settlement time; see the *FX instruments* section of *Chapter 3*, *FX Market Overview from a Developer's Standpoint*), but some may open at a later time. Same with the market close before the weekend: most venues close on Friday at that same time of 5 p.m. in New York, but some even offer weekend trading. We can't consider this weekend trading seriously because the trading volume for weekend deals is negligible, but you may get hold of market data from a venue which provides weekend trading and this weekend data will add quite some confusion to your research process. If you plan to trade exotic currencies, most likely they will only be traded during the work hours of the respective state central bank or just a bit longer.

Besides regular working hours, there are exceptions, mostly around holidays. For example, don't be surprised if you see an early close before or a late open after Christmas.

Third, we must consider how 0:00 time is interpreted. Some data providers treat this time as the start of a new day, while others believe it refers to the previous day. Moreover, some data providers even don't have such a timestamp and the last time of the day in their data is 23:59 (for 1-minute data).

This 0:00 time is quite confusing. When we work with data compressed in bars, the bar's timestamp means the time when the bar closes. Therefore, 0:00 means that the bar closed at midnight. But it still represents price movements that happened before midnight, so they belong to the day that just finished! So, if you want to be absolutely precise when working with time, you may want to add some additional checks to your code that take into account the issues we've just discussed.

Now, let's look at the data we used in our example and see what we actually did. This data is in the New York time zone, so the last time of the week is 17:00 – and this is what we see in the compressed daily data for every Friday. This data provider treats 0:00 as the first time of the new day, so since we divide days by date and do not take time into consideration, the last time of a day is now 23:59.

We may want to modify the new day conditions in the code of the bar-making utility. One of the possible solutions could be a condition like this:

```
if (timestamp.last().date() != timestamp.previous().date() and
str(timestamp.last().time()) != '00:00:00') or (str(timestamp.
previous().time()) == '00:00:00'):
```

If we now run the modified code, we get correctly compressed data, but keep in mind that 0:00 timestamps now denote the end of the day, not its beginning!

Now we have all the data prepared and it's time to try writing the code for our first strategy.

Trend-following strategy – implementation

Since we're going to use the backtesting code that we developed in the previous chapter (see the *Backtesting platform with historical data feed* section in *Chapter 11, Backtesting and Theoretical Performance*), we need to add only small pieces of code that support the required objects.

> **Note**
> Don't forget to change the data source to the file with the daily AUDUSD data that we've just created!

Let's start with adding the `slidingWindow` class to implement moving averages. Obviously, we copy it from the code in the preceding section. The code (as usual with class declaration) goes somewhere after the imports and before the declaration of the first function:

```
class slidingWindow:
    def __init__(self, len):
        self.data = [0 for i in range(len)]
    def add(self, element):
        self.data.pop(0)
        self.data.append(element)
```

As you progress in developing various strategies, sooner or later you will find that many classes or functions are used in most strategies, so you can move them to a separate module and import the module into any strategy prototype.

We add two sliding windows to implement moving averages:

```
data_window_small = slidingWindow(5)
data_window_large = slidingWindow(20)
```

Why 5 and 20 for periods of moving averages? Well, no real reason in particular: when we work with daily data, 5 is usually used to represent a work week and 20 a work month. These values can often be found in technical analysis studies. Other popular periods are 50 (for a quarter) and 200 (for a year). In any case, this is only a draft, so we will be able to modify these values later, after having evaluated the strategy performance.

Then we have the function that actually calculates a moving average:

```
def moving_average(data):
    return sum(data) / len(data)
```

All that we need to modify now is part of the tradeLogic() function. It is the block of code between the trade logic starts here and trade logic ends here comments:

```
####################################
#      trade logic starts here      #
####################################
```

First of all, we retrieve a new closing price and add it to both sliding windows. Then we calculate the moving averages:

```
close = bar['Close']
data_window_small.add(close)
data_window_large.add(close)
ma_small = moving_average(data_window_small.data)
ma_large = moving_average(data_window_large.data)
```

Now the main part: the entry condition. We sell if the close is below the short-period MA and the short-period MA is below the long-period MA. Don't forget that we do that only if we don't have an open short position already (see the *Trading application with live data feed* section in *Chapter 11, Backtesting and Theoretical Performance*):

```
if close < ma_small and ma_small < ma_large and System.
  market_position >= 0:
```

The rest of the trade logic code in the 'Sell' clause remains untouched, and I have reproduced it here only to maintain integrity:

```
order = {}
order['Type'] = 'Market'
order['Price'] = close
order['Side'] = 'Sell'
```

```
    if System.market_position == 0:
        order['Size'] = 10000
    else:
        order['Size'] = 20000
    orders_stream.put(order)
```

And symmetrical for a buy order: we buy when the close is greater than the short-period MA and the short-period MA is greater than the long-period MA:

```
    if close > ma_small and ma_small > ma_large and System.
market_position <= 0:
        order = {}
        order['Type'] = 'Market'
        order['Price'] = close
        order['Side'] = 'Buy'
        if System.market_position == 0:
            order['Size'] = 10000
        else:
            order['Size'] = 20000
        orders_stream.put(order)
    ###################################
    #     trade logic ends here     #
    ###################################
```

This is it. Nothing else needs any modification.

Are you ready to test your first trading strategy? Let's run the code and look at the equity curve.

If you did everything correctly so far, you should see an equity curve similar to the one shown in *Figure 12.3*.

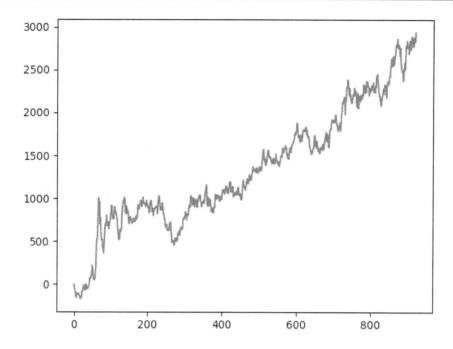

Figure 12.3 – Equity curve of the backtest of the trend-following strategy using AUDUSD daily data

Not a bad start! In *Chapter 11, Backtesting and Theoretical Performance*, we talked about the equity curve and noted that traders (and investors, above all!) are looking for strategies that demonstrate consistent growth over time. Since our equity curve is a representation of our trend-following strategy PnL day by day, we can agree that this strategy indeed demonstrates growth in equity.

However, this result raises further questions. What is the meaning of the numbers on the x and y axes? How do we interpret this result in terms of money or percent growth? Can we say that the growth demonstrated by the backtest is consistent? These and other questions will be discussed in the very next chapter.

Summary

Let's quickly recap what we learned in this chapter. It indeed is the ultimate point where all the knowledge and skills we obtained in previous chapters unite and transform into a working trading application. More than that, in fact, we've got now a scalable *trading platform* suitable for both research and live trading. We suggested a robust design of the platform that keeps the architecture modular and scalable. We learned how to synchronize threads to ensure the correct order of execution of the platform modules while keeping these modules isolated. We saw practical examples of using various data sources that allow the platform to work with both live data feeds and historical data. We completely isolated the trade logic from the rest of the app so now we can develop a strategy using a backtest and then immediately copy and paste the code into the production version of our platform. Finally, using our knowledge of FX markets from previous chapters, we developed a simple trend-following strategy, tested it, and saw a promising result.

Now it's time to analyze our result to get a full understanding of the strategy's behavior and performance.

13

To Trade or Not to Trade – Performance Analysis

In the previous chapter, we developed a simple trend-following strategy, ran a backtest, and generated our first equity curve (a visual representation of the strategy's profits and losses over time). Intuitively, we already know that equity curves of profitable strategies should grow over time, and the steeper the growth, the better. At first glance, our strategy looks fit to this requirement, but of course, it would be better to be able to base our opinions on facts and not just emotions. So, we would like to have a quantitative metric that could be used as an indicator: if its value is greater than something, then the strategy is good. If it's less, then the strategy is not good.

As you might have already guessed, such a single, universal metric does not exist. A trading strategy is quite a complex structure, even if its logic seems simplistic, and its performance should be analyzed from different standpoints. We are interested in knowing not only how much money a particular strategy could make but also how much we should put at stake as risk capital in order to achieve such a gain. Similarly, not only the overall net profit but also how profits (and losses!) are distributed over time matters. Ultimately, we want to be sure that the strategy is indeed tradable: that trades placed in the real market will be more or less similar to those emulated during the backtest.

This chapter is very far from an ultimate guide on trading strategy performance analysis: this subject is so vast that it would require a separate book, if not multiple books. Here, we are going to consider the most essential metrics and see how they help assess a strategy's performance and make our main decision – whether to give this strategy a try or set it aside.

In this chapter, you will learn about the following topics:

- Trade analysis
- Average trade and trading costs
- Measuring performance – alpha and beta revisited

- Net profit versus buy and hold

- Drawdown

- The power of leverage – or how much do I need to trade it?

Trade analysis

As you remember, the difference between trading and investing is, broadly speaking, the number of trades. If you buy and hold a position in an asset for 1 year or more, then it's an investment. If you buy, sell, and buy the same asset or different assets again multiple times during the same year, it's trading.

> **Why a year?**
>
> According to most tax laws, holding a position for 1 year and 1 day qualifies it as an investment, and any profit resulting from this activity is taxed at a discounted rate. If you held the position even for 1 day less than 1 year, it will be considered trading and the resulting profit will be taxed at a full income tax rate. This rule is applicable mostly to equities trading, but at least it makes sense to use 1 year as a reference term.

So, the strategy is actively opening and closing positions during a given period. Regardless of the total net profit (or loss) for the entire period, first, and above all, we are interested in how much each trade contributes to the overall result – at least on average.

Average trade and trading costs

Average trade is one of the most essential yet simplistic metrics: it's just the ratio of the total net profit achieved by a strategy to the total number of trades:

$$Average trade = \frac{Netprofit}{Number\_of\_trades}$$

Why do we need this value?

To answer this question, we should recall a few things from theory again.

In *Chapter 3, FX Market Overview from a Developer's Standpoint*, we considered how markets are organized and learned that there is always a difference between the price at which we can buy and at which we can sell – the spread. Regardless of the type of orders used in the strategy, the market price must move for the distance of the spread *at the very least*, only to move the newly opened position from a negative zone to break even.

Besides that, don't forget the various issues with liquidity and order execution that were considered in *Chapter 10, Types of Orders and Their Simulation in Python*. If the strategy uses market orders, it may encounter slippage, partial fills, or rejects (depending on the TIF specification, see the *Time in force: better control over execution* section in the same chapter). In any case, it's just another cost of trading that should be covered by the strategy.

Finally, don't forget that the broker and the trading venue will charge commissions, and this cost should also be absorbed by the trading strategy.

So, the average trade value should be greater than the sum of the spread, typical slippage, and broker and/or trading venue commissions. Only in this case can the strategy make money in the real market.

Let's now look at real figures, based on the performance of the strategy that we developed in the previous chapter. In order to obtain the necessary values, let's add a few lines to the strategy code. First, we will add a `list_of_orders` property to the `tradingSystemMetadata` class – here, we will save all executed orders. Next, in the `processOrders()` function, we will add the following statement right after the `if order['Status'] == 'Executed':` line:

```
System.list_of_orders.append(order)
```

And finally, at the very end of the backtester's code, right after `plt.plot(System.equity_timeseries)` (see the *Backtesting platform with historical data feed* section of *Chapter 11, Backtesting and Theoretical Performance*):

```
total_trades = len(System.list_of_orders)
print("Total trades:", total_trades)
print("Average trade:", System.equity / total_trades)
```

If you run the backtesting now again with the same data (AUD/USD daily), you should get 37 total trades and an average trade value of about 79.41.

Is that good or bad?

Regarding the number of trades, generally speaking, the greater the number, the better. Why? Because all metrics used to assess the strategy performance are based on statistics, and statistics work best if the size of the dataset is significant. I am not going to go into details about the exact meaning of *significant* in this sense, as it's too complex a subject, but for simplicity's sake, let's take it for granted that we need at least 20-30 data points so that statistical metrics start making sense. From this standpoint, 37 trades look satisfactory.

Now the average trade itself. Its value is 79.41, but in which units? Dollars? Australian dollars? Maybe something else?

Here, we should recall that spot FX is always traded on margin (see the *Trade mechanics: again some terminology* section of *Chapter 3, FX Market Overview from a Developer's Standpoint*) and that the value of 1 pip in money depends on the trading size. In the *Trading application with live data feed* section of *Chapter 11, Backtesting and Theoretical Performance*, we already pointed out that for backtesting, we may want to use a trading size that will make 1 pip equal to $1. This is why we chose a trading size of 10,000 for the backtest and now we can interpret the average trade as *79.41 pips*. Then, we can finally decide whether it's sufficient or not.

Let's sum up all trading costs that we mentioned here: spread, slippage, and commission.

Spread

Spreads depend on the liquidity provider or the broker (the latter often add their own fees into the spread, such a practice is called **markup**), and also on the time of day. An industry average spread for AUD/USD today is between 0.5 and 2 pips with rare increases to 5 and more, typically before economic news. So, it would be safe to suppose that we should subtract 1 pip from the average trade value to account for the market spread during a somewhat less liquid time (remember that our strategy places orders at midnight, when liquidity is thinner than during regular work hours).

> **Note**
>
> If you use the unmodified `emulateBrokerExecution` function in the backtester code, then a spread of 0.5 pips is already included there. You can modify it every time you run a new strategy with a new currency pair, or remove it completely and subtract the spread from the resulting average trade.

Slippage

Slippage mostly depends on the trading size and liquidity in the order book. If the sizes of your orders never exceed top-of-book liquidity, then in the absolute majority of cases, the slippage would be zero. To get a more precise estimate, we need to analyze the top-of-book data at the time of the trade. If you trade with a retail broker, then you may have a hard time getting order book data – normally, brokers do not publish it. If you use a broker as an STP to get access directly to a trading venue, then you will get at least top-of-book data with volumes. Let's do an estimate using LMAX data.

Our strategy places trades only at end of the day, which is midnight (New York time, EST/EDT). This is not the most liquid time, but on average, we can see 50,000 to 200,000 AUD at the top of the book at that time. So, if your order size doesn't exceed 50,000 AUD, then you can safely assume that slippage will be negligible. However, if your order size exceeds 50,000 AUD, then most likely you will experience slippage of up to 1 pip – depending on the actual trading volume. If the trading size exceeds 500,000 AUD, then the slippage may increase to 2 pips and even more.

Which estimate should we use? How can you know which trading size you're going to use?

Let's again recall that the FX markets are traded on margin. This means that you don't need to have the entire amount of money in the broker account to open a position: the broker will provide you with a credit line according to the leverage available according to your status: retail or professional. If you're a retail trader, then most likely you will get a 30:1 leverage. If you're a professional trader, then higher leverage such as 100:1 is available. However, as you will see later in this chapter (see the *The power of leverage – how much do I need to trade it?* section), it is highly unlikely that you're going to use a leverage greater than 10:1. Most likely, it is going to be somewhere in the vicinity of 2:1-5:1. In our example, in order to open a position of 200,000 AUD/USD with a leverage of 10:1, you will need approximately the following:

$$\frac{200000 \cdot AUDUSDrate}{10} = \frac{200000 \cdot 0.6918}{10} \approx \$13800,$$

0.6918 is the average rate of AUD/USD for the last 52 weeks (a work year). In reality, you will need a bit more because the open position should be able to withstand a drawdown (see below in this chapter), but in essence, an estimate of about \$15,000 seems adequate. Without any intention to count money in your pocket, let me suppose that if you're a retail trader, then you will hardly open positions with a size greater than 200,000 AUD, so it is safe to suppose that a slippage of 1 pip would provide a sufficient overhead for our estimate.

> **Note**
>
> The main idea behind all our estimates is to suppose a theoretical worst scenario, something that probably won't be realized in real trading. If the strategy is still able to make money on paper after we have accounted for all possible negative impacts, then it is probable that it's going to make money in real life.

However, if you work with a financial institution, then most likely the average order size can be multiplied at least 10 times, so slippage starts to play quite an important role. I'd suggest subtracting at least 1 pip per 100,000 in the order size to account for slippage in case trades are placed during an illiquid time such as at night.

> **Trading size, slippage, and execution**
>
> In real life, orders whose size exceeds the top of the book are seldom sent directly to the market as market orders to avoid execution at unwanted prices. If you really need to fill a large order, consider rewriting the `processOrders()` function, splitting a large order into parts, and executing them one by one.

Commission

The last part of trading costs seems to be the commission. Typically, a trading venue charges about 25-40 **dollars per million (DPM)**. How do we recalculate it into dollar value for our trades?

The trading size used in the backtest is 10,000 AUD/USD. This means we buy or sell 10,000 Australian dollars or (using an average rate of AUD/USD of about 0.6920) approximately 7000 US dollars. With a rate of 30 DPM, the broker commission would be around $0.21. Now, if we recall that in our backtest $1 equals 1 pip, we can say that the commission makes about 0.21 pips.

So far, we calculated a realistic estimate for the spread, slippage, and broker commission. Is this all we should account for?

No, there is another cost that is very frequently forgotten by many traders: overnight swaps.

Overnight swaps

In the *Economic news* section of *Chapter 6, Basics of Fundamental Analysis and Its Possible Use in FX Trading*, we already mentioned one of the most peculiar features of the FX market: the difference in interest rates between the two currencies in a pair. This difference may be positive and may be negative: for example, if the interest rate of the British pound is 5% per annum and the interest rate of the Japanese yen is 0% per annum, then the difference for GBP/JPY is positive (5%) and the difference for JPY/GBP is negative (-5%).

Once you hold an open position overnight (past the NY bank settlement time), you either receive interest (if the difference is positive) or pay the interest (if the difference is negative). In our example, if you buy GBP/JPY (or sell JPY/GBP, which is the same), then you receive interest, and if you sell GBP/JPY or buy JPY/GBP, then you pay interest.

With our present strategy, we hold AUD/USD for multiple days, sometimes long, sometimes short, so we may receive or pay the interest depending on the side of the position and the current difference in interest rates.

We have to account for these overnight fees, frequently referred to as **swaps**.

> **Note**
>
> Do not confuse swaps with financial instruments, which we discussed in the *FX instruments* section in *Chapter 3, FX Market Overview from a Developer's Standpoint*.

However, it is surprisingly quite a non-trivial task. There are two problems here:

- First, these swap rates change over time because they are based on the interest rates set by central banks (usually referred to as the base rate) and these rates also change. So, we need historical data for base rates at the very least.

- Second, each broker adds their own premium, or markup, to the base rate, and, in most cases, this premium is publicly unknown. Given that brokers do not store historical data for their overnight swap rates, it becomes problematic to reliably restore the history of interest rates differential in a currency pair.

Nevertheless, we can make an attempt. First, we need historical interest rate data. It's a bit less widespread than historical market data, but there are a few resources that provide it free of charge – for example, `Global-rates.com`. Go to `https://www.global-rates.com/en/interest-rates/central-banks/central-banks.aspx` and there you will find links to the Federal Reserve and the Reserve Bank of Australia interest rate data.

As you can see, the data changes quite infrequently, no more than once a month – because decisions on interest rates are made by a special central bank committee and normally they have monthly meetings. We don't need to be absolutely precise in our calculations: in the long run, the overnight swap is going to be just a fraction of a pip, so it's sufficient to sync data for up to a month. I copied the data into an Excel sheet and here's what I got:

RBA		FED		Rates difference
12/06/22	3.10%	12/14/22	4.50%	-1.40%
11/01/22	2.85%	11/02/22	4.00%	-1.15%
10/04/22	2.60%		3.25%	-0.65%
09/06/22	2.35%	09/21/22	3.25%	-0.90%
08/02/22	1.85%	07/28/22	2.50%	-0.65%
07/06/22	1.35%	06/15/22	1.75%	-0.40%
06/07/22	0.85%	05/04/22	1.00%	-0.15%
05/03/22	0.35%	03/16/22	0.50%	-0.15%
11/03/20	0.10%	03/15/20	0.25%	-0.15%
03/19/20	0.25%	03/03/20	1.25%	-1.00%

Table 13.1 – Historical central banks' interest rates for RBA and the Fed

If we subtract the former from the latter, we will get the difference in interest rates for the AUD/USD currency pair. We can see that it changes from as low as 0.15% to 1.4%. Now, the question is how much it means in money.

To calculate that, we should first recall that a year has 365 days and then we should divide the value in the last column of the table by 365. Let's do it with the latest value:

$$Daily\,interest = \frac{-1.4\%}{365} = \frac{-1.4}{365 \cdot 100}$$

Next, we should multiply the daily interest by the trading size. In our example, we trade 10,000 AUD, so we multiply the daily interest by 10,000. Finally, if we want to know the swap value in USD, not AUD, we should multiply the result by the actual exchange rate, that is, the market price of AUD/USD.

I think here it's become obvious that swap rates change not only because central banks change their interest rates but also because the market price of the currency pair changes. For our rough estimate, we may use the 52-week average of the spot price, and thus multiply the final result by 0.68. Thus, in our example, we get:

$$Swap rate = daily interest * 10,000 * 0.68 = -\$0.26$$

How do we interpret this result?

This result means that if we buy 10,000 AUD/USD and hold this position overnight, then we pay 26 cents. Looks negligible, but only because a trading size of 10,000 is quite small: don't forget that the FX market is traded on margin, and even with a retail leverage of 30:1, you need only $300 in the account to be able to open a position of $10,000. Quite often, retail trades are placed with 100,000 of base currency and institutional trades normally *start* with 1,000,000. If you hold a position of 100,000 overnight, you pay $2.6 – not much, but if you do it every night, then it gradually grows into a considerable amount. And if you trade as an institutional trader, then you start paying $26 every night, averaging $130 a week, and so on.

Alright, I hear you saying, *"it's clear that we pay when we are long AUD/USD, but if we're short, we should receive an equivalent amount every night, shouldn't we?"*

Unfortunately, real life is (as always) more complicated than any theory. The issue is that every broker adds their own markup to the overnight rate. There's no surprise in it: brokers also have to borrow to provide you with a credit line, and they can't borrow directly from a central bank, so for them, the interest rate will already be higher. This means that the negative values become even more negative, and positive values become... well, in most cases also negative! I encourage you to check the overnight swap rates with any broker, compare them with our calculated *fair values*, and see the difference. In reality, as of today (at the beginning of January 2023), the best overnight swap rate I could find was -$5.30 for a long position and -$0.30 for a short one for a trading size of 100,000 AUD/USD.

Also, keep in mind that on Wednesday, you will be charged extra because we trade spot, and the spot is delivered on a T+2 basis (again, see the *FX instruments* section of *Chapter 3, FX Market Overview From a Developer's Standpoint*).

We can use an estimate that in the absolutely worst case, we pay about 0.5 pips for the luxury of holding the position overnight. Pips – because, I hope, you remember that using a trading size of 10,000 AUD/USD allows us to interpret the result both in dollars and pips, which is very convenient for further calculations.

And now! Finally! Let's sum up all costs we've discussed so far.

Trading Costs Calculation

Total trading costs per trade = 1 pip spread + 1 pip slippage + 0.21 pips commission + 0.5 pips overnight swap * 20 days in position on average = 12.21 pips.

This is what we must subtract from the average trade, and if the remainder is still positive, then our strategy can make money, at least on paper.

Obviously, now we can see that an average trade of 79 pips is huge because all the costs, even taken with excess, hardly make 15% of the expected return. This is a truly great result, and it's achievable only for long-term trading strategies.

Note

There is a strong relationship between the strategy's position in the market, the average trade value for such a strategy, and the volatility of its returns: the longer we stay in a position, the greater the average trade we can expect and, unfortunately, the volatility of returns for such a strategy will also be greater. This fact can even be proven mathematically as a theorem, but it lies way beyond the scope of this book, so I suggest taking it for granted – for now.

All in all, the trading costs analysis shows that our strategy is very robust in this regard (and believe me, most strategies you will develop yourself in the future won't pass even this first test – but it's normal for research and development). What's next?

Next, we have to revisit a couple of concepts that we already mentioned earlier in the book.

Measuring performance – alpha and beta revisited

In *Chapter 9, Trading Strategies and Their Core Elements*, we touched on two important concepts that are mainly used to analyze performance: alpha and beta. Back then, we looked at them from a slightly different angle: we were in search of opportunities to systematically make profits in the market and considered all these metrics only from that standpoint. However, don't forget that they were originally suggested for evaluating the performance of an investment – if put in simple words, to judge whether the investment outperforms or *beats* the market or not.

Note

I will intentionally simplify the concepts of both alpha and beta and avoid exact mathematical formulae for their calculation. Using them requires good command of the theory of probabilities, and I know from my past experience that it's the very domain of mathematics that causes a lot of confusion to many readers. So forgive me, math purists, but I just want these relatively complex subjects to be understood by everyone.

Let's start with alpha as the more common and simplistic metric.

Alpha in investment and trading

Alpha stands for excess returns; this is the very metric that ultimately says whether you beat the market within the given time span.

Normally, in capital management, alpha is calculated according to the following formula:

$$\alpha = R - R_f - \beta \cdot \left(R_b - R_f\right)$$

Here, R means the return of a portfolio, R_f denotes the so-called *risk-free* rate of return, R_b represents the return of the benchmark, and β represents the volatility of returns (see the following).

Sounds complex?

Well, it's not as complex as it seems at first glance. We only need to understand the meaning of each element of this equation better.

Return, in general, refers to how much money was gained (or lost) per given period of time. Normally, in portfolio investment, returns are estimated by month and by year, in active trading, we also consider daily returns – in some cases, even more granular time frames.

It should be intuitively clear with the return of an investment or a trading strategy, but what is a *risk-free* rate of return? How anything in trading or investing can be risk-free?

Usually, a risk-free return is understood as the difference between the current respective bond yield and the inflation rate. For investments in the United States and denominated in US dollars, we can use Treasury bonds. For investments in the Eurozone and denominated in the euro, usually, German bonds are considered a *risk-free* investment, and so on.

And now we again see a *benchmark*. As we discussed in the *Using currency rates as benchmark* section of *Chapter 9, Trading Strategies and Their Core Elements*, finding a proper benchmark for FX trading can be quite problematic. Therefore, we normally use the change in the price of the currency pair itself to see whether our strategy could do it any better than the market.

If we want to illustrate all of this as simplistically as possible, we could use a linear model of both the market growth and returns with an assumption that $R_f = 0$ (no free lunch ever, right?) and $\beta = 1$ (the volatility of returns is exactly the same as the volatility of the market itself). If the *x*-axis represents time, for example, days, and the *y*-axis represents the return, then alpha happens to be the difference between the values of the two functions:

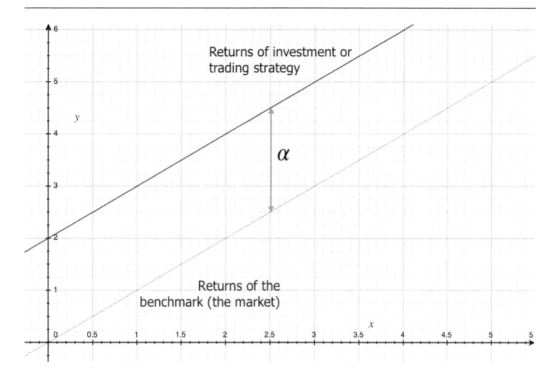

Figure 13.1 – Simplified model of returns and alpha

To make the story about alpha complete, I should note that sometimes, especially analyzing the performance of active trading strategies rather than investment, alpha is supposed to be derived from the classical form of a linear equation:

$$y = \alpha x$$

As in our previous example, this is a very, very simplified model that shows how returns grow over time. If we assume that the market itself grows linearly and its growth rate is equal to 1 (y = x), then any $\alpha > 1$ would mean that the investment's returns grow faster than the market and that the investment actually beats the market. Similarly, any $\alpha < 1$ would mean that the investment's returns grow slower than the market itself. In this case, even if this investment brings some money to an account, it does not beat the market: you can potentially make more by simply buying the market itself (stocks, commodities, and even currencies can constitute the respective market benchmark). This simple assumption is shown in the following figure:

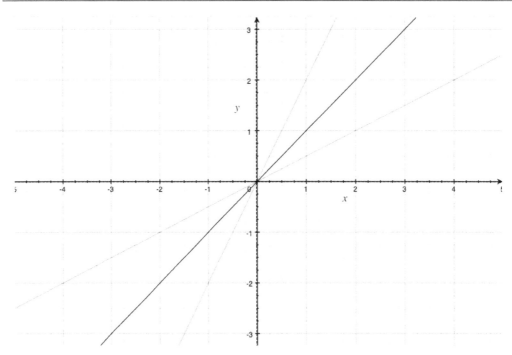

Figure 13.2 – Linear functions with $\alpha = 1$, $\alpha > 1$, and $\alpha < 1$

The benchmark (the market) is assumed to grow at a rate of $\alpha = 1$ (black line). Any function with $\alpha > 1$ (in our example $\alpha = 2$) will grow faster, and any function with $\alpha < 1$ ($\alpha = 0.5$ in our example) will grow slower than the benchmark.

> **Note**
>
> Such an interpretation of alpha is not common and cannot be used in classical capital management theory. I provided this unusual point of view only for your reference.

Now, I hope it's more or less clear with alpha in all its aspects, but what about beta?

Beta

Beta is a measure of the volatility of returns. Remember the analogy of a road trip that we discussed in the *Beta – earn on volatility* section of *Chapter 9, Trading Strategies and Their Core Elements*? Not only the fact that we were able to get from point A to point B matters but also how we got there, so how straight or winding the path was. If we want to illustrate this comparison, we can again use a linear function as the example of a straight path and the same linear function with a periodical component added to it as the example of a path with extra volatility:

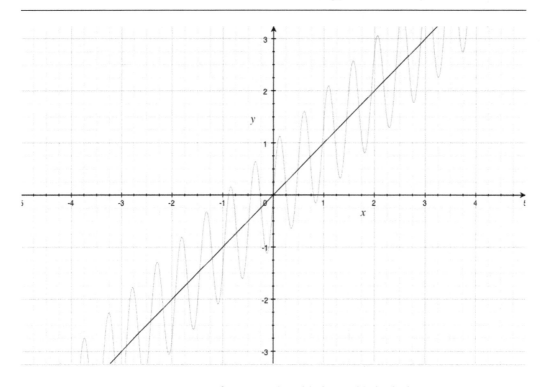

Figure 13.3 – Linear function with and without added volatility

We can see that both functions *get* from point **(0,0)** to **(2,2)**, but the linear one does it *faster*. Now, let's imagine that both graphs illustrate the return on a certain investment. Then, the *x*-axis means time and the *y*-axis means the amount of money earned or lost during a certain period. Therefore, when we see that the curve is growing, this means that money is accumulating in the account, and when we see it going down, this means that the account is losing money.

Now, let's take periodical snapshots of the activity in our sample investments and measure two metrics:

- How much the value changed from the time of the previous snapshot until the time of the current snapshot

- How much the value changed during the snapshot inside a given period of time

In the following figure, I zoomed in and marked the corresponding values on the graph:

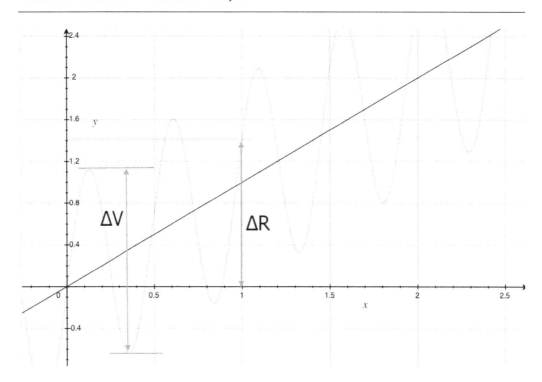

Figure 13.4 – Returns and their volatility in a simplified model

In this example, we check the return (**R**) and volatility (**V**) at every integer value (1, 2, 3, and so on).

Let the difference between the previous value of the return (measured at 0) and the current value (1) be **ΔR**. In our example, $\mathit{\Delta R} \approx 1.4$.

Then we notice that the return first grows (from 0 to approximately 1.3) then falls down to about -0.65, then grows again to 1.6, then falls down to -0.15, and, finally, grows back to about 1.4. So, during the snapshot period from 0 to 1, the function already made several extremes, both maximums and minimums. Let **ΔV** be the difference between a local maximum and the next local minimum, which immediately follows this maximum (not vice versa!) In our example, $\mathit{\Delta V} \approx 1.8$.

The value of **ΔV** is called **drawdown** and is one of the key performance metrics of any investment or trading strategy.

So, how can we now estimate (very roughly, but anyway) the beta of the returns?

We are interested in the ratio of the return to drawdown:

$$\frac{\mathit{\Delta R}}{\mathit{\Delta V}}$$

We want the value of this ratio to be as high as possible. If we have a choice between two or more strategies, then we prefer the one for which the ratio of return to drawdown is greater.

In our example, the obvious choice would be a *linear* strategy because it delivers only gains without a single loss down the road. This means that this strategy has a value of $\Delta V = 0$ and thus the ratio in question is infinite. Of course, it never happens in reality, but it gives a clear idea about the utopian goal of any investor.

The second strategy features a ratio of return to a drawdown of about 0.77. This means that although this strategy makes money, the investor will have quite a few desperate moments until it gets to the positive zone: the volatility of returns of this strategy is greater than the return itself!

The approach that we have just considered is, of course, a very simplified one. In practical applications, beta is normally calculated as the volatility of returns compared not to returns on the same strategy or investment but to a benchmark, as with alpha and other investment performance metrics. Besides that, it would be more correct to evaluate not only the ratio of return to drawdown for the entire investment or trading period but to also calculate them first for a number of smaller periods, then average them, and finally calculate the dispersion of these values, thus understanding how this ratio changes over time or how consistent the volatility of returns is for this given strategy or investment.

However, I promised to keep things simple in this book and not require specific knowledge from the theory of probabilities, so we won't go that far during our first acquaintance with performance metrics. If you want to deep-dive into this very interesting and very complex subject, I recommend starting with a framework article at Investopedia (`https://www.investopedia.com/investing/measure-mutual-fund-risk`) and following all links provided there: very quickly, you will find yourself in the jungles of means, standard deviations, variance, and covariance, but in the long run, it's going to be quite a rewarding experience.

> **Important note**
> The suggested estimate of beta is not the same beta used in the classical capital management formula earlier in this chapter. It is introduced here only to explain the essence of the volatility of returns and better understand the basic performance metrics discussed next.

Alright, we have refreshed our memory about both alpha and beta, but did you notice that so far we have been talking about alpha as a performance metric for investments? Is there any difference between investing and trading, and can we still use alpha to assess the performance of trading strategies?

The main difference between the two is that investing assumes buying an asset and holding it for a long time, while trading means that you actively buy and sell the asset during the same period of time. Therefore, with investment, we can potentially outperform the market by choosing assets that perform better than the broad market (by an index or any other benchmark), and in active trading, we try to outperform the asset itself by holding it for shorter periods of time.

The main problem with using both alpha- and beta-related metrics to analyze the performance of trading strategies is the lack of relevant benchmarks suitable for this purpose. We already mentioned this problem in *Chapter 9, Trading Strategies and Their Core Elements*, and pointed out that it would make more sense to use specific FX benchmarks to assess the performance of FX trading strategies.

However, sometimes it is really difficult to find a suitable benchmark to compare apples to apples: for example, if we try to assess the performance of an intraday strategy that opens and closes multiple positions per day ideally, we should compare it to a similar intraday strategy used as a reference, but finding such a reference will be quite a challenge by itself! So, what do we do in order to adequately assess the performance of a trading strategy given that we don't have a benchmark as such?

Well, this is why most of the performance metrics used to evaluate the trading strategy performance only use that same performance data, sometimes in conjunction with the asset price data. These metrics can be considered *proxies* to *true alpha* or *true beta*, and if put together, they can give quite a comprehensive analysis, which helps answer the main question of trading: whether to put money at stake with this strategy or not.

Let's start with metrics that aim at estimating the alpha of a trading strategy returns.

Net profit versus buy and hold

This is the first thing to check after you have confirmed that the average trade is greater than the required absolute minimum to cover all trading costs. Buy and hold means that we buy the same quantity of the currency that we use in backtest, hold the position for the entire period of the backtest, and then look at the final **profit and loss (PnL)**, on the last bar of the price time series. In our case, we should *buy* 10,000 AUD/USD, hold it for approximately 3 years, and look at the return from this single trade.

I recommend comparing not only the net profits of the strategy and buy and hold but also the equity curves: this will give us an idea about the change in the equity over time in both scenarios.

Let's quickly create the equity curve of a buy-and-hold strategy. As you remember, we isolated the trade logic into a separate function, tradeLogic(), so we only should rewrite the part between the Trade logic starts here and Trade logic ends here comments while keeping the rest of the code untouched. It's a good idea to make a copy of the tradeLogic() function first and give it a proper name – for example, buyAndHold(), before making changes to the code:

```
if System.market_position == 0:
    close = bar['Close']
    order = {}
    order['Type'] = 'Market'
    order['Price'] = close
    order['Side'] = 'Buy'
```

```
order['Size'] = 10000
orders_stream.put(order)
```

As you can see, the only difference between `buyAndHold()` and `tradeLogic()` is that we removed all trade logic and replaced it with a single trade placed on the very first bar. No other trades are placed for the rest of the backtesting.

If we now run the backtest, we will see the equity curve of our hypothetical buy-and-hold *investment*. Note that the *x*- and *y*-axes mean the same as in the simplified illustrations: the *x*-axis represents time – in our backtest, days (because we use daily data in our backtest) – and the *y*-axis represents the returns.

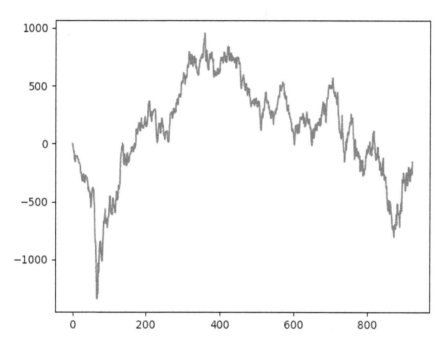

Figure 13.5 – Buy-and-hold returns, AUD/USD

And the output in the console reads as follows:

```
Total trades: 1
Average trade: -153.9999999999997
```

This means that if we bought 10,000 Australian dollars for US dollars 3 years ago (and the historical price data starts in 2020), then we would have had a generous return of -153 dollars (!), which equals -1.53% (!) in 3 years. And this is even without saying that we had a drawdown of almost 1,500 dollars or 15% before we achieved such an incredible result.

Well, I hope you got my sarcasm: now you can see why I always become very skeptical when I hear anything about *investments* in currency markets: even in such a brief timespan of 3 years, it's very hard to find a currency pair that could deliver returns comparable to the *normal* state of a stock market (by *normal* here, I mean the bull market, when stock indices grow every year, quarter, and sometimes even every month. Let's forget about bear markets for now, not to spoil such an idealistic picture). Without actively managing the positions (buying *and* selling), it would be impossible to achieve any acceptable returns in the FX markets. Let's do the switch back – replace the buyAndHold() function with tradeLogic() and run the backtest again:

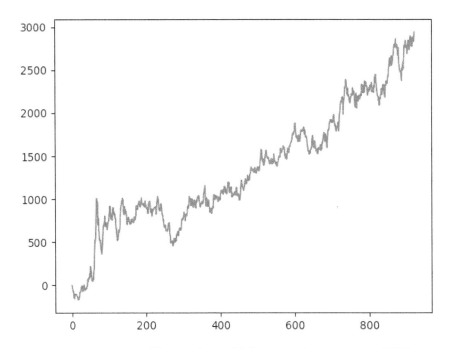

Figure 13.6 – Returns of the sample trend-following trading strategy, AUD/USD

And the console output now reads as follows:

```
Total trades: 37
Average trade: 79.40540540540536
```

This means that for the same test period of 3 years, we made almost $3,000 by trading exactly the same size of 10,000 AUD/USD. Without any comments, it's evident how this result surpasses the buy-and-hold strategy: it equals 30% in 3 years compared to -1.53% for buy-and-hold.

Let's calculate an estimate of alpha for our trend-following strategy. The strategy return is 30%, the *risk-free* rate of return could be estimated at -2.85% (3 years of treasury bills at 4.25% yield minus inflation at 7.1% in 2022), the benchmark return at -1.53%, and given that the beta, or the volatility of returns, is at least no worse than the benchmark (which is obviously the case just looking at the two figures here), then the alpha for our strategy is about 31.53% in 3 years.

So, we can say that the strategy has passed two checks: it has an average trade value that allows the strategy to actually trade (not only on paper), but it also generates alpha (outperforms the benchmark) and its returns are comparable to those of a conventional investment (for example, investing in the S&P 500 ETF would return about 18% in the same 3 years).

Let's now move on to assessing the beta, or the volatility of returns. As noted previously, we are not going to provide the classical definition of beta used in capital management because it requires specific knowledge from the theory of probabilities. Instead, we will consider drawdown, the third most important metric after average trade and overall returns, and show why it can be used as a *proxy* to assess the volatility of returns.

Drawdown

According to an article published on CFI (Maximum Drawdown: `https://corporate financeinstitute.com/resources/capital-markets/maximum-drawdown/`), "A maximum drawdown (MDD) measures the maximum fall in the value of the investment, as given by the difference between the value of the lowest trough and that of the highest peak before the trough." We already saw an illustration of the drawdown in *Figure 13.4* and it is quite easy to understand. However, real equity curves never look like ideal sine waves used for illustration purposes, so drawdown is not a constant value; it changes over time and these changes also may say a lot about the volatility of returns.

So, we want to calculate a new time series according to the following algorithm:

1. Let the first (leftmost) data point in the equity curve be the current historical high (maximum).
2. Compare the next value with the current one.
3. If the next value is greater than the current, let the next value be the new historical high.
4. If the next value is less than the current, store the difference between this value and the current historical high as the drawdown.
5. Finish updating the drawdown when the equity curve makes a new historical high and repeat the entire algorithm.

As you can see, if we work with time series or any other sequences, iterables, arrays, and so on, we can more efficiently realize the same calculation in just two steps:

1. Form a new sequence in which the next element is either equal to the preceding one or greater.
2. Subtract the original sequence from the resulting sequence.

This will give us a sequence of drawdowns.

To better understand what the drawdown is and how it is calculated, let's consider a simple example.

Let's create a list containing a sequence of non-negative values:

```
a = [1,2,4,3,5,8,7,6,2,9,10]
```

Then, prepare an empty list where we're going to store the result:

```
m = [] # m stands for 'maximum'
```

And initialize a variable that is supposed to store the current high (maximum) in the initial list:

```
x = 0
```

Now, we iterate over all elements in the list, a, compare them to the last maximum value, choose the new maximum, update it, and append it to the resulting list, m:

```
for el in a:
    if el > x:
        x = el
    m.append(x)
```

If you did everything correctly, then m should contain the following sequence: [1, 2, 4, 4, 5, 8, 8, 8, 8, 9, 10]. If we now subtract the original sequence, a, from m, then we get the series of drawdowns:

```
[x - y for x, y in zip(a, m)]
```

This returns [0, 0, 0, -1, 0, 0, -1, -2, -6, 0, 0]. This is the list of drawdowns calculated at every data point in the original sequence.

We can verify the result by scanning the data in the original sequence from left to right. The second element in a is greater than the first, so the drawdown is 0 and the latest high is 2. The third element is greater than the latest high, so the drawdown is again 0, and the latest high is updated to 4. The fourth element in a is less than the latest high by 1, so the fourth element in m is -1, and the latest high remains 4. You can continue this calculation and make sure that all the drawdown values are calculated correctly – and that you now fully understand the meaning of the drawdown.

There is a faster way of doing exactly this by using numpy arrays:

```
import numpy as np
a = [1,2,4,3,5,8,7,6,2,9,10]
m = np.maximum.accumulate(a)
dd = a - m
```

This simple code will generate the same sequence of drawdowns as before, the only difference now is that it's going to be a numpy array rather than a native Python list:

```
>>> dd
array([ 0,   0,   0,  -1,   0,   0,  -1,  -2,  -6,   0,   0])
```

Now that we fully understand what drawdown is and how it can be calculated, let's do it for the equity time series of our trend-following strategy.

Firstly, and above all, we should add `import numpy` at the very beginning of the code, among other imports.

Next, let's slightly modify the very end of the backtester code, where `matplotlib plot()` is called:

```
dd = System.equity_timeseries - np.maximum.accumulate(System.
equity_timeseries)
plt.subplot(2,1,1)
plt.plot(System.equity_timeseries)
plt.subplot(2,1,2)
plt.plot(dd)
plt.show()
```

You can see a new command: `plt.subplot()`. It is used to place multiple charts or graphs on the same canvas (see *Chapter 8, Data Visualization in FX Trading with Python*, to refresh your memory regarding the object model of `matplotlib` plots). To save time and space here, I recommend you have a glance at a tutorial at `https://www.w3schools.com/python/matplotlib_subplot.asp` to understand the meaning of `subplot()` parameters.

Now, if you have done everything correctly and run the backtest again (using, of course, the same source price data!), you will now see the same equity curve as before, but with the drawdown chart beneath it:

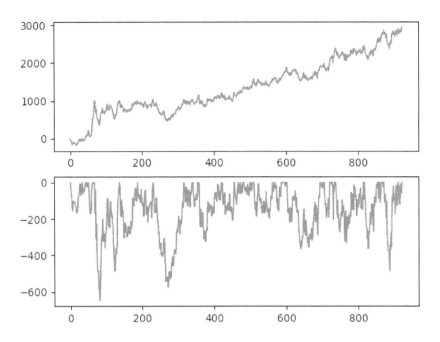

Figure 13.7 – Equity curve and drawdown of the sample trend-following strategy

Now, we know a lot more about our strategy, especially about the risks associated with it. Even without doing precise calculations (which can be quite complex) and taking only a surface look at the resulting graphs here, we can make a number of important conclusions, which we are going to consider in the very next section.

Risk/reward and return on drawdown

First of all, we want to understand whether drawdowns are distributed more or less evenly during the backtest period. This is very important because if there are significant drawdowns that appear at random, then it's a warning sign: this means that there are some occasional processes in the market that are not accounted for by the model used in the trading strategy, and sooner or later, one of these processes may destroy the strategy completely.

Before we proceed, I recommend you refresh your memory about the mean and standard deviation, which we discussed in the *Volatility indicators* section of *Chapter 6, Basics of Fundamental Analysis and Its Possible Use in FX Trading*.

We can quickly analyze the result by running the backtest in an interactive console and entering the following after the initial chart is displayed:

```
mean_dd = dd.mean()
```

This calculates the mean drawdown. The following command returns the standard deviation of drawdowns:

```
std_dd = dd.std()
```

Now, add three lines to the plot: the mean drawdown, mean minus 1 sigma, and mean minus 2 sigma:

```
plt.plot(range(len(dd)), [mean_dd] * len(dd))
plt.plot(range(len(dd)), [mean_dd - std_dd] * len(dd))
plt.plot(range(len(dd)), [mean_dd - 2*std_dd] * len(dd))
```

If you have done everything correctly, you should see something like this in the following figure:

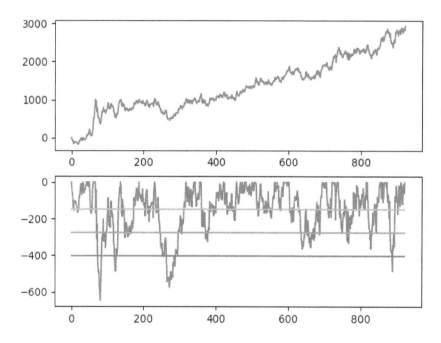

Figure 13.8 – Mean minus 1 and 2 sigma of drawdowns

How do we interpret the result?

Drawdowns that lie outside of 2 sigma (the bottom horizontal line in the chart) are so-called outliers. They deserve special attention because usually, they are caused by reasons not accounted for in the strategy logic. In our case, fortunately, they are not numerous and at least the very first one is easily explained by the market volatility at the beginning of the COVID-19 panic.

Drawdowns between mean and 2 sigma are distributed more or less evenly over time. This means that they are just systematic drawdowns caused by the imperfections of the market model used in the strategy.

Most of the drawdowns are above the mean value and again, they are distributed evenly along the time axis – so, this gives us hope that the market model is adequate for the market.

After an initial visual qualitative analysis, let's go to numbers. The maximum drawdown (which also can be found by typing `min(dd)` in an interactive console or adding `print(min(dd))` to the code) of our strategy is 646 pips. Is it large or small? If you invest $10,000 and temporarily lose $646, this means that you risk about 6.5% of your account. This is a moderate-to-low-risk, which is considered acceptable to most investors.

However, a more important metric is the risk-to-reward ratio. The meaning of this metric is quite intuitive: the less the ratio, the less the volatility of returns and thus the less the overall risk of investing.

Let's do the simple math for our example. The total net profit of our strategy is slightly above 3,000 pips in 3 years. Even if we assume that it generates the same return each year (which is not the case), then on average, it returns about 1,500 pips per annum. This means that by risking $646, we may expect about $1,500, so the risk/reward ratio is about 0.43.

The sacramental question again: is that *good* or *bad*?

Generally speaking, any risk/reward ratio less than 1 is good because this means that you risk less than you may expect to win. There are debates on the *optimal* value of the risk/reward ratio (along with *optimal* values for all other performance metrics) but most authors agree that any value less than 0.5 gives a potential green light to investing in a financial product.

> **Note**
> Strictly speaking, the question about the risk/reward ratio is also closely connected to the problem of benchmarking. Unfortunately, this subject is too wide and too complex to be carefully considered in this book, but the provided rough estimates can work quite well as starting points for your research.

Another metric that is essentially the inverted risk/reward ratio is the return on drawdown. The only difference is that the latter is usually calculated as a percentage and not as a fractional value. The meaning of this metric is also very intuitive: it means the expected premium for the risk – the payoff we expect if we risk a certain amount of money.

In our example, the return on drawdown equals 1,500/646*100 = 232.2% in 2 years. In other words, you may expect about twice the amount of risk you can afford to allocate to this strategy.

At this point, you may exclaim, *"why, but earlier in this chapter, we calculated an alpha of only about 30%, how come now we get such a huge return?"*

This is probably the most confusing part of FX trading and we will consider it in detail in the very next section.

The power of leverage – how much do I need to trade it?

Finally, we are about to answer the main question of any investor: how much do I have to have in my trading account and how much can I expect from it?

Before we continue, let me draw your attention to the following important fact about FX trading.

> **Note**
>
> Do not confuse the return on investment as a performance metric with the actual return on actual investment!

To understand it, we should again recall the essence of margin trading and how it differs from regular investment and trading without margins.

When you invest or trade without margin, you can buy only that amount of assets (equities, commodities, whatever) that cost the amount of money in your account. For example, if you trade stocks, and a stock's price is $100, and you have $10,000 in your account, then you can buy no more than 100 shares of the stock (actually a bit less because of trading costs).

However, if you trade on margin, then you are supposed to have only a fraction of the full required amount, and the rest will be provided as a credit line by your broker. In our example with AUD/USD, if you have 10,000 US dollars in your account and your broker provides you with a retail leverage of 30:1, then you potentially can buy as much as $30 * 10,000/(AUDUSDrate) \approx 440,000$ Australian dollars.

The ability to purchase magnitudes more assets than otherwise possible with the amount in your trading account makes margin trading very attractive to many novice traders. However, leverage is a double-edged sword. Let's do some simple math and see why it may be quite dangerous.

Do you remember that we consistently calculated everything in pips, and not in money? Now we can benefit from this because we only need to adjust the pip value according to the chosen leverage and scale all the performance metrics.

So, when we traded 10,000 AUD/USD, the net return was about 3,000 pips, and the maximum drawdown was 646 pips. If we had the same $10,000 in our account, that would mean that we traded without leverage, and for unleveraged trading, the return indeed would make about 30% while the drawdown would remain acceptably low, around 6.5%.

Now, we trade with a leverage of 30:1. This means that a pip value now equals $30, not $1. Then, the return would make $30 * 3000 = $90,000 – what a handsome profit! If we present this figure as percent growth over the initial investment, we will have an incredible value of 900% in just 3 years. So, margin trading is a great benefit and the way to go, isn't it?

But we forgot about the drawdown. We also have to scale it up, as now 1 pip costs $30. This way, a drawdown of 646 pips translates into $30 * 646 = $19,380.

Oops.

The drawdown now is twice as much as the total initial capital in the account! This means that in reality, we would have never reached the expected return. Moreover, instead of making a profit, we would have lost all money in our account and faced a catastrophe notoriously known as a *margin call*: the situation when the broker calls for adding funds to your account because otherwise, the open position cannot be maintained. Most retail brokers do not wait until clients add funds to their accounts and simply liquidate such a position with a loss. Therefore, if we traded our strategy with a leverage of 30:1, we would have lost all money in the account during the very first drawdown.

So, how do we choose the acceptable leverage?

With margin trading, we normally start from the opposite end. Instead of calculating the projected returns from the strategy metrics, first of all, we try to estimate a leverage that would allow our positions to remain open during the entire trading period.

We know that the maximum drawdown is 646 pips and we have $10,000 in a trading account. Thus, the maximum possible leverage should make the pip value no greater than 10,000/646, which is about $15. Therefore, the absolute maximum possible leverage is 15:1, which is twice as low as the 30:1 offered by the broker.

Now, let's have a critical look at the result.

Can we trade our strategy with leverage of 15:1? Theoretically yes, practically no because in this case, the drawdown would make up 100% of the trading account. I can't imagine any trader, not commenting on investors, who would be able to withstand such a drawdown, even just psychologically.

In reality, the calculation of the right leverage is performed in the following sequence:

1. Define the maximum level of losses. This is not the maximum drawdown of a strategy, but the maximum drawdown acceptable by the investor.
2. Calculate the pip value so that this acceptable level of losses would equal the strategy drawdown.
3. Define leverage as the ratio of the projected pip value to the original pip value.
4. Define the trading size as the original trading size multiplied by the leverage.

Let's calculate the leverage for our strategy with the assumption that an average investor can afford to withstand a drawdown of 10% of the initial investment. Let's also assume that the initial investment is $10,000. Therefore, the maximum loss in the account should not ever exceed $1,000. With a maximum strategy drawdown of 646 pips, the value of 1 pip can be equal to $1,000/646 = $1.54. So, we use leverage of just 1.5:1 (not 15:1, not 30:1, and of course not 100:1 as offered by many brokers!) Now, we recall that a pip value of $1 is obtained when we trade $10,000 per trade. We multiply the original trading size (10,000) by the leverage (1.5) and we get only 15,000 AUD/USD.

And what about returns? Previously we calculated two metrics – alpha and return on drawdown – and they gave two very different values: about 30% in the former case and over 200% in the latter. With our acceptable level of losses of 10% and leverage of 1.5:1, we expect a return of 3,000 pips * $1.5 = $4,500 in 2 years. This equals 45% of the initial investment of $10,000.

Now, let's cover the key takeaways from everything we discussed in this chapter.

> **Note**
>
> Alpha is calculated for an unleveraged investment and gives the lowest estimate of possible returns.
>
> Return on drawdown is calculated for the maximum possible leverage and gives the upper estimate of possible returns (assuming that the drawdown may reach 100% of the initial investment).
>
> The realistic return is calculated based on the chosen risk level and is always between alpha and the return on the drawdown.

Summary

In this chapter, we familiarized ourselves with the most basic yet essential performance metrics. We understand now that there are three main aspects that help assess the strategy performance: trade analysis, alpha-related metrics such as returns, and beta-related metrics such as the volatility of returns and analysis of drawdowns. We learned about the main factors that always have a negative impact on performance, such as spread, slippage, commission, and overnight swaps, and we saw how we can realistically account for them in our assessment.

We have had a surface peek into the basics of capital management and considered alpha and beta, in a simplified form, but at least in a helpful enough way to improve our judgments regarding strategy. Finally, we carefully considered the leverage, saw its double-edged nature, and adopted the correct way of choosing the leverage for markets traded on margin, such as FX.

Of course, this chapter is only an introduction to the vast, complex, but interesting world of capital management and risk assessment, as this entire book is only an introduction to the world of systematic FX trading in general. However, even the basic facts and techniques considered in this book are enough to start your own homework. Hopefully, this homework is going to be perpetual – because any successful trader, in the long run, is a perpetual student of the market.

I encourage you to test any idea you may come across – now that you know how to do it, critically analyze the results – using the approach outlined in this chapter, and continue your studies, using my remarks *"it is unfortunately outside the scope of this book"* as invitations to learn more yourself. One day, you may find that you operate a portfolio of various strategies running in a large number of markets, bringing you both mental satisfaction from decent work and quite a significant material reward.

14
Where to Go Now?

Although the previous chapter sounded like the end of the book, I thought it would be unfair to leave you without giving some guidelines regarding further development of your knowledge and skills in FX markets and creating trading algorithms (algo). Unlike previous chapters, where each chapter was dedicated to a single large topic, this one is a collection of short stories about different aspects of FX algo trading, aiming to provide you with starting points for further research.

Mastering any complex subject requires effort and trading is probably the most time- and labor-consuming activity, which requires a very special attitude combining the mindsets of a scientist and a businessman. Any successful trading strategy or algorithm is a result of many hours of work, of which only 10-20% is spent on actual coding, debugging, and refactoring; the majority of time is always spent on studying the markets, in search of trading ideas and endless trial-and-error proofs of concept. This chapter will give you hints both on finding your own edge in the market and making your trading apps more robust.

Don't forget that we are all perpetual students of the market, and you will keep learning as long as you are in this complex yet exciting business of algo trading.

In this chapter, you will learn about the following topics:

- Implementing limit and stop orders
- The correct way to calculate the number of trades
- From trading ideas to implementation – another sample strategy using limit and stop orders
- Money management and handling multiple entries
- Revisiting strategy performance – more metrics
- More about the risks specific to algo trading
- Classical technical trading setups
- Optimization – the blessing and the curse of algo trading

Implementing limit and stop orders

In *Chapter 10, Types of Orders and Their Simulation in Python*, we considered three main types of orders: market, limit, and stop. However, so far, we have only used market orders in actual codes. Although we noted that a live trading application may not ever use stop and limit orders because they can be emulated on the client side and sent to the market as market orders when necessary, it would be definitely useful to have both types of orders implemented in the backtester to simplify the development of trading strategies.

Let's quickly recall the essence of limit and stop orders.

A **limit order** is always executed at a price equal to the order price *or better*. This means that if the market price is currently 100 and a buy limit order is sent below the market, for example, at 99, then it will be filled only when the price becomes 99 *or lower*. If a buy limit order is sent above the market, for example, at 101, then it will be executed immediately and its price will work as a cap for possible adverse price increase during the order execution.

Similarly, a **stop order** is always executed at a price equal to the order price *or worse*. Using the same example, if a buy stop order is sent below the market, then it is executed immediately, and if it is sent above the market, then it will be executed only when the market price reaches the order level. When executing a stop order, there is no limit on how the price may grow during the execution.

With sell orders, the situation is symmetrical.

When we emulate the execution of limit and stop orders using tick data, we can always check whether a certain tick satisfies the order condition and then assume it as the price at which the order was executed. However, when we work with compressed data, for example, 1 minute, 1 hour, 1 day, and so on, we have no idea at which tick the order would be actually executed. Instead, we assume that if the bar's high or low crosses the order level, then the order is supposed to be filled. *Table 14.1* summarizes all the possible fill conditions for limit and stop orders:

Type of order	Side	Fill condition	Fill price
Limit	Buy	Bar's low < order price	Minimum of the order price and the bar's open
Limit	Sell	Bar's high > order price	Maximum of the order price and the bar's open
Stop	Buy	Bar's high > order price	Maximum of the order price and the bar's open
Stop	Sell	Bar's low < order price	Minimum of the order price and the bar's open

Table 14.1 – Conditions to trigger limit and stop orders and their assumed execution price

You can see that when backtesting using compressed data, the price at which we assume the order was executed is not necessarily equal to the order price. In some cases, it can be the bar's open price. Why?

To answer this question, we should recall that the market price is not continuous, and sometimes adjacent ticks have quite a significant difference in prices between them. In a bar chart, it can be seen as an *empty space* between the bar's closed and the next bar's open. These empty spaces are called **gaps**.

Typically, gaps on bar charts in FX markets can be seen between the close of the market on Friday and its re-opening on late Sunday. Normally, these gaps are not very large, but sometimes they may be quite dramatic, especially if there was some important economic or political news during the weekend. The following graph illustrates a weekend gap for USD/JPY on February 6, 2023:

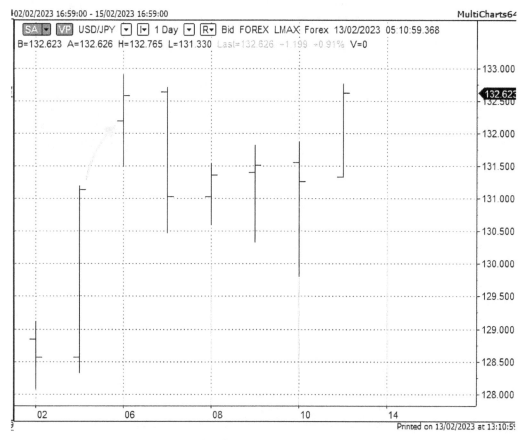

Figure 14.1 – Weekend gap in USD/JPY (chart by Multicharts)

The market closed on Friday, February 3, 2023, at **131.141** and opened on Monday, February 6, 2023, at **132.194**. The difference between these prices is shown by the gray arrow. It is more than 100 pips, which is comparable to the average daily price movement. If on Friday's close we sent a stop order to buy at, say, 131.50, then in reality, this order would have been executed only at 132.194 (and in reality, most likely even worse because of slippage during an illiquid time after the open of the market). If we sold on Friday's close, even if we protected our position with a stop loss – which is in fact just a stop order – well... we could only hope that the position size was small enough not to ruin the trading account with one huge loss.

Anyway, we now can see why we always check whether the order price is beyond the open price of the bar and why we suggest calculating the actual execution price as per the **Fill price** column in *Table 14.1*.

Now that we understand how we can realistically emulate limit and stop orders, let's proceed to coding. We will be working with the backtester code that we developed in *Chapter 11, Backtesting and Theoretical Performance*, and we are going to modify the emulateBrokerExecution() function because the order execution is isolated in it (remember the ideology of keeping the code logic modular? Now, we start to really benefit from this approach).

Presently the emulateBrokerExecution() function contains an implementation only of market orders. Let's add the following block of code directly below it:

```
if order['Type'] == 'Limit':
    if order['Status'] == 'Created':
        order['Status'] = 'Submitted'
    if order['Status'] == 'Submitted':
        if order['Side'] == 'Buy' and bar['Low'] <=
order['Price']:
            order['Status'] = 'Executed'
            order['Executed Price'] = min(order['Price'],
bar['Open'])
        if order['Side'] == 'Sell' and bar['High'] >=
order['Price']:
            order['Status'] = 'Executed'
            order['Executed Price'] = max(order['Price'],
bar['Open'])
```

I hope the code is transparent enough to see that it just implements the logic outlined in *Table 14.1*.

If you want to emulate issues with execution, which are typical for limit orders, then you may want to replace <= with < and >= with > in the code, which check whether the bar's price matches the order price. In this case, you assume that the limit order had a guaranteed fill (see *Chapter 10, Types of Orders and Their Simulation in Python*).

Now, let's add a very similar block to simulate the execution of stop orders:

```
if order['Type'] == 'Stop':
    # print('Begin processing limit order',
```

```
                    Broker.orders_list)
        if order['Status'] == 'Created':
            # Here we actually send orders to the API
            order['Status'] = 'Submitted'


        if order['Status'] == 'Submitted':
            if order['Side'] == 'Buy' and bar['High'] >=
order['Price']:
                order['Status'] = 'Executed'
                order['Executed Price'] = max(order['Price'],
bar['Open'])
            if order['Side'] == 'Sell' and bar['Low'] <=
order['Price']:
                order['Status'] = 'Executed'
                order['Executed Price'] = min(order['Price'],
bar['Open'])
```

The code is absolutely symmetrical to that of limit order simulation.

If you want to emulate slippage, which is typical for stop orders, then you may want to add or subtract a small amount from the executed price. Normally, if we trade liquid markets such as EUR/USD and send orders from 7 am until 9:50 p.m. GMT, we may not add or subtract anything. If we trade less liquid currency pairs, such as AUD/USD, then a slippage of 0.00001 to 0.00005 pips looks reasonable. If you are into more unusual pairs, such as TRY/MXN, then check the order book (if your broker provides such a pair at all!) See again *Chapter 10, Types of Orders and Their Simulation in Python*, for details on stop orders and slippage.

Note an important difference between the way we treat market, limit, or stop orders. A market order's status is set to Executed immediately as soon as the order is received by the emulateBrokerExecution() function, but the status of a limit or a stop order is first set to Submitted. The Submitted status is assigned because once generated, these orders should remain in the orders queue either until they are executed or canceled.

Now that we have added two new types of orders, we should check whether we did everything correctly. As we did in *Chapter 10* to test the execution of market orders, we will use the same source data file, which contains 1-minute bars of EUR/USD. We are only going to read the first 20 bars and execute one limit and one stop order to make sure that they are simulated correctly.

Before we do any testing, let's open the source data file in any text editor, copy the first 21 lines, and paste them into an Excel spreadsheet. Then, we will build a chart using the **Financial** chart type:

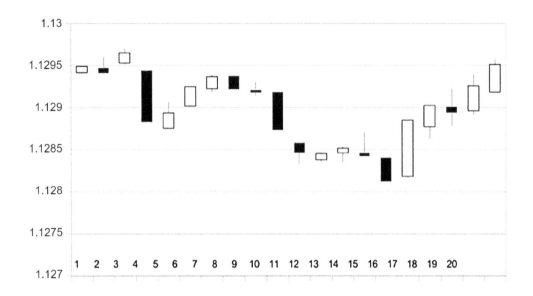

Figure 14.2 – Test chart using the first 20 bars from the EUR/USD source data file

The price data starts from about **1.1295** and falls below **1.1290** on the fourth bar. Great, let's place a buy limit order at **1.1290**. Then, we can see that the price starts growing, but eventually falls below **1.1285**, so let's place a sell stop order at this level – thus emulating a stop-loss (remember that a stop-loss protects an open position from excessive losses and is always placed on the side opposite to the position, so in our example, it will be a sell stop). This stop order should be executed on the 11th bar.

Now, let's get to coding:

1. Firstly, in the getBar() function, we set the maximum number of bars to be read from the file:

    ```
    if counter == 20:
        break
    ```

2. Next, we implement the *strategy* logic so it produces only two orders:

    ```
            if close == 1.12949 and System.market_position ==
    0:

                order = {}
                order['Type'] = 'Limit'
                order['Price'] = 1.1290
                order['Side'] = 'Buy'
                order['Size'] = 10000
                order['Status'] = 'Created'
    ```

```
orders_stream.put(order)

order = {}
order['Type'] = 'Stop'
order['Price'] = 1.1285
order['Side'] = 'Sell'
order['Size'] = 10000
order['Status'] = 'Created'
orders_stream.put(order)
```

If we now try to run the backtest, it will produce no output because we do not process an order status of **Submitted** in the processOrders() function yet. The logic of this processing is quite simple: if the order status is **Submitted**, we should return it to the orders queue.

However, we should be very careful with returning orders to the queue. Don't forget that the processOrders() function uses an internal infinite loop, which retrieves orders from the queue and finishes working only when there is no order left. If we return submitted orders back to the queue inside the same infinite loop, we will never get out of it.

Again, there are different solutions to this problem, and maybe you will suggest a better one, but let's use the most straightforward approach for now. Let's add temporary storage where we will store orders that were processed but not executed, and then put them back in the orders queue after all orders have been processed.

Let's start by adding the self.orders_buffer = [] temporary storage to the constructor of the tradingSystemMetadata class. Then, let's add the following code below the if order['Status'] == 'Executed': logical block in the processOrders() function:

```
if order['Status'] == 'Submitted':
    System.orders_buffer.append(order)
```

This will add the submitted order to the buffer. And finally, we will rewrite the except: clause as follows:

```
for order in System.orders_buffer:
    orders_stream.put(order)
    break
```

The idea is that if there are no more orders in the orders queue, it raises an exception, so we can safely return all submitted orders temporarily accumulated in the buffer back to the queue.

Now, let's run the backtest and look at the resulting equity curve:

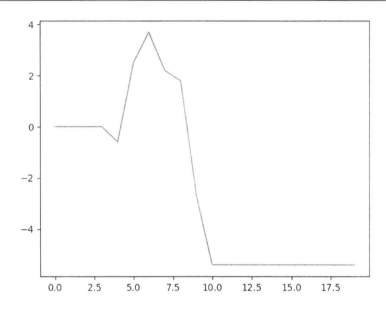

Figure 14.3 – Equity curve

We can see that the buy limit order indeed was executed on the 4th bar (remember that we count from zero), then the equity started to grow, then it dropped, and, finally, the sell stop order was executed on the 11th bar. In the console, we can check the information about the number of trades and the average trade value:

```
Total trades: 2
Average trade: -2.6999999999999247
```

But wait a moment! There's something wrong with it now. According to the price levels at which the orders were executed, the distance between the entry and the exit should be exactly 5 pips, but the average trade is -2.7 pips, which is even not an integer value. What happened? To answer this question, we should revise the way we calculate the number of trades.

The correct way to calculate the number of trades

When we were working with the trend-following strategy in *Chapter 12, Sample Strategy – Trend-Following*, we only opened new positions, and each opening closed the previously open one. This is normal for always-in-the-market strategies. In this case, indeed, the number of trades coincides with the number of executed orders.

In our example with a limit and a stop order, we use two orders to actually perform just one trade: buying and then exiting the market with a profit or loss. Therefore, we should only use the amount of entry orders to calculate the average trade. How can we distinguish between opening and closing orders?

There are multiple ways of doing that. One of the possible options would be adding another key to the order with values of `Entry` or `Exit`, but we will use a different approach: we will add a new attribute to the `tradingSystemMetadata` class, which will hold the actual number of trades, and we will update it only when the market position after the order execution is not zero, that is, the last executed order was not a closing order:

1. First, let's add `self.number_of_trades = 0` to the constructor of the `tradingSystemMetadata` class. This is where we're going to save the number of trades.

2. Next, we need to modify the way we count trades. The right place to do it is when we update the market position in the `processOrders()` function. Presently, we use code that only updates the market position and does not check whether the market position is zero or not after the execution of the last order:

    ```
    if order['Side'] == 'Buy':
        System.market_position = System.market_position +
    order['Size']
    if order['Side'] == 'Sell':
        System.market_position = System.market_position -
    order['Size']
    ```

3. Now, we're going to replace this piece of code with the following:

    ```
    if order['Side'] == 'Buy':
        System.market_position = System.market_position +
    order['Size']
        if System.market_position != 0:
            System.number_of_trades += 1
    if order['Side'] == 'Sell':
        System.market_position = System.market_position -
    order['Size']
        if System.market_position != 0:
            System.number_of_trades += 1
    ```

You can see that this code checks whether the market position changed to non-zero after the trade and only in this case increases the number of trades. Thus, if the last order only closed the position without opening a new one, it won't be taken into account.

4. The only thing to fix now is at the very end of the code, where we print the number of trades and calculate the average trade:

```
print("Total trades:", System.number_of_trades) #
introduced number_of_trades
print("Average trade:", System.equity / System.number_of_
trades)
```

5. If we now re-run the backtest, we will see the correct output:

```
Total trades: 1
Average trade: -5.399999999999849
```

Almost there! The number of trades is correct, but strangely there are 0.4 extra pips in the average trade value – and according to the levels we specified in the strategy logic, the average trade should be exactly -5 pips, not -5.4. Where does the difference come from?

6. To answer this question, we should once again critically revise the processOrders() function. When we developed it to process only market orders generated at the end of a bar, we placed the following three lines before the while True loop, which processes the orders queue:

```
System.equity += (bar['Close'] - System.last_price) *
System.market_position
System.equity_timeseries.append(System.equity)
System.last_price = bar['Close']
```

Therefore, recalculating the equity based on the bar's closing price is the first thing the function does before orders start processing. If we only use market orders, that's fine, we update the System.last_price value when we process the order and it will always coincide with the bar's close. However, now that an order can be executed anywhere between the bar's low and the bar's high, we have an extra amount of **profit and loss (PnL)** each time a limit or a stop order is executed, and this amount equals the difference between the order's executed price and the bar's close. So, we should modify the processOrders() function with the following steps:

1. Let's move the block of three lines that update the equity from the top of the code (before the while True loop) to the end (after the while True loop). See the Stop and limit orders.py code and the processOrders() function.

2. After if order['Status'] == 'Executed', let's add the following line:

```
System.equity += (order['Executed Price'] - System.last_
price) * System.market_position
```

This way, we update the equity value by multiplying the price difference between the previous bar's close (which is stored in System.last_price at the moment of execution of this line) and the price at which the order was executed by the market position, *which existed before the order was executed.* Then, at the end of the `processOrders()` function, the equity is updated once again, this time by calculating the difference between the order price and the bar's close, *multiplied by the new market position.* This gives us a perfectly precise calculation of the strategy equity and, consequently, the value of the average trade.

> **Note**
>
> I intentionally have not published the entire code of the modified backtester here in this book. My goal now is to train you in the mental process of discovering new shortcomings and suggesting solutions. After you're done with all modifications, I recommend downloading my code from GitHub and comparing it – this will give you an excellent opportunity to improve your skills in upgrading code logic, which is the most important and sensitive part of the entire development in algo trading.

3. If we run the final code now, we will get absolutely precise values:

```
Total trades: 1
Average trade: -4.999999999999449
```

Now that we have mastered limit and stop orders, let me give you several hints regarding further development of both backtesting and live trading applications.

From trading ideas to implementation – another sample strategy using limit and stop orders

Let's consider a practical application of the limit and stop orders that we have just implemented. I like using this example because it illustrates the importance of having a trading idea before writing the code and shows that trading ideas do not have to be complex. In practice, the simpler the trading idea, the greater the chance that it will work in production.

As you may remember from *Chapter 3, FX Market Overview from a Developer's Standpoint,* most FX markets undergo a bank settlement procedure, which happens at 5 p.m. New York time. The price at the settlement is very important because it's used to evaluate many other financial instruments and is used for settlement in all cash trades between any parties. So, comparing an intraday price to the last settlement price may give us an idea about the overall sentiment in this market: if it's greater than the last settlement price, then the sentiment is positive – if it's lower, the sentiment is negative.

Next, we may want to suppose that if the overall market sentiment is positive, then we can try opening a long position, and if it's negative, a short position.

Then, we have to decide when we may want to do so. Naturally, it should be the time of the next settlement because, during the day, external factors such as news breaking can move the price up and down many times. However, remember that it's impossible to send an order at exactly 5 p.m. because at that time, the market is closed and the order will be rejected. Besides that, several minutes before the settlement, the liquidity becomes thinner and thinner, so it may be problematic to trade, say, 1 minute before the settlement even with a small trading size. So, we will try entering the market 10 minutes before the settlement time.

And finally, we have to decide how long we stay in the market, or at which price we liquidate our positions. Let's not be greedy and just exit with a small profit of 5 pips. We will use limit orders to exit the position at a certain distance from the entry price – such an order is frequently referred to as a **profit target**. However, if the market develops the opposite way, we should liquidate our position with a loss, so we will use a stop order for this purpose. The question is at which level we place this stop order.

There are many opposite opinions on this subject. Many authors believe that stops should always be smaller than potential profits because otherwise, it looks like you risk more than you can potentially win. Others argue that not only the size of the win and loss matter but their probabilities are also important. Indeed, we can win a game even if the average loss is 2 times the average win if the percentage of wins is greater than 67%.

We have the luxury of quickly testing both approaches: let's first try setting the stop-loss amount the same as the profit target and then increase it to stay at the position for a longer time in the hope that sooner or later, it will reach our profit target level.

As you can see, we build a market model again, as we did in *Chapter 11*, but this time, the model doesn't aim to explain the entire price time series. Instead, this model describes only quite a short-term market process, which may take place in the market at regular intervals. Generally speaking, we can even model the entire price series this way if we find a sufficient amount of regularly appearing market processes.

So, to summarize, the trading algorithm should be as follows:

- At 5 p.m. NY time, we save the close price as the reference.
- At 4:50 p.m. NY time the next day, we compare the price to the reference. If the difference is positive, we buy. If the difference is negative, we sell.
- We set a profit target of 5 pips and a stop loss of 5 pips.
- We stay in the market until either the profit target or the stop-loss is hit.

Is that all?

No. We have to cancel the other order in the *profit target – stop-loss* pair when either of them is executed. Otherwise, the remaining order may be triggered when the market position is flat (zero), and it will open an unexpected and unwanted position that we'll be unable to manage. Orders whose execution depends on the execution of other orders are called **contingent orders**.

Contingent orders

The backtesting and live trading codes developed in this book assume that any order is sent to the broker and then is never modified. However, sometimes you want to change something in an order that has already been submitted but not executed yet. For example, you sent a stop-loss order, but the market conditions changed and you now want to increase or decrease the order price.

Our codes don't support this functionality, and not all brokers support it either. If you want to implement it, the easiest way to do so is to add a unique identifier to each order, and then refer to it in the orders queue when modification is necessary. First, you have to remove the old order from the queue and then issue a new order. This will provide compatibility with virtually any broker because this is the preferred way of modifying orders on the broker's side.

We are not going to implement a universal order management solution that requires the introduction of order IDs and appropriate order handling methods for now, as it is outside the scope of this book. We will add a small piece of code to the `processOrders()` function that clears the entire orders queue as soon as a limit or a stop order is executed. This way, we can effectively implement contingent profit targets and stop-loss orders.

> **Important note**
>
> The suggested workaround only works if we have jsut one pair of contingent orders. If you want to implement a more sophisticated strategy that utilizes multiple contingent orders, there is no other way of doing it than adding order IDs and implementing routines that handle orders individually.

To implement our simple workaround, let's add the following code to the `processOrders()` function at the end of the `if order['Status'] == 'Executed':` branch, right after `System.last_price = order['Executed Price']:`

```
if order['Type'] == 'Limit' or order['Type'] == 'Stop':
    System.orders_buffer = []
    orders_stream.queue.clear()
```

The idea of this code is that if any of the contingent orders have been executed (and remember, we add this to the processing of the **Executed** order status), then we cancel all other orders. Let me repeat once again that this workaround only works if we have just one pair of contingent orders in the orders queue and no other order is in there.

All that we now have to do is add the strategy logic. As always, we only modify the code between the `trade logic starts here` and `trade logic ends here` comments. The code is very simplistic and implements the four-step logic just described:

```
close = bar['Close']
if bar['Time'] == '23:00:00':
    ref_close = close
if bar['Time'] == '22:50:00' and System.market_position
== 0:

    order = {}
    order['Type'] = 'Market'
    order['Price'] = close
    if close < ref_close:
        order['Side'] = 'Sell'
    if close > ref_close:
        order['Side'] = 'Buy'
    order['Size'] = 10000
    order['Status'] = 'Created'
    orders_stream.put(order)

    order = {}
    order['Type'] = 'Limit'
    if close < ref_close:
        order['Side'] = 'Buy'
        order['Price'] = close - 0.0005
    if close > ref_close:
        order['Side'] = 'Sell'
        order['Price'] = close + 0.0005
    order['Size'] = 10000
    order['Status'] = 'Created'
    orders_stream.put(order)

    order = {}
    order['Type'] = 'Stop'
    if close < ref_close:
        order['Side'] = 'Buy'
        order['Price'] = close + 0.0005
```

```
    if close > ref_close:
        order['Side'] = 'Sell'
        order['Price'] = close - 0.0005
order['Size'] = 10000
order['Status'] = 'Created'
orders_stream.put(order)
```

We check whether the price is greater or less than the reference price, open a position with a market order, and immediately send a limit order to take a profit and a stop order to exit with a loss.

I am not going to consider the entire strategy code here because most of it has remained the same as developed in *Chapter 10*, and the modifications that introduced limit and stop orders were considered earlier in this chapter (see the *Implementing limit and stop orders* section). You can download the code from GitHub, analyze the changes made, and run it to make sure you get the correct results.

If we run the code using EUR/USD 1-minute bars as the source data, we will get an equity curve like this:

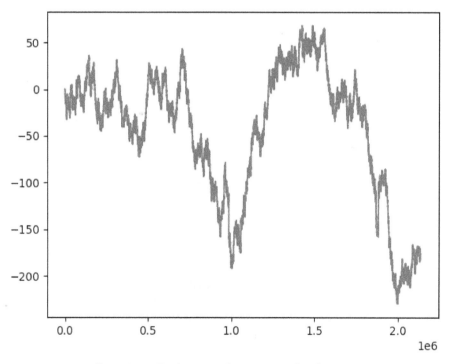

Figure 14.4 – Equity curve of a strategy with tight stops

We will also get the following basic performance metrics: 1,464 total trades with an average trade of about -0.12 pips.

Clearly, the strategy doesn't work, and we even don't have to go through an in-depth analysis of its performance. So, the idea of putting stops at the same distance as profit targets doesn't work. What if we now set the stop at 50 pips instead of 5 and run the code again?

In the following graph, you can see that now the result is dramatically different:

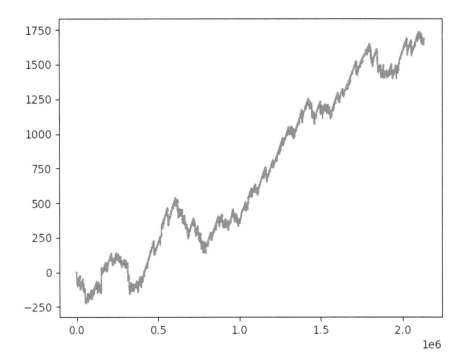

Figure 13.5 – Equity curve of a strategy with wider stops

Now, we have 1,428 trades and an average trade of 1.18 pips.

Is this strategy tradable?

First of all, we need to understand whether the average trade can cover all trading costs. The instrument traded here, the euro versus the US dollar, is by far the most liquid in the FX market and thus normally at the time of the entry, spreads are about 0.00001-0.00002 pips, with at least 100,000 to 500,000 at top of the order book (depending on the trading venue). So, we shouldn't suffer from slippage if we keep the trading size reasonable, and at first glance, it seems like we can actually trade this strategy.

I encourage you to follow all steps considered in *Chapter 13, To Trade or Not to Trade – Performance Analysis,* and make your final decision about this strategy.

> **Hint**
> Don't forget to take into consideration overnight swaps. See how they affect the strategy performance.

However, regardless of whether this strategy is tradable or not, let me emphasize once again the importance of a trading idea behind the code. Trading ideas do not come out of the blue: they are all based on various factors specific to a particular market. I'd even go further and say that *trading ideas are always based on factors that distinguish the market from a random process* in a mathematical sense. That's why we have spent so much time on market fundamentals in this book, and I hope you will be able to find many other trading ideas amid the massive heap of facts that we have considered.

So far, we have been working only with strategies that open new positions only either when the market position is zero or to reverse the currently open position. In this case, the edge of the strategy logic is in its ability to properly time entries and exits. However, there is a whole class of strategies that achieve an edge in managing multiple positions open in the same direction. In this case, we say that a strategy has an edge in terms of *money management*.

Money management and multiple entries

To give you an idea about what money management is and how it may affect strategy performance, let me tell you about probably the most famous – or infamous – kind of money management technique, known as **martingale**.

The origin of martingale is in gambling. Imagine the simplest gambling game of a coin toss. You toss the coin and if it comes up heads, you win; if it comes up tails, you lose. We can use 1 for wins and -1 for losses and the series of tosses can be represented by a sequence as follows:

```
S = {1, -1, -1, 1, -1, 1, 1, 1, -1, -1, 1, -1, ...}
```

If you put at stake an equal amount of money each time you toss the coin, we can multiply the sequence by that amount and write it like so:

```
S1 = {b, -b, -b, b, -b, b, b, b, -b, -b, b, -b, ...}
```

Here, b refers to the size of the bet. Obviously, your total win in the game is the sum of the entire series. In an idealistic model, the results of each toss are independent of each other, and the probability of the coin coming up as heads or tails is strictly 50%. Therefore in the long term, the sum of the series will always be around zero and there is no chance to win this game.

The sum of this series is indeed zero. However, things change dramatically if you start using money management in form of a martingale. After each new loss, you double your stake, and after each new win, you reset the bet size to its initial value. Then, the sequence of wins and losses transforms into the following:

```
S2 = {b, -b, -2b, 4b, -b, 2b, b, b, -b, -2b, 4b, -b, ...}
```

It's clear that now the sum of the sequence is very far from zero; in our example, it is 5b. This means that by using money management, it is possible to win a game with outcomes of equal probability.

At first glance, the martingale looks like the ultimate method to win any game, but there are two pitfalls:

- This method may work only in a game whose outcomes are truly independent. In the theory of probability, processes of this kind are called **stochastic** (see *Chapter 6, Basics of Fundamental Analysis and Its Possible Use in FX Trading*). Financial time series are frequently considered in academic research to be stochastic, at least at the tick level, but we already know that there are certain moments and even relatively long periods when this is not true: for example, after the release of important economic news, it's clear that upticks or downticks will prevail for some time, depending on the resonance of the news (see again *Chapter 6, Basics of Fundamental Analysis and Its Possible Use in FX Trading*).

- Even with a *pure* random walk process, the equal probability of outcomes is achieved only in long term (to be absolutely precise, only in an infinitely long series). If we analyze a short-term subsequence of outcomes, we may see a series of identical outcomes, and no one can guarantee that such a series will definitely end at a certain outcome number – exactly because the probability of a new outcome does not depend on previous outcomes! If you start with just $100 and double your stake with each loss, then you have to put $100 \cdot 2^n$ on the table after the n-th loss in a series. After the 3rd loss, you will have to bet $800, after the 4th loss, $1,600, and so on, and if you are so unlucky to face a series of 10 losses in a row, then you should call your bank and ask them to provide you with a credit line because now you have to bet $102,400!

I hope you understand why the martingale is so popular in books for illustrative purposes but *highly not recommended* for practical use.

In trading, there is a modification of the martingale known as **averaging down**. Let's suppose that we opened a long position, but the market price went down. Instead of liquidating the position or just waiting until the price returns to the initial level, we open long new positions, increasing the trading size and moving the average entry price down. For example, if we originally opened a long position of 1 contract at 100.00 and then added another 1 contract at 90.00, then we actually have a position of 2 contracts opened at 95.00.

Both the martingale and averaging may have only limited uses and normally, traders who use them in any form apply some restrictions to the maximum size of the open position.

Like many other authors, I used the martingale and averaging down for illustrative purposes: only because they give a very clear idea of what money management is about. There are more conservative money management strategies, and some of them are quite sophisticated. If you are interested in learning more about money management strategies and looking for a single source, I'd recommend the ultimate guide written by the money management guru Van Tharp, *Definitive Guide to Position Sizing Strategies*. If you have a more academic interest in the subject or are more inclined to collect information from various sources, I'd recommend starting with understanding the stochastic processes in general (`https://en.wikipedia.org/wiki/Stochastic_process`) and random walks in particular (`https://en.wikipedia.org/wiki/Random_walk`), and then referring to a book by Ralph Vince, *The Mathematics of Money Management: Risk Analysis Techniques for Traders* (`https://www.amazon.com/Mathematics-Money-Management-Analysis-Techniques/dp/0471547387`).

To work with money management strategies, you should be very careful with the order size. Presently, we have worked only with strategies that open a position with a fixed size and then close it before opening a new one. If you increase the position by using multiple orders in the same direction, you should carefully calculate the order size when you try to liquidate a position. If you make a mistake, the strategy will leave one or more positions open, and this may highly adversely impact the strategy's performance. So, generally, the order handling methods mentioned in this chapter are required for the correct implementation of money management strategies.

I would be happy to continue our discussions about the FX markets, systematic, and algo trading at the same level of detail as before, but unfortunately, the book's size is limited, so I will just give you general guidelines on a few more important subjects for your own further studies. They are presented here as separate topics, without any evident logical connection between them.

Strategy performance revisited – more metrics

In *Chapter 13, To Trade or Not to Trade – Performance Analysis*, we considered only the very basic performance metrics. Of course, there are many others that are no less important. I recommend starting with the nice overview from *Quantinsti* (`https://blog.quantinsti.com/performance-metrics-risk-metrics-optimization/`), implementing each metric in the code, and then you can analyze your strategies as market professionals do.

More about the risks specific to algo trading

We have already considered the main risks in any trading: operational, systemic, and transactional. Let's highlight another kind of risk that is specific to algo trading.

When you develop and backtest a strategy using compressed data, along with limit or stop orders, there is a risk that more than one of these orders will be simulated on the same bar. Typically, this happens when the order prices are too close to each other and the data resolution is not granular enough. For example, if you place a limit and a stop order at a distance of 5 pips from each other and run a backtest using daily data, then on most days, both orders should be executed during a single bar. This is what you want to avoid at all costs because the backtester has no idea about how the price has actually moved inside this single bar and therefore no one knows which of the two orders will have been triggered first and which next. So, it is extremely important to correctly choose the data resolution so that the backtesting results are realistic.

> **The rule of thumb for choosing the data resolution**
>
> Always choose the data resolution for which the average range of a bar (the difference between a bar's high and low values) is less than the distance between order prices. If you place limit or stop orders of 100+ pips, then you can use daily data. If you use limit or stop orders of 20+ pips, then most likely, a timeframe of 30 minutes may work. If you use tight stops or limits, as in the previous example, then a 1-minute resolution is the way to go. Remember that only testing using tick data can give you the ultimately correct picture, although this kind of backtest will take a lot of time.

Classical technical trading setups

In *Chapter 7, Technical Analysis and Its Implementation in Python*, we considered a number of classical technical analysis indicators, such as the RSI, a stochastic oscillator, moving averages, and Bollinger bands. We saw that each of these indicators is able to bring into focus a certain property of the price time series: for example, Bollinger bands are a volatility indicator, and moving averages are digital filters that remove higher frequencies from the price data. However, we didn't consider any classical trading setup with any of these indicators. Why?

The answer to this question is twofold. First, these setups can be found in literally any book or internet publication about technical analysis. You can start with an overview of technical indicators at Investopedia (`https://www.investopedia.com/terms/t/technicalindicator.asp`) and then follow the links to articles on specific indicators to see how they are supposed to be used to generate trading signals.

The second and more important reason we don't go into detail on these classical setups here is that none of them can create a profitable trading strategy as they are. You can try building a simple strategy by implementing any of the classical setups, then run it in multiple markets using different data resolutions, and you will see that unfortunately, none of the combinations deliver anything that could be considered satisfactory performance.

Why does this happen? And does it mean that technical analysis indicators are useless for practical trading?

This happens because all of the classical indicators were developed to highlight specific processes that took place in specific markets at a specific time.

For example, Welles Wilder, the creator of the RSI, developed this indicator when he traded commodity futures back in the 1970s. At that time, the market was relatively illiquid and was open for only a few hours a day. Only select traders had access to it and trades were placed either in the pit or by phone – and this is what commodity futures markets used to be in the 1970s. On the contrary, the present-day FX market is open 24/7 and is full of liquidity, with many diverse kinds of market participants, from big banks to retail traders. Its computerized ordering can process thousands of transactions per second. Compare these two markets and you will understand why the indicators of the old days may not indicate what they are supposed to.

The answer to the second question – whether classical technical indicators are useless these days – is negative. We still can use any or all of these indicators *if we understand what exactly they show us.* That's why I tried to focus on their meaning rather than just listing the well-known use cases, such as moving averages crossover (see `https://www.investopedia.com/terms/c/crossover.asp`) or overbought/oversold zones identified with the RSI or a stochastic oscillator (see `https://www.investopedia.com/ask/answers/121214/what-are-best-indicators-identify-overbought-and-oversold-stocks.asp`).

Nevertheless, despite the present-day electronic FX markets being very different from good old pit-traded futures markets, I would highly recommend reading the classic books written by the creators of technical indicators – because, in these books, they explain *why they suggested* a particular indicator, *which market process* they tried to identify using an indicator, and *how we are supposed to profit* from the suggested setups.

Spending a couple of days on thorough reading may be way more valuable than wasting weeks and months trying to fit a particular well-known technical trading setup to a market that it simply doesn't fit by nature. I can recommend starting with a classic by Welles Wilder Jr., *New Concepts in Technical Trading Systems*, in which he carefully explains *how he noticed certain potentially profitable market processes, how he tried to formalize them, how he eventually came to a set of technical indicators,* and *how he actually used them to make profits.* Focus on this *mental process*, not just the numbers, and you will develop a way better understanding of the process of developing a trading strategy.

Keep in mind that behind any formula and any code, there should stand a trading idea, and trading ideas can be found only in the analysis of markets, not in crunching numbers or fitting an irrelevant model to the market. In the next section, we will see why excessive fitting may not only be counterproductive but also dangerous.

Optimization – the blessing and the curse of algo trading

Do you remember how the performance of a simple overnight strategy that we created earlier in this chapter radically changed when we replaced a tight stop of 5 pips with a wider stop of 50 pips?

But this fact raises another important question: why 5 and 50 pips? Why not 6 and 45? Or 10 and 76?

Any quantitative strategy depends on the values of its parameters, and the procedure of finding the best combination of parameters that delivers the best results of the backtesting is called **optimization**.

Optimization is a massive topic. I'd even say it's overwhelmingly vast and complex. At first glance, it looks straightforward: let's find the best combination of parameter values and then run the strategy live with these very values. However, the problem is that we always test and optimize our strategies using past data. And I hope you already understood and remember well that markets are anything but stationary processes. This means that the price behavior may change in the future, and the same strategy with the same *best* combination of parameters will start losing money.

> **Note**
>
> A situation in which a strategy has been optimized using insufficient data or inappropriate logic and then starts losing money in live trading is known as **overfitting** or **curve fitting**. This is considered to be the plague of all algo trading and the reason why many discretionary traders are still skeptical about it.

How to mitigate this specific risk?

There are various workarounds, **forward testing** probably being the most popular. When running a forward test, we first optimize the strategy parameters using only a subset of the entire past market data and then generate the performance report for backtesting, run on another subset of data. For example, if we have data from 2015 to 2023, then we may want to optimize the strategy using data from 2015 to 2017 and then test using data from 2018 to 2023. The backtest using the first subset is then called **in-sample** and the backtest using the second subset is called **out-of-sample**. If the out-of-sample strategy demonstrates performance comparable to that of the in-sample, we can estimate that it will continue working even in the future (although in reality, things may be far more complex).

Another approach is to make a forward test only on a relatively small amount of out-of-sample data, then re-optimize the strategy using newer data, and repeat the forward test on another, newer portion of out-of-sample data, and so on. In our example, we can perform a forward test optimizing the strategy using data from 2015 to 2017, then run a forward test on 2018 only, then re-optimize the strategy using data from 2016 to 2018, run a forward test on 2019, and so on. Such an approach is called **walk-forward optimization**.

As you may have already realized, optimization is an extremely resource- and time-consuming process. Indeed, we need to run a backtest with one set of parameter values, then save the result, modify the parameters, run a backtest again, and repeat. In our sample strategy, if we wanted to find the best values for the stop-loss and profit target between 5 and 50 pips with a step of 5 pips, it would require 100 runs of the entire backtest, which would take hours on most computers. That's why optimization algorithms are mostly developed using compiled versions of Python, such as Cython or Numba.

If you are interested in developing a true understanding of optimization, I'd recommend starting with the concise yet nice introduction by Davide Scassola at *Triality* (https://www.trality. com/blog/an-introduction-to-optimization-algorithms-for-trading-strategies) and then reading Robert Pardo's book, *The Evaluation and Optimization of Trading Strategies* (https://www.amazon.com/Evaluation-Optimization-Trading-Strategies/dp/0470128011).

Final words

Well, any story comes to an end sooner or later, and this book is no exception. Even if you opened it with no idea about FX markets and algo trading, now you have definitely taken yourself to a new level. You have knowledge about FX markets comparable to that of a beginner professional desk trader. You know how to develop trading applications for both live trading and producing reliable backtests. You also know the risks pertaining to trading, for algo trading in particular. You have plenty of roads to go down — in terms of money management, performance analysis, and optimization – but there is one thing I really want you to always remember whatever you do:

Any good trading strategy always has a trading idea behind it. No sophisticated mathematics, no money management, and no optimization will help if the strategy is just a randomly chosen combination of technical analysis studies and parameters. Look for ideas in the market and use the mathematical and programming apparatus to implement, test, and run them – without fear or greed.

Index

Packtpub.com

Subscribe to our online digital library for full access to over 7,000 books and videos, as well as industry leading tools to help you plan your personal development and advance your career. For more information, please visit our website.

Why subscribe?

- Spend less time learning and more time coding with practical eBooks and Videos from over 4,000 industry professionals

- Improve your learning with Skill Plans built especially for you

- Get a free eBook or video every month

- Fully searchable for easy access to vital information

- Copy and paste, print, and bookmark content

Did you know that Packt offers eBook versions of every book published, with PDF and ePub files available? You can upgrade to the eBook version at packtpub.com and as a print book customer, you are entitled to a discount on the eBook copy. Get in touch with us at customercare@packtpub.com for more details.

At www.packtpub.com, you can also read a collection of free technical articles, sign up for a range of free newsletters, and receive exclusive discounts and offers on Packt books and eBooks.

Other Books You May Enjoy

If you enjoyed this book, you may be interested in these other books by Packt:

Hands-On Financial Trading with Python

Jiri Pik, Sourav Ghosh

ISBN: 978-1-83898-288-1

- Discover how quantitative analysis works by covering financial statistics and ARIMA
- Use core Python libraries to perform quantitative research and strategy development using real datasets
- Understand how to access financial and economic data in Python
- Implement effective data visualization with Matplotlib
- Apply scientific computing and data visualization with popular Python libraries
- Build and deploy backtesting algorithmic trading strategies

Developing High-Frequency Trading Systems

Sebastien Donadio, Sourav Ghosh, Romain Rossier

ISBN: 978-1-80324-281-1

- Understand the architecture of high-frequency trading systems
- Boost system performance to achieve the lowest possible latency
- Leverage the power of Python programming, C++, and Java to build your trading systems
- Bypass your kernel and optimize your operating system
- Use static analysis to improve code development
- Use C++ templates and Java multithreading for ultra-low latency
- Apply your knowledge to cryptocurrency trading

Packt is searching for authors like you

If you're interested in becoming an author for Packt, please visit `authors.packtpub.com` and apply today. We have worked with thousands of developers and tech professionals, just like you, to help them share their insight with the global tech community. You can make a general application, apply for a specific hot topic that we are recruiting an author for, or submit your own idea.

Share Your Thoughts

Now you've finished *Getting Started with Forex Trading Using Python*, we'd love to hear your thoughts! Scan the QR code below to go straight to the Amazon review page for this book and share your feedback or leave a review on the site that you purchased it from.

`https://packt.link/r/1-804-61685-0`

Your review is important to us and the tech community and will help us make sure we're delivering excellent quality content.

Download a free PDF copy of this book

Thanks for purchasing this book!

Do you like to read on the go but are unable to carry your print books everywhere?

Is your eBook purchase not compatible with the device of your choice?

Don't worry, now with every Packt book you get a DRM-free PDF version of that book at no cost.

Read anywhere, any place, on any device. Search, copy, and paste code from your favorite technical books directly into your application.

The perks don't stop there, you can get exclusive access to discounts, newsletters, and great free content in your inbox daily

Follow these simple steps to get the benefits:

1. Scan the QR code or visit the link below

https://packt.link/free-ebook/9781804616857

2. Submit your proof of purchase

3. That's it! We'll send your free PDF and other benefits to your email directly